C000145162

One Net, Many Boats

Divine Patterns for the End Times Ekklesia

Steve Harris

One Net, Many Boats - Divine Patterns for the End Times Ekklesia
Published by Global Influencers
PO Box 308, Morningside QLD 4170, Australia
www.globalinfluencers.org
Copyright © 2020 by Steve Harris
All rights reserved

ISBN *(paperback)*   : 978-0-6450343-0-1
ISBN *(eBook)*   : 978-0-6450343-1-8

This book or parts thereof may not be reproduced in any form, stored in a retrieval system, or transmitted in any form by any means - electronic, mechanical, photocopy, recording, or otherwise - without prior written permission of the publisher, except as provided by Australian copyright law.

Cover design by Mercy – www.wotbdesigns.com
Proof Read by Tom Siebert, Christian Editor Connection

Bibles Quoted
Amplified Bible (AMP)
Scripture quotations marked **(AMP)** are taken from the Amplified® Bible (AMP), Copyright © 2015 by The Lockman Foundation. Used by permission. www.Lockman.org

Amplified Bible Classic Edition (AMPC
Scripture quotations marked **(AMPC)** are taken from the Amplified® Bible (AMPC), Copyright © 1954, 1958, 1962, 1964, 1965, 1987 by The Lockman Foundation. Used by permission. www.Lockman.org

Berean Interlinear Bible (BIB)
Scripture quotations marked **(BIB)** are taken from The Holy Bible, Berean Interlinear Bible, BIB Copyright ©2016-2020 by Bible Hub. All Rights Reserved Worldwide. Used by permission.

Berean Study Bible (BSB)
Scripture quotations marked **(BSB)** are taken from The Holy Bible, Berean Study Bible, BSB Copyright ©2016-2020 by Bible Hub. All Rights Reserved Worldwide. Used by permission.

Expanded Bible (EXB)
Scripture quotations marked **(EXB)** are taken from The Expanded Bible. Copyright ©2011 by Thomas Nelson. Used by permission. All rights reserved.

New American Standard Bible (NASB)
Scripture quotations marked **(NASB)** are taken from the New American Standard Bible® (NASB), Copyright © 1960, 1962, 1963, 1968, 1971, 1972, 1973, 1975, 1977, 1995 by The Lockman Foundation. Used by permission. www.Lockman.org

New International Version (NIV)
Scripture quotations marked **(NIV)** are taken from the Holy Bible, New International Version®, NIV®. Copyright © 1973, 1978, 1984, 2011 by Biblica, Inc.™ Used by permission of Zondervan. All rights reserved worldwide. www.zondervan.com

The "NIV" and "New International Version" are trademarks registered in the United States Patent and Trademark Office by Biblica, Inc.™

New International Version – Anglicised (NIVUK)
Scripture quotations marked **(NIVUK)** are taken from the Holy Bible, New International Version® Anglicized, NIV® Copyright © 1979, 1984, 2011 by Biblica, Inc.® Used by permission. All rights reserved worldwide.

New King James Version (NKJV)
Scripture quotations marked **(NKJV)** are taken from the New King James Version®. Copyright © 1982 by Thomas Nelson. Used by permission. All rights reserved.

New Living Translation (NLT)
Scripture quotations marked **(NLT)** are taken from the *Holy Bible*, New Living Translation, copyright © 1996, 2004, 2015 by Tyndale House Foundation. Used by permission of Tyndale House Publishers, Inc., Carol Stream, Illinois 60188. All rights reserved.

The Passion Translation (TPT)
Scripture quotations marked **(TPT)** are from The Passion Translation®. Copyright © 2017, 2018 by Passion & Fire Ministries, Inc. Used by permission. All rights reserved. ThePassionTranslation.com.

Tree of Life Version (TLV)
Scripture quotations marked **(TLV)** are taken from the Holy Scriptures, Tree of Life Version*. Copyright © 2014, 2016 by the Tree of Life Bible Society. Used by permission of the Tree of Life Bible Society.

Definitions are derived from *Strong's Exhaustive Concordance of the Bible*, ed. James Strong (Nashville, TN: Thomas Nelson Publishers, 1977)

Dedication

This book has been written for the Glory of God, and with the leaders and emerging leaders of all denominations in mind. I was particularly focused on the leaders who are working tirelessly and often under difficult and challenging conditions in developing nations. It has been my privilege to stand alongside of many of you and to work with you. You inspire me in so many ways and you are continually in my prayers. I honour you for your daily and often very costly sacrifices.

I pray that this book will inspire and help you to embrace the great and mighty shift that is occurring in the realm of the Spirit regarding the role of the 21st century ekklesia. The spirit of the LORD is hovering over many nations at this time, including yours; and He wants to use your ekklesia for His Glory and to transform your nation from grassroots to government. May the strategies that are discussed within these pages inspire and equip you and the people entrusted to your care to become the "greater things" Christians that Jesus spoke of in **John 14:12**.

The nation of Papua New Guinea was very much in my heart while writing. I believe that Papua New Guinea is called to be a template nation – a nation that implements the Divine patterns and templates that God is revealing at the present time, which in turn will lead to revival and national transformation and set an example for other nations to follow.

This book is especially dedicated to the wonderful people of Papua New Guinea and to the spiritual leaders from many different streams who have sacrificially sown the seeds of revival there over many generations.

This book is also for every believer in every nation who has a cry in their heart that tells them that *"there must be more"* to their Christian experience and destiny. My heartfelt prayer is that this book will help you to understand the "more" on a personal level, and also help you to see the bigger picture; Christ working in you and through you can transform a nation as you faithfully serve the LORD within your sphere of influence.

May your own personal transformation impact your local ekklesia as well as your families, friends, Kingdom businesses and ministries, and may you all rise to greater heights as you pursue the fullness of your destiny in Christ.

The vital role that intercessors and worshippers have been given to advance the Kingdom of God has not always been understood or acknowledged. This book attempts to address that by underscoring and explaining the important and strategic roles of Holy Spirit led intercession and worship, particularly in the times in which we are living. If you are privileged to be called to one of these roles, I acknowledge, affirm, and honour you. Know that God is going to use you powerfully to establish and then maintain the foundation for the coming revival.

Acknowledgements
and
Appreciation

To my King, my LORD, my God, Saviour, Redeemer and Best Friend, there is no life, no light, and no love without You. Thank you for the matchless gift of joyful, abundant and eternal life in You.

To my dear grandmother Helen - you are the one who faithfully sowed the seeds of eternal life into my heart. I am forever grateful to you and I know you will be cheering from Heaven to see your grandson releasing this book for the Glory of our beloved Jesus.

To my beloved sons Steve & Elias - thank you for all of your love, friendship and support. I love & treasure you both. To my granddaughters, Charlotte and Emmie, my precious treasures from Heaven - you fill my life with so much joy, love, laughter, song and dance.

To Chris Joannou, Jorge Munoz, Wye Yi Wong, Yoke Haye Foong, Pastor Josephine Tsai, and Elizabeth Ndili, for being such amazing friends and supporters over many years.

To Pastor David Cheng Lip Kiong and Pastor David Kueh - thank you for the extremely significant role that you played in my life. Pastor David, you are sorely missed by many, but our loss is Heaven's gain.

To Graham and Heather, Ricky and Ronderlynn, Ali and Jen, Louise, Sharlene, Aaron, Rani, Yivan, Morgan, Kerry, Melwyn and Naveena - a special heartfelt thank you to each of you, for journeying with me here at the Australian home base from the very start, when Global Influencers was in its embryonic phase.

Your support and encouragement, your mighty prayers and selfless service have sown the seeds for what is now a global network. I cannot thank you enough.

To the members of Global RestoreNet, our incredible global prayer team - each and every one of you is amazing, mighty, precious, and powerful. Thank you for your dedication and sacrifice.

To Prakash, Tabita, Paul, and all of our leaders in other nations, when I look at all that we have achieved together I am in awe of our God, and filled with such admiration, love and respect for all of you. Thank you for your outpoured lives that serve as an example to believers everywhere of what a true disciple of Christ can and should be.

To Bruce and Cheryl Lindley – thank you for modelling and pioneering apostolic and prophetic leadership for so many.

To Chris Petersen, Peter and Katie Dunstan, and Glen and Anna Gerhauser, thank you for arriving in my life at just the right time. I believe that God has connected us all for such a time as this. Thank you for being so real and for overflowing with Jesus. *"You shall know them by their fruit"* (**Matthew 7:16a**).

To Joseph and Margaret Walters, thank you for demonstrating such a humble, beautiful model of apostolic parenting at a national level.

Thank you to Isaac Joseph for sowing the prophetic prayer seed that helped to birth this book.

To Thomas and Barana Abe, and Joseph and Margaret Gabut, thank you so much for your friendship, and also for your exemplary leadership. The way that you all have sown your lives into your nation at the very highest levels and also at the grassroots level, with such Godliness, humility, integrity, and excellence over an extended period of time, is an example to us all. It is an absolute honour and a privilege to know you and to walk with you in the fields of God's choosing.

Tom and Barana, because of your leadership, our apostolic centre at Gamogagolo PNG is maturing and growing in ways that we believe every apostolic centre and hub should.

Endorsements

Apostle Steve Harris has captured and epitomizes the true spirit and heart of Kingdom apostolic life and ministry.

Apostle Harris demonstrates the simplicity, humility, and practicality of Christ, and the signs following that accompany his ministry attest to that.

I personally have been genuinely impacted by the ministry of this modern apostle, and by the kindness, love, simplicity, and sincerity of his life.

He is a true apostolic father in the faith.

Apostle Joseph Walters
Chairman, Body of Christ, Papua New Guinea

I have known Steve Harris for decades and have witnessed, firsthand, his passion and desire to see the Father's Kingdom come here on the earth. He has given his life to this.

Using every resource at his disposal, Steve has invested his very being into inviting all he meets into a loving, vital relationship with the LORD that results in life transformation.

What you are about to read is not merely a theoretical idea to be discussed, but a burning message to be received. The intensity with which it is written is an overflow of a life filled with white-hot passion for Jesus.

As you read, don't do so just with your mind, but also open up your heart, and allow the Holy Spirit to impart to you not only ideas, but an anointing and grace to BE the end times ekklesia.

Paul "Skip" Smith
National Church Engagement, Alpha Australia

One Net, Many Boats is a book for Christians that are tired with the "normal" Christianity that is not transforming communities and nations. Churches are winning souls, but there is still widespread corruption and moral decadence in countries that profess to be Christian nations. What are the biblical patterns to take the Gospel into important spheres of influence such as government, politics, businesses, entertainment, and society at large to see real transformation?

This book is convicting, Holy Spirit-inspired, and power-packed with testimonies of Heavenly encounters and healing miracles, as well as divine patterns and principles for the true ekklesia to effectively advance God's Kingdom into all spheres of human culture.

One Net, Many Boats is a timely release during a challenging crisis the whole world is facing in this new decade. It is a must-read for true disciples of our Lord Jesus Christ who are passionate, ready to die to self, and willing to be shaken and realigned to advance God's Kingdom for the Glory of the soon coming King.

Thomas Dirona Abe
Founding Chairman and Leader,
Gamogagolo Worship and Ministry Centre
Global Influencers PNG Central leader
Former CEO of State-Owned Statutory/Commercial Entities

Today, God is raising up a new kind of leader. These leaders have a heart like David rather than the heart of Saul. They long to please One - their Heavenly King.

I know Steve Harris personally, and his authentic heart has blessed me. Steve is one of those rare treasures - he's like David. He is a worshipper, warrior and servant.

His book *One Net, Many Boats* takes you up the mountain of God, unveiling the heavenly blueprints that are in the Lord's heart for his church, the ekklesia.

Glen Gerhauser
Holy Fire Ministry Training School & Church on the Park
www.brisbanefire.com

This book by Steve Harris is a clear prophetic call to the Church today to engage with the Holy Spirit in renewed love and obedience, to engage with one another in renewed unity, and to engage with those outside the Church in renewed passion.

Steve's book is a worthwhile addition to your pastoral library; it is easy to read, and easy to understand. Steve builds his thoughts in a structured revelation of what God has shown him, both in dreams and visions, as well as in Scripture. His heavy use of Scripture is refreshing as he moves from point to point. He brings a revelation of what God is saying to the Churches today, adding personal examples and illustrations, and projecting outcomes.

One Net, Many Boats is a call to join hands with our brothers and sisters to seek Christ in a transformational relationship for the good of those who have yet to experience God's love.

Ron Simms
National Leader, Full Gospel Australia
www.fullgospelaustralia.org.au

For those with a heart to hear what the spirit is saying to the church, *One Net, Many Boats* is a blueprint for this new era in church history.

With a masterful use of Scripture, and illustrated by the use of personal heavenly encounters, Steve speaks of a period coming of great revival and harvest, combined with a reformation of the ekklesia, and the transformation of the world throughout the seven mountains.

Steve provides a blueprint for an inclusive apostolic hub, which includes both a 24/7 Kingdom prayer and worship centre, as well as a Kingdom resource centre to resource and equip the churches and ministries throughout a nation.

Steve underscores all this with the need for a deeper level of intimacy with God, which he so profoundly lives on a day-to-day basis. This is a must-read for any student of Scripture keen to understand the period we are living in, and the way forward into the new era.

Peter Dunstan
Co-Founder: Breakfree Australia

"One Net Many Boats" is an amazing gift to the body of Christ.

Christian leaders need to understand what God is saying to the church as well as discern how to effectively function in this new wineskin as apostles, prophet, pastors, teachers and evangelists.

Steve Harris has written an excellent resource to equip leaders to do both effectively, with Biblical insights and strategic patterns to enable leaders to go forward and to emerge into the fullness of their calling and ministry to others.

Every believer also needs to understand how God wants them to function in this new era. This is a great resource for every Christian. I know you will be blessed by the 'new era equipping anointing' released by God through this book.

Bruce Lindley
Founding Apostle, ARC Global Apostolic Community
www.arcglobal.org

Table of Contents

Part 01 - Foundations

Part 02 - Restoration

Part 03 - Transformation
(Ancient Paths and 21ˢᵗ Century Paradigms)

Part 04 - Final Thoughts

Part 05 - Resources, References, and Further Reading

Foreword

I am humbly honoured and privileged to write the foreword to mark the timely release of this brilliant book, *One Net, Many Boats,* during this time and season.

I first met Steve Harris by divine appointment in 2017 during one of his teaching seminars in Papua New Guinea. I come from a Salvation Army, Baptist, and United Churches background. Later in my Christian walk I was exposed to various Pentecostal churches and speakers from overseas.

In all of my thirty-six years as a Christian, I have never met a Pentecostal preacher operating in all the five-fold ministry gifts who is as humble and full of agape love as Pastor Steve. We immediately connected with each other from day one. His soft-spoken, down-to- earth demeanour and genuine love for the grassroots people are a result of his deep walk with the LORD.

His Kingdom leadership seminars have resonated well with Christians from mainline churches and all denominations, because of his Christlike love, communication and character. Christlike character is what unites the body of Christ; not background, titles, positions, gifts, or eloquence.

One Net, Many Boats is a must-read for any 21st century Christian who is passionate about the Lord Jesus Christ and the advancement of His Kingdom into all spheres of human culture.

It is vital for the Church to understand the need for the restoration of the two-fold Great Commission that is the mandate of the ekklesia and outlined in this book, an individual mandate to win souls **(Mark 16:15)** and a corporate mandate to disciple the nations **(Matthew 28:19-20)**.

The latter is crucial if Christians are to take back domains and spheres currently influenced by the enemy, and truly experience revival on a national scale.

This book is packed with amazing experiences of Heavenly encounters, testimonies, healing miracles, and Kingdom principles.

Pastor Steve has been there, experiencing and living genuine Heavenly encounters, and he is able to lead people to their own place of encounter with the Risen Christ.

This book helps us to embrace Divine patterns and strategies that enable us to live in our kingly authority as supernatural disciples and God's Ambassadors here on earth, impacting communities and nations for the fulfilment of the Gospel of the Kingdom.

Let this book awaken and bless you as a child of God with a clear vision and new sense of purpose to be a carrier of God's presence, and to make a difference in a world that is facing great shaking and uncertainty in this new decade.

Thomas Dirona Abe
Founding Chairman and Leader,
Gamogagolo Worship and Ministry Centre
Global Influencers PNG Central leader
Former CEO of State Run Statutory & Commercial Entities

Introduction

Matthew 13:51-52 (AMP)
*51 "Have you understood all these things
[in the lessons of the parables]?"
They said to Jesus, "Yes."*

*52 He said to them, "Therefore every scribe
who has become a disciple of the Kingdom of Heaven
is like the head of a household, who brings out
of his treasure things that are new and fresh
and things that are old and familiar."*

Treasures Old and New

In Old Testament times, a scribe would be appointed by God to act as secretary of state, and to prepare and issue decrees in the name of the king. [1]

There is a balance that the scribe mentioned in **Matthew 13:52** who has become a disciple of the Kingdom of Heaven understands. His role was prophetic in real time, as he was seeing the unfolding of what was written in the Law, and the fulfilment of the Prophets and the Psalms right in front of his eyes through the life of Jesus **(Luke 24:55)**.

His role was to give understanding of the new to those who were well versed in the old - and to present both as holy treasures. This is also what Jesus did through the parables. He explained what was completely fresh and new, and in many senses completely beyond human understanding, with stories about familiar and well-understood events from everyday life.

Would a scribe writing at the time of Christ have fully understood that Jesus was God in the flesh, and that right before him stood the Creator God of the universe in human form ? What would the scribe - the steward of old and new treasures - have made of the miracles that were occurring on a daily basis before his own eyes ?

How would he have responded to Jesus, the Great High Priest **(Hebrews 4:14)** doing things that it was forbidden - according to the "Old Treasure" - for the priest to do; such as healing on the Sabbath, and touching dead bodies - causing defilement according to the Law of Moses **(Numbers 19:11; Haggai 2:13)**, in order to raise the dead **(Luke 8:54** – Jairus's daughter**)?**

He may not have fully understood, yet he recognised that the new was just as valuable as the old had always been, and in fact the new gave added value to the old, and vice versa.

And so, he brought both – the old and familiar, as well as the new and fresh - out of his treasure room to share with his esteemed guests.

Even today, there are times for the followers of Christ that the "old" and the "new" would seem to be incompatible – that is, until God releases His divine revelation and understanding through the Holy Spirit, the One entrusted with teaching us all things. **(John 14:26)**

We are living in a time when God is doing brand new things, and there is a tendency when He does this for His people to either run after the new and completely forget or reject the old and the blessing contained therein; or to reject the new and stay with the old, missing the revelatory blessing that is brought through the fresh outpourings of the Holy Spirit.

As human beings, we tend to mistrust what we do not understand; and we usually do that for what seem to be all the right reasons at the time. For example, some who rejected the deity of Jesus when He walked upon the earth were absolutely certain that they were obeying and pleasing God the Father by doing so.

Embracing the new and fresh things of the Spirit, while respecting the old and familiar, is healthy and wise. The generations of God's servants who have gone before us have sown powerful seeds through their faithful planting of the Word of God.

Those seeds are now being watered, multiplied and given fresh meaning through the powerful, end times moving of the Spirit of God.

The old and familiar ways have helped us to form our character as individuals and as a world wide body of believers, and have given us firm foundations in the Word of God. The new and fresh ways of the Holy Spirit, and the paradigms that He is revealing for the benefit of His ekklesia, can enable, equip, and accelerate us to carry the Gospel of the Kingdom to the ends of the Earth in unprecedented ways, and bring entire nations into the fullness of all that God has for them.

There are Divine patterns and templates that will facilitate the unity that is required to release God's commanded blessing to His ekklesia, and to bring transformation to the nations of the world. While the paradigms may be ancient, it is the current era that represents the fullness of time in which to implement them.

Now is the time for God's people to arise as one, and to be equipped to usher in the restoration of all things. May we be attentive to the Spirit of God, and also open to embrace and facilitate any adjustments and realignments that are necessary within our own spheres of influence, so that our ekklesias and networks can become more effective vehicles to release the absolute fullness of the Gospel of the Kingdom to the very ends of the Earth, and into every sphere of human culture.

This is a time when more and more people are experiencing Heavenly encounters. I have been blessed throughout my Christian walk to experience God in this way, but have not felt that it was time to write about those experiences until now (2020). My heartfelt prayer is that the Heavenly encounters that are shared within the pages of this book will inspire you to step across the Heavenly thresholds that you will encounter during your private devotional times, into a deeper and more passionate walk with the LORD.

Throughout this book the word "ekklesia" is used rather than the word "church", which is the usual English translation of the Greek word ἐκκλησία *(ekklesia)*.

I have done this because now more than ever before, there is an urgent need for all believers to expand and adjust our current understanding of "church" to align with what Jesus meant when He told Peter that *"upon this rock I will build my ekklesia"* (**Matthew 16:18**). The ekklesia that Jesus said He would build – in partnership with us - is called to transform nations from grassroots to government across every sphere of society, as well as to win souls.

May all that has been lost to the ekklesia over time be completely revived, renewed, and restored in our day and in our time. May we learn to be as wise as the Kingdom scribe, celebrating all that has gone before, embracing what is now here, and eagerly anticipating that which is yet to come.

My prayer for you is that through the testimonies, teachings, and strategies contained within the pages of this book, you will receive and rejoice in treasures that are both old and familiar, and also new and fresh; and that together they will greatly enrich your life, and also broaden and accelerate your God-given calling and purpose, and the supernatural effectiveness of your ekklesia, and all for the Glory of Almighty God.

Steve Harris
Founder
Global Influencers

Part 01

Foundations

1 Corinthians 3:11 (NASB)
*For no man can lay a foundation other than
the one which is laid, which is Jesus Christ.*

Chapter 01

The Fulfilment
of
God-Given Vision

Habakkuk 2:1-4 (NKJV)
[1] I will stand my watch
And set myself on the rampart,
And watch to see what He will say to me,
And what I will answer when I am corrected.

The Just Live by Faith
[2] Then the Lord answered me and said:
"Write the vision and make it plain on tablets,
That he may run who reads it.

[3] For the vision is yet for an appointed time;
but at the end it will speak, and it will not lie.
Though it tarries, wait for it;
Because it will surely come, it will not tarry.

[4] "Behold the proud, his soul is not upright in him;
But the just shall live by his faith."

The prophet Habakkuk was given some vital keys regarding the establishment and fulfilment of God given vision. During my own walk with God, I have seen time and again that as soon as I began to write down the visions that God had given to me about soul harvest, healing miracles, and the raising up of mercy and justice ministries amongst the poor, suddenly, there would be an avalanche of fulfilment, eternal fruit, and even revival ... **Habakkuk 2:1-4** fulfilled.

Because I chose to obey and write down all the visions and burdens that He had placed within my heart, at the stage when there was truly no more to show for any of it than just things that were hoped for, and things that were not yet seen - almost from one day to the next, the things that had been "hoped for" suddenly "were", and the things that been "not seen" had suddenly taken on physical form and were being gloriously fulfilled. And others were also running with and fulfilling the God-given vision, and growing in Christ and becoming personally fulfilled as a result.

There is a powerful, vitally important Divine principle that is at work here. Simply *because* everything has been written down clearly according to the Heavenly vision, God will *breathe upon it* and He will cause others to run with it, and *it will take shape and grow* ... and all for His Glory, and for the fulfilment of His wonderful purposes to the very ends of the Earth.

Here are seven keys that we can receive from **Habakkuk 2:1-4** :-

1 - Prioritise the "waiting and watching."

2 - Stand your watch - do not give up !
    Be alert, attentive, and vigilant.

3 - Learn to listen and obey – especially the small, sometimes frustrating steps that will often lead to the larger steps, provided that we "stay the course."

4 - Learn to hear 100 percent clearly from the LORD, to discern what is God and what is not God; and be prepared to wait until you "know that you know" that it is Him.

5 - Write down the vision and make it very plain so that others may run with it.

6 - "Though it tarry" – understand that to God, *"a day is as a thousand years, and a thousand years is as a day"* **(2 Peter 3:8)**. From our perspective, His timing seems so very different to human timing and priority – and yet, His timing is always perfect.

We must take great care not to run ahead (i.e., try to "force" our destiny to happen on our terms through works of the flesh) or to fall behind (become inattentive or insensitive to His voice) where the timing of God is concerned. Also, we should be open to the fact that vision given to us may be for others to fulfil. It may be our role to simply impart it.

Many lessons are learned, and many valuable character attributes are formed, as we learn to neither run ahead nor lag behind God's perfect schedule, and as we also learn to resist the temptation to abbreviate or embellish it ! In other words, be prepared to patiently wait for the establishment and fulfilment of the God-given vision, God's way.

7 – Learn to live by faith. May *"the substance of things hoped for"* and *"the evidence of things not* **(yet)** *seen"* **(Hebrews 11:1-2)** be sufficient to sustain our belief in the vision, as you learn to wait more and more upon God and as you learn to place more and more of your trust in Him.

Divine patterns and blueprints consist of revelation that has been birthed in a place of supernatural encounter with the Divine Godhead. They will be understood, embraced, and activated by people who live in close, ever-deepening communion with Him.

Hebrews 8:5 (NKJV)
... who serve the copy and shadow of the heavenly things, as Moses was divinely instructed when he was about to make the tabernacle. For He said, "See that you make all things according to the pattern shown you on the mountain."

Things revealed to you in the Throne Room of Heaven
will come to pass on the earth.

Though they may be not "yet" seen, they will be, if we prioritise the watching and waiting; resolutely stand our watch; learn to listen and obey; learn what is God and what is not; write down the vision; accept God's way and God's timing; and live by faith.

We will gain Divine approval and see an increase of supernatural fruitfulness if we learn to embrace and honour our God-given visions in this way.

Hebrews 11:1-2 (AMP) - The Triumphs of Faith
¹ Now faith is the assurance (title deed, confirmation)
of things hoped for (divinely guaranteed), and the evidence
of things not seen [the conviction of their reality
- faith comprehends as fact what cannot be experienced
by the physical senses]. ² For by this [kind of] faith
the men of old gained [divine] approval.

Habakkuk was the messenger.

He faithfully wrote down what he saw and heard from Heaven, and he released it so that others could run with it.

The contents of this book are based upon the glorious promises and encouragements contained within the Bible, and also drawn from my own experiences, which include Heavenly encounters and earthly missions (to the Throne Room and to the nations), planting ekklesias and apostolic hubs, and much more.

As an ever-amazed ambassador of an always wonderful God, I have seen the fulfilment of much of what is written here, in and through my own life.

I also know that an equal part of what has been received, written down, and shared here by faith, has not, as yet, been seen; but it will be, as you, the reader, are drawn by the Holy Spirit to run with the Divine patterns that are presented here. God will fulfil them in and through your own Christ-surrendered life.

Selah, and Amen.

Chapter 02

One Net, Many Boats

Recently, as I was worshipping, I saw, in the Spirit, a massive mantle of Glory that was circular in shape, dropping down from Heaven.

As it descended, it covered a large region of the earth. I saw some local ekklesia leaders and network leaders standing at one edge of the mantle and trying to pick it up by lifting the edge, but they were unable to do so on their own.

I saw some other local ekklesia members, standing at another point along the edge of the mantle, also holding the edge of the mantle and trying to lift it up. However, it was simply too large, and too heavy.

I then saw other people streaming in from all over the world. There were representatives of every major people group, and also people from every generation – from children to great-grandparents. It was a beautiful sight to behold with such a wonderful diversity of cultures and generations.

This amazing sight was accompanied by the glorious sound of everyone's voices lifted harmoniously in a multitude of languages to worship the LORD as one. Effortlessly, they positioned themselves at equidistant points around the edges of the mantle, and together they held it in their hands.

And suddenly – the mantle of Glory was able to be lifted up.

God spoke. This is what He said :-

> *"This mantle is too 'weighty' with Kabod [2] Glory,*
> *Divine attributes and design, and generational*
> *responsibility, for one person or single group to carry.*
>
> *The glorious mantle of revival was never intended to*
> *be carried by individuals alone, but rather by people of all*
> *nations, denominations, and generations working together."*

Once the edges of the mantle had been lifted up, it suddenly changed into a fishing net, and I saw that the people groups who had been holding the edges were suddenly standing in waist deep water. Still worshipping as one, they began walking toward the centre of the net.

As the distance between them decreased, the circle grew tighter, and a multitude of good-sized fish of many different kinds started jumping out of the water.

It was a bumper catch – and not a single fish slipped through the net.

I also saw that as the various groups came closer to each other, the different anointings and mantles that each group carried were literally "rubbing off" (one meaning of "anointing" is "to rub" [3]) on each other.

Every group grew in strength, anointing and Godly stature from the "rubbing" with every other group. It was supremely beautiful because of the Divine unity that was being released through the blending of the diverse anointings that were carried by the different generations and people groups.

Agape relationships formed and strengthened, leading to vigorous upwards (spiritual connection), inwards (character development), and outwards (multiplying fruitfulness and relationships) growth, for every group.

One net, many boats : this is a prophetic picture of what
the end times ekklesia will look like, and how it will function.

And - an abundant and joyful harvest will come as we learn to work together, directed by the glorious anointing and Divine blueprints and strategies of Almighty God.

Matthew 14:33 (AMP)
Then those who were in the boat worshipped Him
(with awe-inspired reverence), saying,
"Truly You are the Son of God."

Isaiah 4:5 (NKJV)
Then the LORD will create above every dwelling place
of Mount Zion, and above her assemblies, a cloud
and smoke by day and the shining of a flaming fire by night.
For over all the glory there will be a covering.

Being truly led by the Spirit of God leads to true unity. And unity is the single human activity based on individual choice, upon which God commands His blessing.

Psalm 133:1 &3b (NKJV)
¹ Behold, how good and how pleasant it is
for brethren to dwell together in unity!
... ³ᵇ For there the LORD commanded the blessing
- Life forevermore.

May we be truly, joyfully, and gloriously unified across all nations, denominations, and generations as we embrace the end times leading of the Holy Spirit.

And may the coming revival be much more than a Holy visitation, but rather, a Holy habitation that transforms societies and nations from the inside out, and from grassroots to government, as we stand shoulder to shoulder with God and with each other in the harvest fields of His choosing.

Zephaniah 3:9 (NIV)
"Then I will purify the lips of the peoples,
that all of them may call on the name of the Lord
and serve him shoulder to shoulder."

Chapter 03

Glorious Regiments

John 1:50-51 (AMPC)
⁵⁰ Jesus replied, "Because I said to you,
I saw you beneath the fig tree,
do you believe in and rely on and trust in Me ?
You shall see greater things than this!"

⁵¹ Then He said to him,
"I assure you, most solemnly I tell you all,
you shall see heaven opened, and the angels of God
ascending and descending upon the Son of Man!"

Psalm 91:11-12 (AMP)
¹¹ For He will command His angels in regard to you,
To protect and defend and guard you in all your ways
[of obedience and service].
¹² They will lift you up in their hands,
So that you do not [even] strike your foot against a stone.

Jesus said :

"I assure you, most solemnly I tell you all, you shall see" ...

The Bible clearly teaches the existence of angels as mighty, created spirit beings, whose chief duties are to worship and serve God.

They are not a race, reproducing themselves, but are a company created to minister to the heirs of salvation.[4]

In both the Old and the New Testaments there are accounts of angels ministering to the people of God. Nearly all of the great men of the Bible exhibited a belief in the existence of angels.

The LORD Jesus Christ Himself spoke often of the angels, and was also ministered to by them **(Mark 8:38, 13:32; Matthew 13:41; John 1:51; 2 Thessalonians 1:7; Hebrews 12:22).** [5]

I remember one particular occasion when I was woken up in the middle of the night by the LORD to pray and to worship. As soon I began to worship, the realms of Glory were opened and I found myself immediately taken up. The Glory was so thick, and His Presence was so strong, I was trembling, shaking, and completely overwhelmed. After a little while, when I was able to adjust to the intensity of His Presence, I noticed that in the midst of the Glory there were some very intense golden "spots" where the Glory seemed to be much thicker than it was everywhere else.

Suddenly, the Spirit of the LORD picked me up and "zoomed me in" closer to one of the golden "spots." As I drew nearer, I could see that the "spots" were actually square in shape.

He picked me up again and brought me in closer – right into the middle of one of the squares. I was astounded to see that what had appeared to be "spots" from a distance were in fact glorious regiments of angelic beings. There were 10,000 assembled in each formation, standing 100 wide and 100 deep, and all covered in the Glory of God.

At this point, the LORD spoke to me and said, "Son, these glorious regiments are commanded by me. They are activated in response to the prayers of My people. When they begin to pray with the full Divine authority that is their birthright in Me, I release and activate my regiments in response to their prayers, to help them fulfil their glorious assignments to the very ends of the earth.

Tell my people to prepare, because **Now is the Time**."

The last statement that the LORD made – "Now is the Time" – was with a voice of such Divine majesty and authority that the atmosphere became charged and filled with His powerful Presence, and everything shook.

I was there in that Glorious realm for a long time, absorbing the power of the revelation, completely undone in the Presence of the Almighty, and doing my best to absorb the full implications of what had been revealed.

Now is the time. The LORD is inviting us to co-govern the affairs of the Earth in Divine partnership with Him through Spirit-led worship and intercession and the implementation of Divine strategies.

The angelic hosts are standing ready to be released to *"protect, defend, and guard us in all our ways of obedience and service"* **(Psalm 91:11)**, beginning in the Throne Room and ending in the nations.

May He equip and empower us all to see what He is doing in the realms of the Spirit, so that His Kingdom may come and His will be done in all its fullness to the very ends of the Earth.

Matthew 26:53 (NIV)
"Do you think I cannot call on My Father,
and He will at once put at my disposal
more than twelve legions of angels?"

Revelation 14:6 (NIVUK)
"Then I saw another angel flying in mid-air,
and he had the eternal gospel to proclaim
to those who live on the earth
– to every nation, tribe, language and people."

Psalm 2:7-8 (NKJV)
[7] *"I will declare the decree :*
The Lord has said to Me,
'You are My Son, today I have begotten You.
[8] *Ask of Me, and I will give You the nations for Your inheritance,*
And the ends of the earth for Your possession."

Chapter 04

Overflowing With the Fullness of God

Transformation of ekklesias, and then of our nations through the transformed ekklesia, begins with the transformation of ourselves. Every time two or three gather in His Name (or as the AMPC beautifully renders *"are ... drawn together ... into His Name"*), Jesus says that He, as the great "I AM", will be right there in our midst.

> **Matthew 18:20 (AMPC)**
> *For wherever two or three are gathered*
> *(drawn together as My followers)*
> *in (into) My name, there I AM in the midst of them.*

It is so important that our personal "Divine Patterns" are in place if we are going to be used by the LORD to implement His corporate "Divine Patterns" for the end times ekklesia.

Filled to Overflowing

We are called to be filled to overflowing with the life and love of Christ on a personal level and on a corporate level. We are called to build Christ-centred communities that overflow with rich and abundant supernatural expressions of His life, His truth, His hope, and most importantly, His love.

John 10:10b (AMP)
I came that they may have and enjoy life,
and have it in abundance [to the full, till it overflows].

Romans 5:5 (AMP)
Such hope [in God's promises]
never disappoints us, because God's love
has been abundantly poured out within our hearts
through the Holy Spirit who was given to us.

Our communities are called to be so full of Jesus that His life, truth, light, and love permeate not only the regions in which they are planted, but also the networks to which we belong. We are called to influence every sphere of human culture through the overflowing abundance of supernatural life that we carry.

Matthew 15:14-16 (NKJV)
14 "You are the light of the world.
A city that is set on a hill cannot be hidden.
15 Nor do they light a lamp and put it under a basket,
but on a lampstand, and it gives light to all
who are in the house.

16 Let your light so shine before men, that they may see
your good works and glorify your Father in heaven."

God always intended His ekklesias to be places where people know that they will personally encounter the Living God - not where they will only hear about Him.

Hebrews 2:12 (NKJV)
"I will declare Your name to My brethren;
In the midst of the assembly I will sing praise to You."

Revelation 1:13 (NKJV)
...and in the midst of the seven lampstands
One like the Son of Man, clothed with a garment
down to the feet and girded about the chest
with a golden band.

Revelation 2:1 (NKJV)
"To the angel of the church of Ephesus write,
'These things says He who holds the seven stars
in His right hand, who walks in the midst
of the seven golden lampstands:'"

Deeper Encounters and Greater Things

No matter where we are in our walk with God, and no matter how long or short a time we have walked with Him, there will always be a place of deeper encounter that He has prepared for us.

Psalm 17:15 (AMP)
As for me, I shall see Your face in righteousness;
I will be [fully] satisfied when I awake
[to find myself] seeing Your likeness.

Psalm 42:7-8 (NKJV)
[7] Deep calls to deep
at the [thundering] sound of Your waterfalls;
All Your breakers and Your waves have rolled over me.
[8] Yet the Lord will command His lovingkindness
in the daytime, and in the night His song will be with me,
A prayer to the God of my life.

Philippians 3:12 (NKJV)
Not that I have already attained,
or am already perfected; but I press on,
that I may lay hold of that for which
Christ Jesus has also laid hold of me.

How close are we to becoming the *"Greater Things Christians"* that Jesus spoke about in **John 14:12** – the ones who would do greater works than He did ?

John 14:12 (NASB)
Truly, truly, I say to you, he who believes in Me,
the works that I do, he will do also; and greater works
than these he will do; because I go to the Father.

Levels of Engagement

What is our level of engagement with the Almighty? Does He call us His friends ? Are we living in His Presence and/or under an established Open Heaven ? If someone asked us what Jesus was like (not just who He is) would we be able to tell them, based upon our own personal experiences of Him, and glorious encounters with Him ?

When the apostle Paul spent time with people, he did not present himself with *"superiority of speech"* or *"lofty words of eloquence."*

Rather, wherever he went God demonstrated His Word through miraculous displays of His power. This is because Paul lived his life in intimate relationship with God, continually immersed in His Presence.

> **1 Corinthians 2:1-5 (AMP)**
> **- Paul's Reliance upon the Spirit**
> *¹ And when I came to you, brothers and sisters,*
> *proclaiming to you the testimony of God [concerning salvation*
> *through Christ], I did not come with superiority*
> *of speech or of wisdom [no lofty words of eloquence*
> *or of philosophy as a Greek orator might do];*
>
> *² for I made the decision to know nothing*
> *[that is, to forego philosophical or theological discussions*
> *regarding inconsequential things and opinions while]*
> *among you except Jesus Christ, and Him crucified*
> *[and the meaning of His redemptive, substitutionary*
> *death and His resurrection]. ³ I came to you in*
> *[a state of] weakness and fear and great trembling.*
>
> *⁴ And my message and my preaching were not*
> *in persuasive words of wisdom [using clever rhetoric],*
> *but [they were delivered] in demonstration*
> *of the [Holy] Spirit [operating through me]*
> *and of [His] power [stirring the minds of the listeners*
> *and persuading them], ⁵ so that your faith would not rest*
> *on the wisdom and rhetoric of men, but on the power of God.*

If we and the people whom we lead are to become ambassadors of Christ **(2 Corinthians 5:20)** who truly represent Him in all of His glorious fullness, then we must learn what it means to have "Christ in us the hope of glory" **(Colossians 1:27)**. We must not limit the ways that He can work through us because of our unbelief, lack of knowledge of His ways, or lack of intimate relationship with Him.

> **2 Corinthians 5:20 (AMP)**
> *So we are ambassadors for Christ,*
> *as though God were making His appeal through us;*
> *we [as Christ's representatives] plead with you*
> *on behalf of Christ to be reconciled to God.*

> **Colossians 1:27 (NKJV)**
> *To them God willed to make known what are the riches*
> *of the glory of this mystery among the Gentiles:*
> *which is Christ in you, the Hope of Glory.*

Intimacy with God will demolish unbelief and also increase our knowledge of Him and of His ways. Intimate relationship will transform us from Glory to Glory **(2 Corinthians 3:18)** and transform us into the "Greater Things Christians" of **John 14:12**, by leading us into the place of personal Divine encounter with our Creator God.

> **2 Corinthians 3:18 (AMP)**
> *And we all, with unveiled face, continually*
> *seeing as in a mirror the glory of the Lord,*
> *are progressively being transformed into His image*
> *from [one degree of] glory to [even more] glory,*
> *which comes from the Lord, [who is] the Spirit.*

There Is Always More

There is a danger for all of us that we can fall into routines that are devoid of new life in terms of our spirituality, without even realising it. If this happens, it can cause us to fall well short of what God intended for us, leaving our destinies on hold, and generating a feeling of unfulfillment in our daily lives. This is why daily "fresh manna from Heaven" is so important, and so enjoyable !

If we are going to lead others into the fullness of all that God has for His end times ekklesia, we need to be living in a place of genuine encounters with the LORD ourselves, as we cannot lead people to places we have not been.

As we enter a new decade and an exciting new era in God, we are all being given a Divine opportunity to examine everything that we have become "accustomed" to doing, and to readjust our lives as necessary to ensure that all we are doing is perfectly aligned with God's end time purposes.

There is a cry going up all over the world from believers' hearts that says, "LORD, there must be more!"

In response to this, there is a Heavenly outpouring that is beginning, which will result in unprecedented renewal, restoration, and realignment of individuals, ministries, and nations.

I believe that a large part of the "more" will be released, individually and corporately, as individuals choose to engage on a deeper level than ever before with the LORD, until we reach a point where we are continually overflowing with His fullness, through daily, living, fresh encounters with Him.

It's not about finding the "next big thing" - it's about rediscovering our first love with "the One who is all and is in all" **(Colossians 3:11)** and watering the foundational roots of our faith through deepening intimacy with the Lover of our souls.

Everything we need and everything we desire is found in Him.

> **John 7:37-38 (AMPC)**
> *^{37} Now on the final and most important day of the Feast,*
> *Jesus stood, and He cried in a loud voice,*
> *"If any man is thirsty, let him come to Me and drink!*
> *^{38} He who believes in Me*
> *[who cleaves to and trusts in and relies on Me]*
> *as the Scripture has said, from his innermost being*
> *shall flow [continuously] springs and rivers of living water.*

Isaiah 12:2-3 (AMPC)
² Behold, God, my salvation!
I will trust and not be afraid,
for the Lord God is my strength and song;
yes, He has become my salvation.
³ Therefore with joy will you draw water
from the wells of salvation.

Personal and Corporate Revival

Only when the internal wells are unstopped, and the rivers of living water are flowing, can we be activated into the fullness of our roles within the Kingdom of God.

Listen carefully and reverently to His voice. The Lamb of God is speaking profoundly, one on one, to each and every one of His precious children. Press in until you receive your glorious treasure.

Revival begins in us. An ekklesia in revival consists of individuals who are living in revival, and already overflowing with Jesus, coming together in unity to glorify the Risen Christ, and becoming further equipped to take Him to those who need Him the most.

Meetings that are led by people who are in personal revival will cause multiplication of the life of Christ within for all who participate. The prevailing mindset will change from people coming to watch and listen, and returning home unchanged, to people coming fresh from their personal God-encounters, to encounter Him again with joy in the corporate setting, and to be further activated to transform their communities through the living overflow of Christ in them, who alone is the hope of glory for all **(Colossians 1:27)**.

The other side of this is that revival can certainly be "messy" and unpredictable. I have had the privilege of ministering in the midst of a few sustained revivals. In amongst the outpouring of souls, miracles, and glorious Presence, other things can occur that will offend tradition and offend the flesh.

However, if we shut down the unknown for fear of what "might" happen, we run the very real risk of missing what God had planned, and we can fall into a routine in our corporate gatherings that is not pleasing to the LORD.

Isaiah 29:13 (NLT)
And so the Lord says,
"These people say they are mine.
They honour me with their lips,
but their hearts are far from me.
And their worship of me is nothing
but man-made rules learned by rote.

God doesn't want ever that to happen to us, and so He continually and graciously orchestrates opportunities that allow us to renew, refresh, and revive everything related to our walk with Him.

He is just that good !

Let us allow the spotlight of the LORD to examine us, our motivations, and our ministries. That can be an uncomfortable experience, but it is absolutely necessary if we are going to represent Him with integrity.

Let us "follow the Glory" across the river and into the land of the fullness of His promises for us, for the sake of the emerging generations, and for our nations (**Exodus 13:21-22; Joshua 3 ff.**).

Exodus 13:-21-22 (NKJV)
[21] *And the Lord went before them by day in a pillar*
of cloud to lead the way, and by night in a pillar
of fire to give them light, so as to go by day and night.

[22] *He did not take away the pillar of cloud by day*
or the pillar of fire by night from before the people.

Are you crying out for the "more" of God ? Are you longing for deeper encounters, greater things, and for personal and corporate revival ? Then draw away from the busyness of everyday existence and seek the Face of the Almighty.

The Divine pattern given by God for the Tabernacle of Moses was designed so that the outer courts were lit with natural light, and the Holy Place was lit with candle light; but the Holy of Holies was illuminated only by the Glory of God.

The outer court was noisy, the Holy Place was more intimate, but the Holy of Holies was the place of deeply intimate, face to face encounter with the Almighty.

Do not be satisfied with spending time in the outer courts, where God and His Glory are not visible, and where the flesh and the cares of this world can still distract us. Go deeper.

For anyone who wishes to be an overflowing carrier of the Presence and Glory of the Most High God, the directions to the Throne Room are found in **Revelation 4:1** where Jesus said :-

> *"Come up here and I will show you*
> *what must take place after this."*

Jesus went up on to the mountain, and He called those whom He wanted; and they came to Him **(Mark 3:13).**

It is time for you to find your holy mountain **(Psalm 43:3)**, your tent of meeting **(Exodus 40:34)**, your sanctuary, your place of encounter with the Living God **(Psalm 96:6)**, and to abide there, until you hear Him calling to you with His Divine instructions for your life and ministry.

Let's determine that we will be a people who are desperate for the "more" that God longs to release in us and through us.

Let us become the people who are known as the ones who are overflowing with His fullness, day and night.

Let's meet Him on His holy mountain and see what He will say to us when we meet with Him there. May we be prepared to become living sacrifices in His service, embrace the "more" and go wherever He chooses to send us, to do whatever He will call us to do.

Exodus 40:16 (NKJV)
*Thus Moses did; according to all
that the Lord had commanded him, so he did.*

LORD, overflow us continually with Your Holy Presence.

Amen.

Chapter 05

Habitation or Visitation ?

There is such a sense in every nation that I've visited recently that the Glory of the LORD is hovering over the face of the earth, just as the Spirit of God hovered over the unformed earth in **Genesis 1:1-2**. The Holy Spirit and the accompanying Glory are hovering now, prior to being poured out on all flesh as per **Joel 2:28-29**.

There is a sense that we are approaching a spiritual "tipping point." God is watching and waiting, looking for a people who will rise up to worship Him in Spirit and in truth and with serious, desperate hunger.

When we set aside the time just to be with Him and to love Him with no requests other than He would take us deeper into His heart, our desperate hunger sows into the Heavenly realms and in response, God rains His Glory down, all over the dry & dusty & thirsty & hungry land & people.

Especially for those who have sown with tears that mirror the LORD's compassion for this world that has gone so far astray, you can expect to reap with joy.

> **Psalm 126:5-6 (NASB)**
> *⁵ Those who sow in tears shall reap with joyful shouting.*
> *⁶ He who goes to and fro weeping, carrying his bag of seed,*
> *Shall indeed come again with a shout of joy,*
> *bringing his sheaves with him.*

As a child you may have gone camping in one of the old style canvas tents. And somebody would say,

"Whatever you do, don't touch the tent !"

And being a child, of course as soon as someone had said that, you would have to touch the tent just to see what would happen.

With those old canvas tents, as soon as you touched them, they would begin to leak. At first, it would just be small drips. But then the drips would turn into a trickle, then a torrent, and then a waterfall. And soon, everyone & everything inside the tent would be soaked !

In **John 17** Jesus speaks about sharing the Glory that His Father gave to Him ... with us.

> **John 17:22-23 (NASB)**
> *²² The glory which You have given Me*
> *I have given to them, that they may be one,*
> *just as We are one; ²³ I in them and You in Me,*
> *that they may be perfected in unity,*
> *so that the world may know that You sent Me,*
> *and loved them, even as You have loved Me.*

God is always looking for people who are hungry enough to defy tradition and who are bold enough to reach up and touch the tent of God **(Isaiah 4:5)** - and even reach right up through it - so that the tent of God will leak, a drip of Glory will become a trickle, then a torrent, and then a waterfall.

The Glory of God will flood down in response to our hunger and then begin to cover the earth as the waters cover the sea.

> **Isaiah 4:5 (TPT)**
> *Then Yahweh will create over all of Mount Zion*
> *and over every gathering a cloud of smoke by day*
> *and a glow of flaming fire by night.*
> *And all this manifestation of dazzling glory*
> *will spread over them like a wedding canopy.*

Habakkuk 2:14 (AMP)

"But [the time is coming when] the earth shall be filled
With the knowledge of the glory of the Lord,
As the waters cover the sea."

God *will* pour out His glory. For those of us who are fortunate enough to be living in the 21st century, I believe we have been positioned in our own fullness of time, right at the very beginning, at the "tipping point" of the last and greatest outpouring of the Holy Spirit.

Just as Christ was sent into the world in His own fullness of time **(Galatians 4:4)**, so have all of us who are alive now been positioned by the Almighty into ours.

We're positioned on the edge of the time of the latter rain and the former rain falling together as seen and recorded by the prophet Joel.

Joel 2:28-29 (NKJV)

²⁸ *"And it shall come to pass afterward*
That I will pour out My Spirit on all flesh;
Your sons and your daughters shall prophesy,
Your old men shall dream dreams,
Your young men shall see visions.
²⁹ *And also on My menservants and on My maidservants*
I will pour out My Spirit in those days."

Once the latter and the former rains start, they won't stop.

The time of the latter and the former rains has the potential to become a time of the habitation of God's tangible Presence rather than a visitation - provided that we are prepared and equipped to run in the path of His commands with set-free hearts.

Psalm 119:32 (NIV)

I run in the path of Your commands
For You have set my heart free.

The Latter and the Former Rain Together

Joel 2:23 (NKJV)
Be glad then, you children of Zion,
and rejoice in the Lord your God;
For He has given you the former rain faithfully,
And He will cause the rain to come down for you –
The former rain, and the latter rain in the first month.

The rains that begin in the autumn in Israel are known as the *yoreh*, or the "early" (former) rains, since they signify the start of the rainy season. These early rains are reason to be glad after a hot, dry summer, and they will prepare ground so that it can be broken up ready to work the fields. Towards the springtime, around the time of Passover, Israel will have the latter rains, known as the *malkosh*, necessary for the ripening of the barley and grain.[6]

The latter rain that falls is much heavier than the former rain. It not only matures the crops that were planted in autumn, but the latter rain also allows for a second planting so that there are multiple harvests, and an overlap between the seasons of sowing and reaping.

Spiritually, the former and latter rains represent outpourings of the Holy Spirit, and most Bible scholars agree that the fulfilment of the former rain occurred on the Day of Pentecost when the 120 in the upper room were baptised in the Holy Spirit.

The fruit of that single Divine encounter was that through those 120 radically empowered people, the Gospel, accompanied with confirming signs and wonders, spread rapidly throughout the Mediterranean region.

That first outpouring literally turned the paradigms and established ways of the world upside down, as the disciples fearlessly went from place to place, filled to overflowing with the love and power of the Spirit.

The Scriptures tell us that they acted contrarily to the ways of the world and the decrees of the earthly rulers, and that they proclaimed the existence of *"another King – Jesus."*

Acts 17:6-7 (NKJV)
⁶ But when they did not find them,
they dragged Jason and some brethren
to the rulers of the city, crying out,

"These who have turned the world upside down
have come here too. ⁷ Jason has harboured them,
and these are all acting contrary to the decrees
of Caesar, saying there is another king - Jesus."

If we travel all the way back in time to the Garden of Eden, we can see that right through the Old Testament, well prior to the times of personal salvation or the outpouring of the former (spiritual) rain of the Holy Spirit, devout individuals experienced open Heaven visions, encounters with angels and the four living creatures, and even met with God Himself.

Below are just a few of the marvellous encounters that occurred. They were like a Divine planting of seeds of expectation for the generations that followed, giving us a deep hunger for our own personal Divine encounters, and for the coming spiritual revival that has been prophesied.

Moses

Exodus 33:9 (NKJV)
And it came to pass, when Moses entered the tabernacle,
that the pillar of cloud descended and stood at the door
of the tabernacle, and the Lord talked with Moses.

Enoch

Genesis 5:24 (NKJV)
And Enoch walked with God;
and he was not, for God took him.

King David

Acts 2:25 (NKJV)
For David says concerning Him:
"I foresaw the Lord always before my face,
For He is at my right hand, that I may not be shaken."

Psalm 17:15 (NKJV)
As for me, I will see Your face in righteousness;
I shall be satisfied when I awake in Your likeness.

Isaiah

Isaiah 6:1 (NKJV)
In the year that King Uzziah died,
I saw the Lord sitting on a throne, high and lifted up,
and the train of His robe filled the temple.

Ezekiel

Ezekiel 1:1 (NKJV) - *Ezekiel's Vision of God*
Now it came to pass in the thirtieth year,
in the fourth month, on the fifth day of the month,
as I was among the captives by the River Chebar,
that the heavens were opened and I saw visions of God.

Jesus in our Midst

John 1:14 (NASB)
And the Word became flesh, and dwelt among us,
and we saw His glory, glory as of the only begotten
from the Father, full of grace and truth.

If men and women who did not have the indwelling Spirit of God could have such powerful face-to-face encounters with Him, what then should we expect when the latter rain and the former rain fall together as prophesied in the book of Joel ?

We already have Christ living inside of us **(Galatians 2:20; Colossians 1:27)**. And we live in a time when the heavens have been opened above us, and for us **(Revelation 3:7-8, 20-21, 4:1-2)**.

We should expect a heavy outpouring – a spiritual *yoreh* and *malkosh* of God's Spirit.

We should expect wave after global wave of spiritual seedtime and bumper harvests of souls to occur simultaneously. We should expect everything that was experienced by the Old Testament believers in Yahweh in terms of supernatural experience to be multiplied in intensity, frequency, and distribution; and we should expect the unexpected.

> **1 Corinthians 2:9-10 (AMPC)**
> *⁹ But, on the contrary, as the Scripture says,*
> *What eye has not seen and ear has not heard*
> *and has not entered into the heart of man,*
> *[all that] God has prepared (made and keeps ready)*
> *for those who love Him [who hold Him in affectionate*
> *reverence, promptly obeying Him and gratefully*
> *recognizing the benefits He has bestowed].*
>
> *¹⁰ Yet to us God has unveiled and revealed them by*
> *and through His Spirit, for the [Holy] Spirit searches*
> *diligently, exploring and examining everything,*
> *even sounding the profound and bottomless things*
> *of God [the divine counsels and things hidden*
> *and beyond man's scrutiny].*

Not only that, but it is very likely that old and familiar Bible passages will be understood in brand new and fresh ways as we learn to receive from the LORD on new levels and also to operate under the anointing of the latter and the former rain together.

Remember **Matthew 13:51-52**. In **verse 51**, referring to His teaching through parables, Jesus asked, *"Have you understood everything that I've explained to you?"*

While the disciples answered *"yes"*, their understanding was limited by their experience of God and their paradigm (world view) that they had held up until they met Jesus.

How differently they must have understood the teachings of Jesus once they knew that He had risen from the dead - and once He had appeared to them in glorious risen form !

So it is for us. As the latter rain begins to fall with the former rain, we should expect our understanding of many of the Biblical passages – particularly the ones prophesying about the end times - to become extended and amplified.

This is because much of the Bible was written prophetically about the very times in which we live, and can only be fully understood through the lens of modern history, and also from within the context of increased manifestations of the glory of God.

We should be like the Bereans **(Acts 17:11)** searching the Scriptures for verification of the new and fresh ways in which the old and familiar will be revealed by the Holy Spirit; and then rejoice in the abundant fulfilment of the precious Word of the LORD.

Acts 17:10-11 (NKJV) - Ministering at Berea
[10] Then the brethren immediately sent Paul and Silas away by night to Berea. When they arrived, they went into the synagogue of the Jews.

[11] These were more fair-minded than those in Thessalonica, in that they received the word with all readiness, and searched the Scriptures daily to find out whether these things were so.

Heavenly Declarations

Right since the beginning of time, the angels and cherubim and seraphim and elders and living creatures and all the heavenly hosts have surrounded the Throne of God and declared His Glory and Majesty and Splendour and all His attributes. And they will do that forever **(Revelation 4 ff.)**.

Recently, during a deep time of prayer and worship. I was allowed just a little glimpse into that realm. It was glorious beyond description. And, it seemed as though the declarations of who God is were becoming louder, so loud that they were going to be discerned by the saints living on the earth who are attuned to the frequencies of Heaven through their continual seeking of Him through prayer and worship.

By "attuned to the frequencies of Heaven", I mean those who have developed the ability to see what God is doing and hear what He is saying in the Heavenly realms, which comes, over time, through making the conscious decision to continually abide with Him.

The progression of the antiphonal call and response of prayer and worship between Heaven and Earth, which is an integral part of the final and global harvest, is recorded in **Revelation 5** and is worthy of further study.

The rain is beginning to fall … Oh LORD, open our eyes to see, interpret, and apply with latter and former rain clarity, the fullness of all that you have for us during these exciting days !

God wants and needs His children to develop their relationship with Him to the point where they are spiritually positioned to receive all that He has planned for them to receive during the coming outpouring, which will be unlike anything this world has ever experienced.

Obadiah said that *"the day of the LORD is near for all nations"* **(Obadiah 1:15)**.

Surely, he was seeing our times when he penned those words.

I don't want to miss the mighty, end times outpouring. Do you ?

Jesus Standing in Our Midst

Hebrews 2:11-12 are remarkable verses. They state that Jesus – the Risen Christ- will declare His Father's Name to us, and then worship His Father from the midst of the congregation, as we worship Him.

> ### Hebrews 2:11-12 (AMP)
> [11] *Both Jesus who sanctifies and those who are sanctified [that is, spiritually transformed, made holy, and set apart for God's purpose] are all from one Father; for this reason He is not ashamed to call them brothers and sisters,*
>
> [12] *saying,*
> *"I will declare Your (the Father's) name to My brethren (believers), In the midst of the congregation I will sing Your praise."*

I had the privilege of ministering with Pastor Benny Hinn from the piano for a short season. One of the things that I loved the most about ministering with him is that Pastor Benny has a beautiful understanding of what I like to call the "**Hebrews 2:12** Moment" - that moment when the Risen Christ walks into a meeting.

Our beloved Jesus longs to stand right in the midst of His house, with His people, singing praises to His Father ...

We were in Jayapura, at the Saturday night meeting with 1.1 million people in attendance. (645,000 had attended the previous evening's crusade).

Suddenly, Jesus was there. The Glory of God swept down the mountain behind the platform, through the choir, through the worship leading team of four (Pastor Benny, another singer, and two of us on keyboards), over the platform, and into the crowd.

Well over 100,000 people were born again over the two nights, and countless people were miraculously healed as the Spirit of God fell.

Hebrews 2:12 moments are extraordinarily wonderful, incomparable, and glorious. Yet – it is a habitation of the LORD that the world so desperately needs. God help us to order our steps and to align ourselves with Your Heavenly timetable.

Understanding the difference between a visitation and a habitation of the LORD will influence our personal and corporate decision making.

When someone visits, they come and then they go.

When someone inhabits, they come – and they stay.

God does not want to simply visit us, or visit our once a week gatherings. He wants His Glory to fill us and overflow through us, filling the Earth and permeating every level of society.

> **Numbers 14:21 (AMP)**
> *... but indeed as I live, all the earth*
> *will be filled with the glory of the Lord.*

Abiding Permanently

I have heard people make the statement "we need a habitation of God, not a visitation."

And I have asked the LORD about why we have visitations rather than habitations of His Presence.

His answer was sobering. He said :- "If my people want Me to abide permanently with them, then they need to learn to abide permanently with Me.

The reason I only visit is because even though I long for their permanent abiding with me, even though I have opened a door for humanity to abide permanently with Me that no man can shut **(Revelation 3:7-8,20; Revelation 4:1)**, the majority of My people prefer to remain just casual visitors with Me."

Jesus declared the existence of the open door that no man could shut **(Revelation 3:7-8)**. He then told us that He was knocking at the door **(Revelation 3:20)**; and then He issued the command to pass through it and "come up here" **(Revelation 4:1)**. The open door is awaiting, the banqueting table has been set, and the King is saying *"come and dine with me"* **(Song of Solomon 2:4)**. Selah.

Revelation 3:7-8 (NKJV) - The Faithful Church
⁷ "And to the angel of the church in Philadelphia write,
'These things says He who is holy, He who is true,
"He who has the key of David, He who opens
and no one shuts, and shuts and no one opens":
⁸ "I know your works. See, I have set before you
an open door, and no one can shut it; for you have a little
strength, have kept My word, and have not denied My name."

Revelation 3:20 (NKJV)
Behold, I stand at the door and knock.
If anyone hears My voice and opens the door,
I will come in to him and dine with him, and he with Me.

Revelation 4:1-2 (NKJV) - The Throne Room of Heaven
¹ After these things I looked, and behold,
a door standing open in heaven.

And the first voice which I heard
was like a trumpet speaking with me, saying,
"Come up here, and I will show you things
which must take place after this."

² Immediately I was in the Spirit;
and behold, a throne set in heaven,
and One sat on the throne.

Song of Solomon 2:4 (AMPC)
He brought me to the banqueting house,
and his banner over me was love
[for love waved as a protecting and comforting banner
over my head when I was near him].

It Is Time

The clarion call is resounding in the Spirit realm.
God is calling His remnant to attention and to action.

At the beginning of 2020, we stepped into not just a new year, but a decade of unprecedented Heavenly blessings, Holy Spirit outpourings, and Divine encounters.

For the remnant - those who are spiritually hungry, thirsty, serious, and not satisfied with religious observance but instead are longing for deepening Divine relationship - and who are aligned and tuned into Heaven's frequencies, and listening intently, this is what God says :-

**"Days of reverential awe and wonder are coming to my remnant.
I will move as I have never moved before.
Prepare, my bride, prepare."**

Revelation 19:7 (TPT)
*Let us rejoice and exalt him and give him glory,
because the wedding celebration of the Lamb has come.
And his bride has made herself ready.*

Deuteronomy 4:32-36 (NKJV) *(emphasis mine)*
[32] *"Indeed, ask now about the former days that were
before you, from the day that God created man on the earth,
and ask from one end of the sky to the other.*
***Has there ever been such a great thing as this,
or has anything like it been heard?***

[33] *Has a people ever heard the voice of God speaking
from the midst of the fire, as you have heard - and lived?*
[34] *Or has any god ever tried to come to take for himself
a nation from within a nation - by trials, by signs
and wonders, and by war, and by a mighty hand and
an outstretched arm ,and by great terrors - like all that
Adonai your God did for you in Egypt before your eyes?*

[35] *You were shown, so that you might know that
Adonai is God - there is no other besides Him.*

*³⁶ From the heavens He made you hear His voice
to instruct you, and on earth He caused you to see
His great fire - you heard His words from the midst
of the fire. "*

**"Days of Open Heaven, days of Holy Fire, days of unprecedented
outpouring of the latter and the former rain together are coming.
Gather the oil jars - the hungry ones - and worship Me - your
Creator God - until I come."**

It is time for the Bride to prepare herself in earnest
for the coming habitation of the Bridegroom. Amen.

Genesis 1:1-2 (NKJV)
¹ In the beginning God created the heavens and the earth.

*² The earth was without form, and void;
and darkness was on the face of the deep.
And the Spirit of God
was hovering over the face of the waters.*

Joel 2:24 (NKJV)
*The threshing floors shall be full of wheat,
And the vats shall overflow with new wine and oil.*

Revelation 21:3 (NKJV)
*And I heard a loud voice from heaven saying,
"Behold, the tabernacle of God is with men,
and He will dwell with them, and they shall be His people.
God Himself will be with them and be their God. "*

Ephesians 5:27 (TPT)
*All that he does in us is designed
to make us a mature church for his pleasure,
until we become a source of praise to him
- glorious and radiant, beautiful and holy,
without fault or flaw.*

Chapter 06

Consecration

Joshua 3:5 (AMP)
Then Joshua said to the people,
"Sanctify yourselves [for His purpose],
for tomorrow the Lord will do wonders
(miracles) among you."

A few years ago, I had the great privilege of ministering in a fairly remote village in Papua New Guinea.

It wasn't the easiest place to reach. Getting there involved a three hour bumpy drive on roads filled with large and deep potholes and other hazards, another hour driving over rugged hills with deep, muddy ruts where the vehicle track used to be; and finally, a trip by motor canoe up a swollen, fast-flowing river, which was reached by clambering and sliding down a very steep and muddy river bank. It often rains at that exact moment !

The village meetings were attended by about 1,000 people over a five day period. The main meetings had up to around 500 people attending at one time.

There was a wonderful mix of people from denominations as diverse as Catholic, Seventh Day Adventist, Salvation Army, Assemblies of God, Uniting Church (called United church in PNG) and other Pentecostal and non-Pentecostal believers, as well as many who did not yet have a personal relationship with Christ.

The people came from many different villages, and some came from Port Moresby and beyond. There was a wonderful unity in the village and campsites, and because of the unity, God commanded powerful blessings in our midst.

We commenced on Wednesday evening and had a total of eight meetings through to Sunday morning. God had instructed me to lead the people on a journey of repentance and consecration up until Thursday night when **Joshua 3:5** became God's heart cry to His people.

On Thursday morning, I had taught on "Ephphatha" (Aramaic for "be opened") and the Spirit of God fell powerfully as people cried out to God for spiritually open hearts, spirits, eyes, and ears.

The Glory of God was there in the middle of the jungle ! Four people with heart conditions and a man paralysed down one side were healed on Thursday morning. The paralysed man had a face-to-face encounter with Jesus as he was being healed. The Presence of the LORD was very thick. Crowds were already in the hundreds and building.

The Spirit of God had moved powerfully right from the start of Wednesday night. But the Fire of God began to fall in earnest during the Thursday night meeting.

I declared what I saw and heard in the Spirit - that if we would all consecrate ourselves as per **Joshua 3:5**, then on Friday, Jesus would walk through the building and heal the sick.

It was a bold statement to make, and if I hadn't heard from the LORD, it would have been foolish at least or arrogant at worst to speak it out. Over the years I have learned to be obedient and I've also learned that when we obey, God honours our obedience. Being disobedient and not allowing the release of Divine blessing is not something that would be easy to live with.

After the meeting on Thursday night, people could be heard throughout the camp and the village, crying out to God and worshipping through the night until the sun rose on Friday morning. The fact that it was pouring rain all night did not hinder anyone from seeking God.

I walked around and saw people lying face down in the mud, soaked by the relentless downpour, and crying out to God in repentance – hungry, thirsty, desperate people knowing that they needed another level of consecration if they were to experience a deeper level of encounter with the Almighty.

On Friday morning during the worship, the Heavens opened and the sound of Heavenly worship was heard by everyone. It was stunning.

We experienced a "**Hebrews 2:12** moment" when Jesus walked into this meeting, and everyone knew it. It was an extraordinary time of face-to-face encounter with the LORD for many who were there.

There had been people with heart conditions healed on Thursday morning, and there were some more miracles on Friday morning; and also a man who came forward to give his life to Christ.

But God was holding back the floodgates, waiting for His people to rend the Heavens with their cries of repentance.

On Friday afternoon, it rained heavily for about three hours. I was wondering if the meetings would be washed out due to the flooding & the length and intensity of the storm - but the rain turned out to be prophetic for what God was about to do in the Spirit.

Friday evening arrived. This was the one. Jesus had said that He would walk through the building healing the sick if the people consecrated themselves. We experienced incredible worship with the Glory of God poured out in our midst, followed by a very intense and protracted spiritual battle with a few demon-possessed people being used by the enemy to try to distract from the glory of what God was doing. It was all happening.

After that battle had been won in the Spirit, about twenty five people came forward to give their lives to Jesus. And then, the miracles began. Ten deaf people were completely healed: eyes, hearts, kidneys, lungs, backs, arms, legs were all healed.

A man leapt up out of his wheelchair and began to walk and leap and praise God, and a mute man's tongue was loosed and he began to speak.

Many worshipped all through the night again after the Friday evening meeting, in gratitude for all that God had done...and there was much more to follow.

On Saturday morning, everyone was on fire and so expectant after all of the astounding miracles that they had witnessed on Friday night.

There were more Heavenly sounds released during the worship - angelic voices, and Heavenly trumpets. The Presence of God was overwhelming. There was a massive outpouring of Glory, and more miracles. I taught on supernatural discipleship and people streamed forward, wanting to have their spiritual eyes and ears opened so that they could be supernaturally activated to see what God was doing and hear what He was saying.

On Saturday evening, I spoke on "What is the Baptism of the Holy Spirit?" and "What is Salvation?." Around 150 people came forward to receive Jesus. After that, scores of people were baptised in the Holy Spirit, followed by more extraordinary miracles.

The lame walked, the deaf heard, damaged eyes were healed and opened, demon-possessed were set free and born again, and much more.

There were also some very powerful "meetings between meetings" involving pastors and leaders. Their hunger for more of God was so evident. There was a session held with the worship team that left them all weeping and crying out to God. The Spirit of the LORD was hovering over His people and stirring all the hungry hearts.

Glory, Glory, Glory to God !

There is so much more that could be said ... because each encounter, each miracle, has a ripple effect starting with the person who receives it, and then touching their families, their villages, their churches, their communities and beyond.

One week after returning to Australia, I spoke to the local pastor who confirmed that the Spirit of God has ignited the villages in the region. Hallelujah !

On Sunday morning after a final service where once again God moved powerfully, it was time to leave.

The people lined up along both sides of the river to say farewell, and they stood by the river bank, waving until our boat disappeared out of sight around a bend in the river.

> **Psalm 65:5-6 (TPT)**
> [5] *You answer our prayers with amazing wonders*
> *and with awe-inspiring displays of power.*
> *You are the righteous God who helps us like a Father.*
> *Everyone everywhere looks to you,*
> *for you are the Confidence of all the earth,*
> *even to the farthest islands of the sea.*
> [6] *What jaw-dropping, astounding power is yours!*
> *You are the Mountain-Maker who sets them all in place.*

The wonderful events described above should in no way be taken for granted.

However, I believe that they are very close to the "normal" benchmark that God seeks to establish for the 21st century ekklesia. Remember, we are called to be the "Greater Things Christians" of **John 14:12**.

Consecration was very much a part of everything that occurred during the meetings described above. But we also need to understand that consecration is not a one-time event.

I can guarantee that the ones who lay face down in the mud and the rain, crying out to God in repentance until sunrise, were not praying for the very first time in their lives; otherwise, their prayers would have ceased after five or ten minutes. Their actions clearly demonstrated how a desire to consecrate ourselves to the LORD will affect our desire to pray, and also the amount and the quality of time that we devote to our "alone time" with God.

God will respond when His people genuinely consecrate and humble themselves and pray and seek His face. He will not only meet with us and forgive us and walk amongst us; He will heal our land.

2 Chronicles 7:14-15 (AMP)
[14] ... and my people, who are called by My Name,
humble themselves, and pray and seek (crave, require
as a necessity) My face and turn from their wicked ways, then I
will hear [them] from heaven, and forgive their sin
and heal their land. [15] Now My eyes will be open and
My ears attentive to prayer offered in this place.

Consecration is best expressed through a life that is in step with the footsteps of God; through a heart that beats as one with His; and through a continual lifestyle of repentance, humility, and surrender. God will seek you out and draw near to you if you choose to live   this way.

Isaiah 66:1-2 (AMP) - Heaven Is God's Throne
[1]This is what the Lord says,
"Heaven is My throne and the earth is My footstool.
Where, then, is a house that you could build for Me?
And where will My resting place be?
[2] For all these things My hand has made,
So all these things came into being [by and for Me],"
declares the Lord.

"But to this one I will look [graciously], to him who
is humble and contrite in spirit, and who [reverently] trembles
at My word and honors My commands."

James 4:6-8 (NASB)
[6] But He gives a greater grace. Therefore it says,
"God is opposed to the proud, but gives grace
to the humble." [7] Submit therefore to God.
Resist the devil and he will flee from you.
[8] Draw near to God and He will draw near to you.
Cleanse your hands, you sinners;
and purify your hearts, you double-minded.

Consecration requires us to be ready and willing to be *"poured out as a drink offering"* if that is what God requires from us.

> **Philippians 2:17 (AMP)**
> *But even if I am being poured out as a drink offering*
> *on the sacrifice and service of your faith*
> *[for preaching the message of salvation],*
> *still I rejoice and share my joy with you all.*

Consecration must precede Divine visitation and Divine habitation.

The command and response is clear.

As we consecrate ourselves, God will respond **(see Joshua 3:5).**

His response to those who choose to consecrate themselves is beautiful; *He* will consecrate the *place* where you meet with Him – He will consecrate *you,* and He will *"come and dwell"* in our midst.

> **Exodus 29:44-45 (NKJV)**
> *[44] So I will consecrate the tabernacle of meeting and the altar.*
> *I will also consecrate both Aaron and his sons to minister*
> *to Me as priests. [45] I will dwell among the children of Israel*
> *and will be their God.*

When we sanctify ourselves and consecrate ourselves, God *will* pour out His Glory in unprecedented ways.

> **2 Chronicles 5:11-14 (AMP)**
> **- The Glory of God Fills the Temple** *(emphasis mine)*
> *[11] When the priests came out of the Holy Place*
> *(for all the priests who were present had sanctified themselves*
> *[separating themselves from everything unclean], without*
> *regard to their assigned divisions),*
>
> *[12] and all of the Levitical singers, Asaph, Heman, and Jeduthun,*
> *with their sons and relatives, clothed in fine linen, with*
> *cymbals, harps, and lyres were standing at the east end*
> *of the altar, and with them a hundred and twenty priests*
> *blowing trumpets [13] in unison when the trumpeters and singers*

were to make themselves heard with one voice
praising and thanking the Lord, and when they raised
their voices accompanied by the trumpets and cymbals
and [other] instruments of music, and when they praised
the Lord, saying,

"For He is good, for His mercy and lovingkindness
endure forever,"

then the house of the Lord was filled with a cloud,
[14] so that the priests could not remain standing to minister
because of the cloud; for the glory and brilliance
of the Lord filled the house of God.

The Presence and the Glory of God will find and fill empty, submitted, and surrendered hearts. In other words, God is looking for the heart that not only enjoys receiving from Him (a believer's heart) but also the heart that is sold out to following Him, that has counted the cost, and is willing to pay the price (the disciple's heart). (see **Philippians 3:7-14**)

John 3:30 (NKJV)
He must increase, but I must decrease.

Galatians 2:20 (NKJV)
I have been crucified with Christ; it is no longer
I who live, but Christ lives in me; and the life which
I now live in the flesh I live by faith in the Son of God,
who loved me and gave Himself for me.

Isaiah 50:5 (AMP)
The Lord God has opened My ear,
And I have not been rebellious
Nor have I turned back.

King David asked the question *"who may ascend into the hill of the LORD"* and *"stand in His Holy Place?"* and the response from the LORD is those with *"clean hands and pure hearts"* and one whose speech and actions reflect Godly integrity.

Psalm 24:3-4 (NASB)
[3] Who may ascend into the hill of the Lord?
And who may stand in His holy place?
[4] He who has clean hands and a pure heart,
Who has not lifted up his soul to falsehood
And has not sworn deceitfully.

I remember reading **Psalm 24:3-4** as a young Christian and thinking that I was doomed to never approach the Throne of Glory, until I realised that it was the direction of my hands (towards God in worship) and the intention of my heart (to please my Creator in all things) that God was most interested in.

God will orchestrate the continual testing our hearts, to reveal to us the areas that require further consecration to Him. If we recognise and humbly submit to His testing, the rewards will be great, both for ourselves and also for those whom we are called to serve.

Deuteronomy 8:2-5 (NASB) - God's Gracious Dealings
[2] "You shall remember all the way which the Lord your God
has led you in the wilderness these forty years, that He might
humble you, testing you, to know what was in your heart,
whether you would keep His commandments or not.

[3] He humbled you and let you be hungry, and fed you
with manna which you did not know, nor did your fathers know,
that He might make you understand that man
does not live by bread alone, but man lives by everything
that proceeds out of the mouth of the Lord.

[4] Your clothing did not wear out on you, nor did your foot swell
these forty years. [5] Thus you are to know in your heart that
the Lord your God was disciplining you just as a man
disciplines his son. "

It is our heart's intention and direction, much more than its perfection that draw the attention of the LORD to us. But God will perfect us if our heart's intention and direction are continually towards Him.

Let's set the GPS of our heart towards the Throne Room of Glory; and let us determine to consecrate ourselves, for God truly desires to work in us and through us, and to do great and mighty things in our midst for His glory.

Hebrews 4:16 (TLV)
Therefore let us draw near to the throne of grace
with boldness, so that we may receive mercy
and find grace for help in time of need.

Leviticus 20:7 (AMP)
You shall consecrate yourselves therefore,
and be holy; for I am the Lord your God.

Psalm 51:5-7, 10-11 (NASB)
⁵ Behold, I was brought forth in iniquity,
And in sin my mother conceived me.

⁶ Behold, You desire truth in the innermost being,
And in the hidden part You will make me know wisdom.

⁷ Purify me with hyssop, and I shall be clean;
Wash me, and I shall be whiter than snow.

¹⁰ Create in me a clean heart, O God,
And renew a steadfast spirit within me.

¹¹ Do not cast me away from Your presence
And do not take Your Holy Spirit from me.

Daniel 11:32 (NKJV)
Those who do wickedly against
the covenant he shall corrupt with flattery;
but the people who know their God
shall be strong, and carry out great exploits.

Chapter 07

Repentance, Forgiveness, Humility, and Unity

John 17:22-24 (NKJV)

22 "And the glory which You gave Me I have given them, that they may be one just as We are one: 23 I in them, and You in Me; that they may be made perfect in one, and that the world may know that You have sent Me, and have loved them as You have loved Me.

24 Father, I desire that they also whom You gave Me may be with Me where I am, that they may behold My glory which You have given Me; for You loved Me before the foundation of the world."

This is a relatively short chapter, with a very long title ! But the truths contained within it are absolutely foundational for the spiritual, mental, emotional, and even physical health of individuals, ekklesias, and networks of ekklesias. If we do not learn to walk in genuine repentance, forgiveness, humility, and unity, the foundations of every other area of our lives and ministries will to some extent be flawed, and our effectiveness for the Kingdom of God will be limited.

Recently, I visited a small village in Papua New Guinea, where we had planted an apostolic ministry centre and training hub earlier the same year, to conduct some meetings.

During our second day of meeting together, the tangible, visible Glory of God manifested and stayed with us for 48 hours – throughout all the meetings for the duration of the weekend – giving us a small but very glorious taste of what Divine habitation could be like.

I saw and heard things in the Spirit that I'd never seen or heard before in more than thirty years of ministry. In some of the photos taken during the meetings, the Shekinah Glory was clearly visible as balls of very bright light resting on or hovering over people, and sometimes as beams of light.

People came to the meetings from villages all over the district. Some came from much further afield and had travelled more than a day to be in attendance.

The blessing of **Psalm 133** that is directly connected to unity, was poured out in response to the coming together, in love, of leaders and members of the Catholics, Seventh Day Adventists, United Church, Salvation Army, Assemblies of God, and other Pentecostal and Evangelical believers.

The thick, tangible, visible Glory of God began to manifest after all of the pastors and leaders from the various denominations listed above were asked to pray for one another. God was releasing His commanded blessing in response to their willingness to demonstrate repentance and humility towards each other.

Many people came forward to give their lives to Christ. They bowed down without being asked to; the Presence of God had released an awestruck reverence in all of us. After receiving Jesus, most were slain in the spirit, and many began having face-to-face encounters with the Almighty, right there in the Glory. Many who had just been born again received the additional blessing of the Baptism of the Holy Spirit almost instantly.

There were many miracles that occurred, and others who after prayer entered into a process of healing. People were set free from demonic possession and oppression.

I will never forget the experience of standing in the midst of God's Glory, and of how easy it became to lead people to Jesus, then into the Baptism of the Holy Spirit, and then to receive miracles, when there was such a Holy and tangible Presence of God being manifested.

The King of Glory was there in all of His overwhelming beauty and majesty.

Throughout our time together over those few days, the Holy Spirit kept bringing us back to the themes of repentance, forgiveness, humility, and unity. And every time we explored them further, He would pour His Spirit out in even greater measure. Why? Because genuine expressions of repentance, forgiveness, humility, and unity are absolutely crucial elements that will precede any enduring move of God.

Jesus said :-

> **Matthew 5:23-24 (NKJV)**
> [23] *"Therefore if you bring your gift to the altar,*
> *and there remember that your brother has something*
> *against you,* [24] *leave your gift there before the altar,*
> *and go your way. First be reconciled to your brother,*
> *and then come and offer your gift."*

One of the major barriers to unity within the wider Body of Christ is the hardening of our hearts - that is, lack of humility - towards those who think or act differently than we do in matters of our Christian faith. Whereas, true humility by its very nature will give birth to lasting unity.

We want God to accept the gift of our consecrated hearts on the altar of holy sacrifice, so that He can send His holy fire on to that altar and consume us with His holy love.

Yet pride and unforgiveness, the polar opposites to humility and forgiveness, often create barriers that can hinder our prayers, rob our joy and our peace, and can lead to all kinds of "spiritual heart disease."

No one likes living in conflict, or having unresolved disputes.

If we would choose to love rather than to insist upon what we believe to be our "rights" (even what we may believe to be God-given rights) or on being "right", I believe that the move of God would already be here – and it would be unstoppable.

If in doubt as to what is right in terms of our own actions, we just need to check the Word of God, and repent of any wrong attitudes or actions that have hurt others and damaged our own souls. Having said that, we must, on the other hand, be extremely careful to never misuse God's Word to legalistically impose our position upon another person or group.

Let's be clear. Without repentance, asking someone else to pray for you to be delivered of a bad attitude will never change that bad attitude.

Repentance means "a change of mind" (Greek = **μετάνοια** (metanoia))[7], implying a completely new way of thinking, and therefore acting. Repentance is a genuine change in the inner person, and it is something that we must initiate and take responsibility for.

Repentance is necessary if we are to change our way of thinking about, and our actions towards, other individuals and groups.

Repentance leads to forgiveness and humility, and forgiveness and humility lead to unity.

Remember we are looking at Divine patterns for the end times ekklesia. There is a massive harvest of souls that is coming – there are literally *"multitudes in the valley of decision"* **(Joel 3:14)** on a scale that has never been seen from the beginning of time until now.

There are so many diverse people groups to win. Standing shoulder to shoulder and working together in love, is the only way to bring in the end times harvest net that will be literally bursting at the seams with souls. Humility and forgiveness will give birth to the agape love that needs to flow between us all.

Repentance, forgiveness, humility, and unity are inextricably linked.

A heart that Almighty God will choose to be consecrated for His purposes, consumed with holy fire and used as a vessel of revival in His hands, cannot be harbouring pride or unforgiveness, or be involved in critical judgement towards others.

The hour is late. We must put all of our offenses aside, nailing them to the Cross, and learn to celebrate rather than criticise our differences. Let's celebrate the foundational truths that we have in common, and reconcile at every level possible, for the sake of our nations.

That all sounds so wonderfully simple, and yet - we all know that unity isn't easy.

But take heart. Unity is more than possible. If we do our part (repent and humble ourselves) God promises to do His part, which is to command His blessing upon our unity, when we achieve it **(Psalm 133:1-3)**.

That means that God believes that we can do it !

We have seen the supernatural fruit of unity over and over again in many of our meetings in Papua New Guinea and other nations over a sustained period of time. In every case, the supernatural fruit flowed into the surrounding villages and regions. Even the tiniest taste of God's commanded blessing has been glorious almost beyond measure and, more importantly, has brought lasting change to many lives.

> **Romans 8:29-31 (NKJV)**
> *[28] And we know that all things work together for good to those who love God, to those who are the called according to His purpose. [29] For whom He foreknew, He also predestined to be conformed to the image of His Son, that He might be the firstborn among many brethren. [30] Moreover whom He predestined, these He also called; whom He called, these He also justified; and whom He justified, these He also glorified.*
>
> *[31] What then shall we say to these things ? If God is for us, who can be against us ?*

The preceding verses in **Romans 8** tell us that we are predestined to become like Jesus, conformed to His image, which at the very core means to become like Him in character.

The condition is that we allow "all things" - the circumstances of our lives - to work together to achieve the Christlikeness that God wants us to reflect. He particularly uses adversity, and situations that are uncomfortable or distasteful to us, to achieve that.

The Christlike choices that we make within those difficult scenarios will cause us to bow lower and lower before the LORD in poured-out worship, repentance, and humility - with powerful results.

There is a very sobering and frightening opposite to humility that is recorded in Scripture.

In the case of Pharaoh, because of pride, he intentionally hardened his heart so many times against God and His people that ultimately, the Scriptures record in **Exodus 11:10** that *God hardened Pharaoh's heart*, with catastrophic results.

> **Exodus 11:10 (NKJV)**
> *So Moses and Aaron did all these wonders*
> *before Pharaoh; and the Lord hardened Pharaoh's heart,*
> *and he did not let the children of Israel go out of his land.*

What a disastrous point of no return, for Pharaoh personally, and for the nations and people who were subjected to his rule and influence. His desperation to hang on to his personal empire eventually caused Pharaoh – and his empire - to fall permanently.

Our own motivations can, over time, slowly and almost imperceptibly drift from God-serving to self-serving if we are not spiritually vigilant and drawing daily from the fresh manna and oil of the LORD.

May we retain the soft hearts that replaced our old, stony hearts at the moment of salvation, so that God can continue to have His way in us at all times.

LORD, help us to repent of anything, particularly hardness of heart towards yourself or towards others, that would stop us from being able to fully consecrate ourselves to You, and to enter unreservedly, into Your Presence and Your end time purpose for our lives, our families, our ekklesias, our networks, and our nations.

Set us free from anything that would hinder unity or hold us back in any way from your glorious fullness; and please do not allow us, or those entrusted to our care, to arrive at the God-forsaken, barren place that Pharaoh did. We ask you for the heart-gifts of repentance, humility, forgiveness, and unity.

Hebrews 4:7 (NKJV)
... again He designates a certain day,
saying in David, "Today,"
after such a long time,
as it has been said:

"Today, if you will hear His voice,
Do not harden your hearts."

Proverbs 28:14 (NKJV)
Happy is the man
who is always reverent,
But he who hardens his heart
will fall into calamity.

Ephesians 5:21 (NIV)
Submit to one another
out of reverence for Christ.

Part 02

Restoration

Isaiah 2:2 (AMP)
Now it will come to pass that
In the last days the mountain of the house of the Lord
Will be [firmly] established as the highest of the mountains,
And will be exalted above the hills;
and all the nations will stream to it.

Chapter 08

Keeping Our Gates, Guarding Our Hearts

"Therefore, Guard Your Heart and Mind in Me"

It's difficult to put this encounter into words. I had been out all day in a quiet place, worshipping the LORD and listening as He spoke to me prophetically about various things.

I came home and was going to go to bed but instead was drawn to the living room.

As I crossed the threshold of the room, I was startled by a very loud Heavenly sound, which led to the following Heavenly encounter.

I heard them before I saw them. I heard the sound of metal on metal, swords being drawn, and the clash of armour. I looked up and was astounded to see huge warrior angels, at least thirty feet tall.

They stood at ground level, in a group of four. They were facing outwards, and the ankles of each touched the ankles of the one standing adjacent, so they formed a huge square, which I stood in the middle of.

Then there was another group of four, standing on the shoulders of the first, and so on. There were thousands upon thousands of them and they were facing outwards, looking north, east, south, and west and surrounding me in a battle formation.

They extended from the earth all the way up to Heaven, and up above them and all around them was the Glory of God.

The distance was immense, so much so that the topmost angels seemed tiny, even though I knew that they were huge.

They were so big that the square defined by their legs was at least twenty feet across.

They were brilliant and metallic and golden in appearance, because they were shining with the reflected, outpoured, Majestic Glory of the LORD.

I heard the sound of metal on metal as they drew their swords out of their sheaths and raised their shields in front of their chests. I was speechless. I could not speak for a long time.

I lifted my hands and worshipped God; then I dropped to my knees, and then I fell on my face.

Afterwards, I asked God, "LORD, what does this mean ?"

He replied :-

> *"These have been assigned, to protect your access*
> *to My Throne Room. Their protection cannot*
> *be breached from the outside - only from the inside.*
> *Therefore, guard your heart and mind in Me."*

This experience lasted from Saturday evening through to the following Sunday evening. I revisit this Heavenly encounter daily; and when I do, I can still see them, thousands upon thousands, facing north, east, south, and west, standing in tight formation, each directly above the other, stretching from the earth all the way up to the Throne Room.

This is the Established Open Heaven, a protected portal and an open door into the Realms of Glory.

I pray regularly for all the people whom I am called to love, and as I see them in the Spirit, I pick them up and place them under this established Open Heaven and ask God to bless and protect them, to teach them to guard their hearts and minds in Christ Jesus; so that the same Open Heaven may be established over their lives, and over the lives of those whom they are called to love. I pray that all the blessings of the Open Heaven will flow into them and through them.

I pray that once their personal gates are well kept, that they will in turn be vigilant to keep the gates of their families, villages, ekklesias, districts, provinces, cities, and nations.

On the day that I was led by the Holy Spirit to include the above testimony in this book, I prayed all of the above for everyone who would read it, and for all the beloveds within your sphere of influence to also receive the blessing that flows from it. Amen.

Psalm 91:4,11-12 (NIV)
[4] He will cover you with his feathers,
and under his wings you will find refuge;
his faithfulness will be your shield and rampart.
[11] For he will command his angels concerning you
to guard you in all your ways;
[12] they will lift you up in their hands,
so that you will not strike your foot against a stone.

Revelation 3:7b-8 (NKJV)
[7b] 'These things says He who is holy, He who is true,
"He who has the key of David, He who opens
and no one shuts, and shuts and no one opens":

[8] "I know your works. See, I have set before you an open door,
and no one can shut it; for you have a little strength,
have kept My word, and have not denied My name."

Revelation 4:1-5 (NKJV) - The Throne Room of Heaven

*¹ After these things I looked, and behold, a door
standing open in heaven. And the first voice which I heard was
like a trumpet speaking with me, saying,
"Come up here, and I will show you things
which must take place after this."*

*² Immediately I was in the Spirit; and behold,
a throne set in heaven, and One sat on the throne.
³ And He who sat there was like a jasper and a sardius stone in
appearance; and there was a rainbow around the throne, in
appearance like an emerald. ⁴ Around the throne
were twenty-four thrones, and on the thrones
I saw twenty-four elders sitting, clothed in white robes;
and they had crowns of gold on their heads.*

*⁵ And from the throne proceeded lightnings, thunderings,
and voices. Seven lamps of fire were burning before
the throne, which are the seven Spirits of God.*

Philippians 4:5-9 (NKJV)

*⁵ Let your gentleness be known to all men.
The Lord is at hand.*

*⁶ Be anxious for nothing, but in everything
by prayer and supplication, with thanksgiving,
let your requests be made known to God;
⁷ and the peace of God, which surpasses
all understanding, will guard your hearts
and minds through Christ Jesus.*

*⁸ Finally, brethren, whatever things are true,
whatever things are noble, whatever things are just,
whatever things are pure, whatever things are lovely, whatever
things are of good report, if there is
any virtue and if there is anything praiseworthy
- meditate on these things.*

Proverbs 4:23-27 (TPT)
²³ So above all, guard the affections of your heart,
for they affect all that you are.
Pay attention to the welfare of your innermost being,
for from there flows the wellspring of life.

²⁴ Avoid dishonest speech and pretentious words.
Be free from using perverse words no matter what!

Watch Where You're Going

²⁵ Set your gaze on the path before you.
With fixed purpose, looking straight ahead,
ignore life's distractions.

²⁶ Watch where you're going!
Stick to the path of truth,
and the road will be safe
and smooth before you.

²⁷ Don't allow yourself to be sidetracked
for even a moment or take the detour
that leads to darkness.

Keeping Our Personal Gates

There is not a single day that goes by where I do not remember the incredible experience documented above. It has shaped me and changed me forever. There was also a Divine empowerment that came from it. I noticed a significant increase in fruitfulness, in the number of souls and number and intensity of miracles, and increased glorious encounters during worship, individually and corporately, due to the wonderful blessings of the Open Heaven.

This encounter serves as a daily reminder and conviction in my heart, mind, spirit, and soul of just how crucial it is to keep our personal gates if we are going to live in the Glory, which empowers us to be effective (and also joyful) servants of our King.

The Bible says that *"the peace of God that passes all understanding"* will *"guard our hearts and our minds through Christ Jesus. "*

That peace will only be obtained, and then maintained, when we have learned to guard the gates of our hearts and minds, being extremely careful, as per **Proverbs 4:23-27**, about the things that we allow in, and how we allow our thoughts, mindsets, emotions, and priorities to be shaped.

Entering God's Gates

God invites us to enter His gates with thanksgiving and His courts with praise, and to enter the Holy of Holies with boldness. This is possible because the blood of Jesus opened the way for us. For the one with clean hands and a pure heart, who has learned to keep their own gates, the progression of intimacy, starting at the gates of the outer court, progressing to the inner court/Holy Place, and finally into the Holy of Holies (the place of face-to-face encounter with the LORD), is a joyful, powerful, and humbling journey.

Psalm 100:4 (NKJV)
Enter into His gates with thanksgiving,
And into His courts with praise.
Be thankful to Him, and bless His name.

Hebrews 4:16 (NKJV)
Let us therefore come boldly to the throne of grace,
that we may obtain mercy and find grace
to help in time of need.

Hebrews 10:19 (AMP) - A New and Living Way
Therefore, believers, since we have confidence
and full freedom to enter the Holy Place
[the place where God dwells]
by [means of] the blood of Jesus ...

Ephesians 2:18 (NKJV)
For through Him we both have access
by one Spirit to the Father.

Living Gateways of the LORD

The Bible also tells us that we are His living gateways, meaning that we are intended to be the receivers, carriers, and releasers of His Presence and His Glory. He longs to move powerfully in us and through us.

Psalm 24:-6-9 (TPT)
⁶ They will stand before God,
for they seek the pleasure of God's face,
the God of Jacob.

Pause in his presence

⁷ So wake up, you living gateways!
Lift up your heads, you ageless doors of destiny!
Welcome the King of Glory, for he is about
to come through you.

⁸ You ask, "Who is this Glory-King?"
The Lord, armed and ready for battle,
the Mighty One, invincible in every way!

⁹ So wake up, you living gateways, and rejoice!
Fling wide, you ageless doors of destiny!
Here he comes; the King of Glory is ready to come in.

The Upper Citadel

2 Samuel 5:6-10 (TLV) - Securing Jerusalem
⁶ Now the king and his soldiers marched to Jerusalem
against the Jebusites, the inhabitants of the region.

But they said to David, "You'll never get in here!
Even the blind and the lame could ward you off,"
thinking, "David can't get in here."

⁷ Nevertheless, David did capture the stronghold
of Zion (that is, the City of David).

*⁸ On that day David said, "Whoever would conquer the
Jebusites must strike through the water shaft to those 'lame and
blind' whom David's soul despises." That is why they used to
say, "The blind or lame couldn't get into the house."*

*⁹ So David occupied the stronghold and renamed it
the City of David. Then David fortified it all round
from the Millo inward. ¹⁰ David continued to grow
stronger, for Adonai Elohim-Tzva'ot was with him.*

1 Chronicles 11:4-9 (TLV)
*⁴ Then David and all Israel went to Jerusalem - that is
Jebus, where the Jebusite inhabitants of the land lived.
⁵ Now the residents of Jebus said to David, "You cannot
get in here!" Nevertheless David captured the stronghold
of Zion, which is now the city of David.*

*⁶ David had said, "Whoever strikes down the Jebusites
first will be commander-in-chief." So Joab son of Zeruiah went
up first, so he became commander. ⁷ David lived
in the stronghold; for this reason it is called the city of David.
⁸ He fortified the city all around, from the Millo
to the surrounding walls, and Joab repaired the rest
of the city. ⁹ David grew more and more powerful
because Adonai-Tzva'ot was with him.*

The Jebusites had become complacent, thinking that the upper citadel
of their city was impregnable, and that even *"the blind and lame"*
(2 Samuel 5:6) could defend it. And while it was seemingly unable
to be breached from the outside, it certainly could be breached from the
inside. Their complacency made them blind to the weakness in their
defenses. David saw that entry could indeed be made through the water
shaft, and Joab led the way.

The Jebusites also completely underestimated the cunning and
persistence of David and his men. They were 100 percent determined
to gain entrance and to capture the entire city, not just the lower reaches;
and so, they found a way where many had previously tried and failed
to do so.

We need to understand that the enemy is prowling around like a roaring lion **(1 Peter 5:8)** just looking for that one chink in the armour – the one weakness in our defenses - that will allow him to breach our walls, open our gates, and come inside so that he can occupy our "upper citadel" and wreak havoc in our souls, and in our nations.

It is easy to underestimate his schemes, and while our focus should be upon the LORD, we must not become the victims of complacency, which could lead to the failure to maintain our spiritual defenses in a state of constant readiness.

Once David and his men had conquered Jerusalem and occupied it, one of the first things that he proceeded to do was to fortify it. He recognized that if he and his men had been able to breach the defenses, sooner or later another enemy would appear who would be able to do the same thing. He did not rely on yesterday's victories, yesterday's strategies, yesterday's fortifications, or yesterday's prayers to keep the gates of his city.

David did not want to lose what he had gained – a city, a kingdom, and a dwelling place for his God **(Psalm 132:3-8** and called "resting place" in verse 8)**, something that he was passionate about and determined to achieve.

Psalm 132:3-8 (BSB)
³ "I will not enter my house
or get into my bed,
⁴ I will not give sleep to my eyes
or slumber to my eyelids,
⁵ until I find a place for the LORD,
a dwelling for the Mighty One of Jacob."

⁶ We heard that the ark was in Ephrathah;
we found it in the fields of Jaar.
⁷ Let us go to His dwelling place;
let us worship at His footstool.

⁸ Arise, O LORD, to Your resting place,
You and the ark of Your strength.

Many years later, during the spring season *"when kings march out to war"* **(2 Samuel 11:1)**, David chose not to march out to war, but instead decided to stay home.

He left his "soul gates" swinging wide open; and adultery entered in.

One sin led to another, and soon, all that he had worked so hard to build began to slip away.

God faithfully kept His generational promises that He had made to David's lineage, but David's own kingdom had been breached from the inside, and although he repented, things were never quite the same for him in terms of the peace and stability that had been established in partnership with the LORD.

We are the temple of the Holy Spirit **(1 Corinthians 6:19-20)**, and the ones with whom God seeks to dwell **(Isaiah 57:15, 66:1-2)**. We must keep our gates with reverent diligence.

> **1 Corinthians 6:19-20 (NKJV)**
> *¹⁹ Or do you not know that your body*
> *is the temple of the Holy Spirit who is in you,*
> *whom you have from God,*
> *and you are not your own?*
>
> *²⁰ For you were bought at a price;*
> *therefore glorify God in your body*
> *and in your spirit, which are God's.*

Strongholds

Psalm 59:17 (NASB)
O my strength, I will sing praises to You;
For God is my stronghold,
the God who shows me lovingkindness.

Psalm 94:22 (NASB)
But the Lord has been my stronghold,
And my God the rock of my refuge.

Psalm 144:2 (NASB)
My lovingkindness and my fortress,
My stronghold and my deliverer,
My shield and He in whom I take refuge,
Who subdues my people under me.

The LORD is our true stronghold, our fortress and our deliverer.

But, just as Joab found the way in and breached the upper citadel from the inside, so the enemy is seeking to do the same to us. He wants to keep us, and our nations, captive to his lies, and if we give him access to create strongholds in our minds where war can be waged against us **(2 Corinthians 10:3-6; Matthew 12:29)**, that is exactly what he will do.

2 Corinthians 10:3-6 (NKJV)
[3] For though we walk in the flesh,
we do not war according to the flesh.
[4] For the weapons of our warfare are not carnal
but mighty in God for pulling down strongholds,
[5] casting down arguments and every high thing
that exalts itself against the knowledge of God,
bringing every thought into captivity
to the obedience of Christ,
[6] and being ready to punish all disobedience
when your obedience is fulfilled.

Matthew 12:29 (NKJV)
*Or how can one enter a strong man's house
and plunder his goods, unless he first binds
the strong man? And then he will plunder his house.*

How strong is your spiritual house ?

How strong are your fortifications ?

How well do you keep your personal gates and those of your sphere of influence ? Let the strong man who seeks to destroy you be well bound and unable to breach your defenses, lest he come in and bind you and plunder your house. Let us be the ones who have so effectively strengthened ourselves in the LORD that He has become our wall of Holy fire with His Glory in our midst.

Zechariah 2:5 (AMP)
*For I,' declares the Lord,
'will be a wall of fire around her
[protecting her from enemies],
and I will be the glory in her midst.'"*

God-Appointed Gatekeepers

God searches the earth for those who will stand in the gap for the sake of the land **(Ezekiel 22:30)** and to act as gatekeepers - as intercessory agents of restoration and reconciliation **(Isaiah 58:12)**.

Ezekiel 22:30 (AMP)
*I searched for a man among them who would
build up the wall and stand in the gap before Me
for [the sake of] the land, that I would not destroy it,
but I found no one [not even one].*

Isaiah 58:12 (AMP)
*"And your people will rebuild the ancient ruins;
You will raise up and restore the age-old foundations
[of buildings that have been laid waste];
You will be called Repairer of the Breach,
Restorer of Streets with Dwellings.*

God is looking for a focused, equipped, Spirit-empowered remnant who are willing to pay the price, who will submit to the choosing processes of the LORD, and then arise and keep the gates and repair the broken walls of humanity.

These are the emerging remnant who have learned to walk in the kingly authority that is their birthright. The power of their prayers, decisions, decrees, and declarations will keep their personal gates, and also those of their spheres of influence. They will know which spiritual doors and gates have been opened and shut by the LORD **(Revelation 3:7-8)** and they will pray in alignment with that.

They will also discern other spiritual doors that have been opened and need to be shut, and they will win every spiritual battle that needs to be won. The decrees of these spiritual gatekeepers will be extremely powerful to enact spiritual shifts.

> **Job 22:28 (AMP)**
> *"You will also decide and decree a thing,*
> *and it will be established for you;*
> *And the light [of God's favour]*
> *will shine upon your ways."*

The following verse speaks of the gates of Jerusalem being rebuilt, re-hung, and re-consecrated to the LORD. The gates of our souls, families, flocks, ministries, Kingdom businesses, networks, and nations must be well kept, and consecrated to the LORD.

As it was for Jerusalem, in some cases they may need to be completely rebuilt, and then re-hung, and finally re-consecrated.

> **Nehemiah 3:1 (NKJV)**
> **- Rebuilding the Wall** *(emphasis mine)*
> *Then Eliashib the high priest rose up*
> *with his brethren the priests and built the Sheep Gate;*
> ***they consecrated it and hung its doors.***
> *They built as far as the Tower of the Hundred,*
> *and consecrated it, then as far as the Tower of Hananel.*

At a national level, I believe that keeping the gates of our nation should be the domain of the apostles, prophets, intercessors, and worshippers working closely together **(Ephesians 2:20; Psalm 68:24-25)**.

This clears the way for the pastors, teachers, evangelists, Kingdom economists, Kingdom entrepreneurs, and all those placed into leadership positions by God across every sphere of human influence (government, education, media and communications, economics, family, arts and entertainment, and spirituality) to fulfill their purpose unhindered by spiritual interference.

Seek the LORD and ask Him to identify the gates that He has assigned you to keep.

There is so much more that could be written on the subject of keeping our gates.

In the context of this book, it is simply necessary to emphasize and underscore the importance of keeping our gates at every level; of being continuously vigilant **(1 Peter 5:8)**; and of "patrolling and keeping" the boundaries of our personal metrons and of our nations **(Zechariah 1:7-11, 6:7)**.

The keeping of our spiritual gates is an essential Divine pattern that needs to be understood and activated by the nation-transforming, end times ekklesia. God will increase the revelation on this subject as we move further into the end times.

This is because the Divine strategies that enable the keeping of the gates of our metrons – from personal to national - will become ever more crucial to facilitate Kingdom advancement.

> **1 Peter 5:8 (NKJV)**
> *Be sober, be vigilant;*
> *because your adversary the devil*
> *walks about like a roaring lion,*
> *seeking whom he may devour.*

Zechariah 1:7-11 (AMP) - Patrol of the Earth

*⁷ On the twenty-fourth day of the eleventh month
(Feb 15, 519 b.c.), which is the month of Shebat,
in the second year of [the reign of] Darius,
the word of the Lord came to Zechariah the prophet,
the son of Berechiah, the son of Iddo, as follows:*

*⁸ In the night I saw [a vision] and behold,
a Man was riding on a red horse, and it stood
among the myrtle trees that were in the ravine;
and behind Him were horses: red, sorrel
(reddish-brown), and white.*

*⁹ Then I said, "O my lord, what are these?"
And the angel who was speaking with me said,
"I will show you what these are."*

*¹⁰ And the Man who stood among the myrtle trees
answered and said, "These are the ones whom
the Lord has sent to go throughout the earth and patrol it."*

*¹¹ And the men on the horses answered the Angel
of the Lord who stood among the myrtle trees and said,*

*"We have gone throughout the earth
[patrolling it] and behold, all the earth sits at rest
[in peace and free from war]."*

Zechariah 6:7 (AMP)

*When the strong horses went out,
they were eager to patrol the earth.
And the Lord said, "Go, patrol the earth."*

So they patrolled the earth [watching and protecting it].

Chapter 09

Day and Night, Night and Day

Day and Night, Night and Day
Let the Incense of our Prayers
Arise for the Nations
And
Let the Holy Fire of God
Burn in the Nations

Revelation 5:8 (AMP)
And when He had taken the scroll,
the four living creatures and the twenty-four elders
fell down before the Lamb (Christ),
each one holding a harp and golden bowls
full of fragrant incense,
which are the prayers of the saints (God's people).

Jeremiah 1:10 (AMP)
"See, I have appointed you this day
over the nations and over the kingdoms,
To uproot and break down,
to destroy and to overthrow,
To build and to plant."

**The only way to permanently
uproot and break down,
to overthrow and utterly destroy
the usurping principalities of darkness,
and to release the justice
and righteousness of Christ
throughout a nation,
is to light a permanent Holy Fire
of worship and intercession
that burns day and night
to the Glory of God.**

Leviticus 6:13 (AMP)
*The fire shall be burning continually on the altar;
it shall not [be allowed to] go out.*

Luke 18:7 (NASB)
*Now, will not God bring about justice for His elect
who cry to Him day and night,
and will He delay long over them?*

Jeremiah 32:27 (AMP)
*"Behold, I am the Lord, the God of all flesh;
is there anything too difficult for Me?"*

Jeremiah 1:10 speaks about nations, and the release of justice and righteousness throughout a nation. But national change starts at an individual level.

During my first twenty years as a missionary, God called and sent me to nations where Christians were persecuted because for their faith, and to places that were well off the beaten track - even for missionaries.

I remember many times where I would take out the map of a particular nation that He was calling me to, lay it out on the floor, lie down on top of it, spread my hands out, and just weep and begin to intercede for it. I'd start in the early evening and would often still be praying when the sun came up.

I'd been invited to one particular nation via a middle-of-the-night phone call. I said to the person inviting me, "Give me a few days to pray about it." I began to pray as soon as the phone call had finished.

After about an hour of prayer, the Heavens opened up, and in the vision that followed, I saw multitudes of people. They were extremely poor, hungry for food, and hungry for the truth, with their hands held up high above their heads, and they were weeping.

The Presence of the LORD overwhelmed me, and as I looked at the multitude, He simply said "Steve, I love them – will you go ?"

I dropped to the floor, weeping, and I lay in a pool of tears until the sun rose. I had my answer, and I sent a text message to the person who had invited me, saying, "Please send me the dates."

Day and night prayer opened doors into difficult nations and opened the Heavens above every meeting that we held, whether it was two of us praying together on a train, or a meeting with hundreds attending.

God answers earnest, fervent prayer. I know that day and night prayer was the reason that so many were saved, healed, delivered, and set free during those trips. Even during monsoon season with rain bucketing down, roads and towns flooded, and everything muddy and waterlogged, people would still somehow find a way to get themselves to the meetings, and into the poured-out Presence of God, expecting and receiving their miracles.

One particular meeting that was held in the middle of a flood, in a mud and thatch hut that somehow was not washed or blown away, became a place of encounter for everyone who was there. God sent His Glory and His Holy Fire into that place as soon as hands were laid on the first person. There were literal piles of bodies on the floor as people were powerfully touched by the LORD. Many had face-to- face encounters with Him in that heightened state of spiritual awareness.

And then, the miracles began. An 84 year old tribal man, who was hundreds of kilometers from home, was carried in to the meeting by some friends. He was deaf and lame. After prayer he was slain in the Spirit.

While he was on the floor, God opened his ears and healed his deafness. Then I took hold of his hands and said, "In Jesus' Name, get up and walk" – and he did. He jumped, he danced, he cried, he hugged me, he sang – he was happy !

In that same meeting, a man who'd had a stroke about fifteen years previously, and who was completely paralyzed on his right side, was able to walk and use his right hand after prayer. His right leg was shrivelled, and again after prayer, God grew it – He created brand new muscle and flesh instantly. At the end of the meeting, the man walked out of there unassisted, and he thanked me for what had happened by shaking my right hand with his right hand, which he had been unable to be use for fifteen years, until Jesus touched him.

God healed more who were lame, and more who were deaf. He healed heart conditions, serious back problems, everything that was wrong with people's arms and legs, and He healed tuberculosis. He healed fear, and He healed issues of blood. Scores gave their lives to Jesus, and scores were gloriously baptized in the Holy Spirit. The Holy Fire and Glory of God filled the atmosphere.

Suddenly it was 10pm – it was still pouring rain – flood waters surrounded the hut, and the mosquitoes came and joined the meeting. But I honestly cannot think of anywhere else that I would have rather been.

The next day we travelled to a remote rural location. We met in a mud and bamboo building, with a very high iron roof, beautiful mud floor, fantastic acoustics, and a congregation consisting at first of mostly women and children, although a lot of men arrived later - they'd been working in the fields.

A few hours later, all but a handful of people had been prayed for, and all but one had been 100 percent healed. Hearts, lungs, arms, legs, backs, stomachs, epilepsy, and cancer - people who had been afflicted for years, all met Christ the Healer that day.

There was a little girl who had been born deaf and dumb. Her big sister - about nine years old - had brought her to the meeting.

Both were barefoot and wore ragged dresses. I picked the little girl up and just held her, and prayed quietly for her. As I did that, God healed her. She'd never heard before, and then suddenly there she was in my arms, looking around with amazement as she experienced the wonder of sound for the first time in her life. Then, I touched her lips with my index finger, and she opened her mouth and began to speak !

Another young lady in her mid-20s had a painful brain tumor. It was grade 4, and it caused her so much pain she could not speak; she could only groan. She had little time left to live. After prayer, the swelling and the pain disappeared. She believed that she was 100 percent healed, and it was confirmed, two days later by the doctors at the hospital, that the tumour had completely disappeared.

There were hundreds of other miracles during that meeting, with many people receiving multiple miracles. All Glory to God.

> **Psalm 77:12-14 (NIV)**
> *12 I will consider all Your works*
> *and meditate on all Your mighty deeds."*
> *13 Your ways, God, are holy.*
> *What god is as great as our God?*
> *14 You are the God who performs miracles;*
> *You display Your power among the peoples.*

Sometimes, people would be too sick to come out to a meeting. On another occasion in a tribal area, there was a man named Daniel who was too sick to leave his bed. He'd suffered from various infirmities for many years. After teaching the group who were gathered there about the power of corporate prayer, I gathered everyone together and asked them to stretch out their hands as I prayed for Daniel over the phone. This all had to be done through a series of interpreters, and it was difficult at times. I commanded him to get out of his bed and walk in Jesus' Name.

Supernatural strength came into his body, and he got up and walked. This was the first time he'd been able to walk for three years. He was walking and jumping and weeping and giving thanks to God. Daniel also suffered from partial blindness, continual migraines, kidney stones, and angina, which caused severe chest pains and shortness of breath. Over the phone, God healed all of his conditions, one by one.

Hallelujah ! As you can probably imagine, Daniel became a very happy man. His sister, who was in the meeting with us acting as one of the interpreters, confirmed the next day after she met with him face to face that he was completely healed.

> **Acts 3:6-8 (NKJV)**
> *⁶ Then Peter said, "Silver and gold I do not have,*
> *but what I do have I give you:*
> *In the name of Jesus Christ of Nazareth, rise up and walk."*
> *⁷ And he took him by the right hand and lifted him up,*
> *and immediately his feet and ankle bones received strength.*
> *⁸ So he, leaping up, stood and walked and entered the temple*
> *with them - walking, leaping, and praising God.*

There have been hundreds of meetings that were just like the ones described above in terms of the Presence, Glory, and supernatural moving of the LORD. Through these experiences, I have learned and been reminded time and again of the power of day and night prayer to open the doors into nations, and to open Heavens within those nations. I have often spent three to four months in prayer and preparation for one trip of a few weeks' duration.

Christ is the Healer, and He is always ready to do "His part" – but we must also do "our part". We cannot do His, and He will not do ours. He is the King of Kings and LORD of LORDs. The kingdoms of the earth belong to Him, and He will pour out His Spirit and cover the Earth with His Glory as the waters cover the sea - but we must do "our part."

James 5:16-18 speaks of earnest, effective, and fervent prayers availing much.

> **James 5:16-18 (NKJV)**
> *¹⁶ Confess your trespasses to one another,*
> *and pray for one another, that you may be healed.*
> *The effective, fervent prayer of a righteous man avails much.*
> *¹⁷ Elijah was a man with a nature like ours, and he prayed*
> *earnestly that it would not rain; and it did not rain on the land*
> *for three years and six months. ¹⁸ And he prayed again, and the*
> *heaven gave rain, and the earth produced its fruit.*

Throughout the Gospels, Jesus shows us what earnest and fervent prayers look like; and then in **Hebrews 7:25** we see that even now, He *"always lives to make intercession for them (us)."*

> **Hebrews 7:25 (NKJV)**
> *Therefore He is also able to save to the uttermost*
> *those who come to God through Him,*
> *since He always lives to make intercession for them.*

National Prayer, National Change

When we speak of national change, we're speaking about much more than wonderful meetings as described above. But those powerful encounters with the LORD and the countless changed lives stand as testimonies both to the awesome love and power of our God, and they demonstrate what He will do in response to day and night prayer.

If God will open such wonderful doors, and do such great and mighty things in response to the day and night prayers of just one ordinary man, can we even begin to imagine what will He do when entire fellowships, networks, and nations are engaged in filling the golden bowls of Heaven with the incense of their day and night prayers **(Revelation 5:8)** ?

I believe that in the days that are coming, we will see an exponential increase in miracles at the individual level, at the corporate level, and at the national, governmental level - as God's people join together earnestly and fervently to seek Him day and night.

Will we be blessed if we do not engage in day and night prayer ?

To some extent, yes. But, will our nations be blessed and transformed and enter revival and reformation at every level if we do not engage in corporate 24/7 prayer ? I don't think so. National change will start at an individual level – with individual hearts committed to being set alight with the Holy Fire of the LORD, and to burn day and night for Him.

One of the major expressions of the Restoration of the Tabernacle of David is 24/7 prayer and worship that will ultimately release the Glory of God on a national level. This restoration is clearly connected with the end times harvest of souls.

Acts 15:15-17 (NKJV) *(emphasis mine)*
¹⁵ And with this the words of the prophets agree,
just as it is written:
¹⁶ 'After this I will return
And will rebuild the tabernacle of David,
which has fallen down;
I will rebuild its ruins, and I will set it up;
*¹⁷ **So that the rest of mankind may seek the Lord,***
Even all the Gentiles who are called by My name,
Says the Lord who does all these things.'

And again, Jesus tells us that it is day and night prayer that will release His justice **(Luke 8:17)**. So, day and night prayer would appear to be at the heart of both the end times harvest, and the end times transformation of nations.

Travail – Painful but Wonderful

The LORD experienced anguish in His soul as He bore the responsibility for our sins **(Isaiah 53:11)**.

The ekklesia is going through labour pains now before the coming of the Lord. Those labour pains are in part the travail and burdens and compassion of the LORD expressed through His people - intercession that is so deep it hurts. It is also the travail of God's people that will continue until the ekklesia becomes the Glorious Bride that Christ is returning for **(Galatians 4:19)**.

The creation is experiencing travail of its own, as it awaits the emergence of that mature and glorious Bride, and the redemption, healing, and deliverance that the LORD will bring through her **(Romans 8:19-22.26)**.

Isaiah 53:11 (AMP)
As a result of the anguish of His soul, He shall see it
and be satisfied; By His knowledge [of what He
has accomplished] the Righteous One, My Servant,
shall justify the many [making them righteous
- upright before God, in right standing with Him],
For He shall bear [the responsibility for] their sins.

Galatians 4:19 (AMP)
My little children, for whom I am again
in [the pains of] labor until Christ
is [completely and permanently] formed within you ...

Romans 8:18-22, 26 (NKJV)
[18] For I consider that the sufferings of this present time
are not worthy to be compared with the glory which
shall be revealed in us. [19] For the earnest expectation of the
creation eagerly waits for the revealing of the sons of God.

[20] For the creation was subjected to futility, not willingly,
but because of Him who subjected it in hope; [21] because
the creation itself also will be delivered from the bondage
of corruption into the glorious liberty of the children
of God. [22] For we know that the whole creation groans
and labors with birth pangs together until now.

[26] Likewise the Spirit also helps in our weaknesses.
For we do not know what we should pray for as we ought,
but the Spirit Himself makes intercession for us
with groanings which cannot be uttered.

The only way to permanently uproot and break down, to overthrow and utterly destroy the usurping principalities of darkness, and to release the justice and righteousness of Christ throughout a nation, is to light a permanent Holy Fire of worship and intercession that burns day and night to the Glory of God.

Chapter 10

Altars

There was a time almost thirty years ago when a pioneering Australian apostle laid hands upon me while I was living in Canberra (Australia's capital city) and said :-

> *"God is calling you to build an altar of sacrifice to Him. It is not a physical altar, but it is a time and a place when you will regularly meet with Him. And the LORD says that as you obediently do that, He is going to send Holy Fire down upon that altar, and that fire will be established in you and move through your life wherever you go.*
>
> *As you worship Him and minister His word in softness and simplicity, great power and great authority will be made manifest to the ends of the earth for His Glory.*
>
> *All that you need to do is keep the fire burning through your sacrifices of prayer, praise, and worship to your King."*

I am so grateful for that humble, mighty servant of the Living God, the word of God that he shared, and for the accompanying holy, burning Presence that left me trembling and shaking on the ground, where I stayed for a few hours encountering God with fiery intensity.

I had already established a prayer time and a prayer place in my life, but from that day onwards, something changed. I intensified my prayers and my seeking, and soon, there was a new level of anointing that began to manifest through my life and ministry.

Not long after that I was invited to be a part of revivalist Rodney Howard-Browne's worship team for a series of meetings that lasted for ten days and nights at the Brisbane Entertainment Centre, a venue holding around 10,000 people. The meetings were packed, the Presence of God was incredible, large numbers of people were born again, and there were many outstanding healing miracles, including scores of people healed from cancer.

Many people saw into the Heavens and experienced Divine encounters of every kind during those meetings. In some of the meetings, the Glory Cloud of God manifested overhead.

During those ten days and nights, I also began to realize just how much the sacrifice of prayer and worship had begun to open doors in my life that otherwise would have remained closed. God opened doors to citywide and global ministry, all of which was infused with His fiery Presence and often with signs and wonders and other supernatural fruit accompanying the outpouring of His Spirit.

I could tell you of literally hundreds of meetings in various nations where the only prayer that came out of my mouth was the word "fire" and miracle after miracle resulted from the anointing that God had promised to release, if I would only keep the fire burning in my own personal prayer and worship time.

It all began in the Secret Place, the place of encounter, on my knees and on my face at the sacred meeting place; at the altar of sacrificial praise, worship, and intercession.

Royal Priesthood, Holy Nation

The Bible tells us that we are royal priests, and a holy nation :-

> **1 Peter 2:9 (TLV)**
> *But you are a chosen people, a royal priesthood,*
> *a holy nation, a people for God's own possession,*
> *so that you may proclaim the praises of the One*
> *who called you out of darkness into His marvellous light.*

Scripture also encourages us not to neglect our priestly duties.

2 Chronicles 29:11 (TLV)
"My sons, now do not be negligent,
for Adonai has chosen you to stand before Him,
to serve Him, and to be His ministers
and to burn incense to Him."

In other words He has chosen us to minister to Him by standing before Him and burning incense to Him, which is symbolic of our heartfelt prayers rising to the Throne of God.

Revelation 5:8 (AMP)
And when He had taken the scroll, the four living creatures
and the twenty-four elders fell down before the Lamb (Christ),
each one holding a harp and golden bowls full of fragrant
incense, which are the prayers of the saints (God's people).

The four living creatures and the twenty four elders fall down before Jesus, the Lamb of God, with their offering in their hands.

What is their offering ?

Our prayers (the incense rising from the golden bowls), and our worship (golden harps). These are the only two things that originate from outside the realm of Heaven, that are offered before the Throne of Heaven. It is humbling, and also greatly empowering, to see our prayers and worship from the same perspective that our Creator does.

We are further instructed from God's Word that *"the fire on the altar"* should not be allowed to be extinguished. It is to be a continuous flame.

Leviticus 6:13 (AMP)
The fire shall be burning continually on the altar;
it shall not [be allowed to] go out.

Living Sacrifices

An altar is the spiritual place where we lay ourselves down as a living sacrifice to our Creator. There is usually fire associated with that sacrifice, and the fire consumes the sacrifice.

Our God is a consuming fire **(Hebrews 12:29)**, and He is the One who once more is shaking the Heavens and the Earth. The Bible tells us that only that which cannot be shaken shall remain.

Oh, how we need to fortify ourselves in the LORD, as individuals, families, ekklesias, communities, and nations. How we need to run in and surrender ourselves, as never before, at the altar of sacrificial prayer and worship, so that we can withstand the turbulence of the days in which we are living ! God says that He will shake the nations, but also that in the midst of the shaking He will fill the temple with His Glory.

But this is not a temple made with human hands.

We are His temple now ! **(1 Corinthians 6:19)**

> **Haggai 2:6-7 (NKJV)**
> *⁶ "For thus says the Lord of hosts:*
> *'Once more (it is a little while) I will shake heaven and earth,*
> *the sea and dry land; ⁷ and I will shake all nations,*
> *and they shall come to the Desire of All Nations,*
> *and I will fill this temple with glory,' says the Lord of hosts. "*

> **1 Corinthians 6:19 (NKJV)**
> *Or do you not know that your body*
> *is the temple of the Holy Spirit who is in you,*
> *whom you have from God, and you are not your own?*

> **Hebrews 12:26-29 (NKJV)** *(emphasis mine)*
> *²⁶ whose voice then shook the earth;*
> *but now He has promised, saying,*
> *"Yet once more I shake not only the earth,*
> *but also heaven. "*

²⁷ Now this, "Yet once more,"
indicates the removal of those things
that are being shaken, as of things that are made,
that the things which cannot
be shaken may remain.

²⁸ Therefore, since we are receiving a kingdom
which cannot be shaken, let us have grace,
by which we may serve God acceptably
with reverence and godly fear.

*²⁹ **For our God is a consuming fire.***

Heaven's Response

Heaven's response to the *continuous* prayers and worship
that John saw and recorded in **Revelation 5:8** is shown
in the verses that follow :-

Revelation 5:9-10 (NKJV) *(emphasis mine)*
*⁹ **And they sang a new song,** saying:*
"You are worthy to take the scroll,
And to open its seals;
For You were slain,
And have redeemed us to God by Your blood
Out of every tribe and tongue and people and nation,
*¹⁰ **And have made us kings and priests to our God;***
And we shall reign on the earth."

Kings and priests (rendered as *"kingdom of priests"* in other
translations) are intended to operate in the full delegated authority
of Heaven. And the Kingdom of Heaven is intended to manifest upon
the earth through God's people, the ekklesia, again with the full
delegated, or legislated, authority of Heaven.

As the fire of heaven comes down upon the altar of your devotions,
prepare yourself for the full manifestation of His glorious authority, and
for His fullness to flow in love through your life and through your
ekklesia.

The Altars that Need to be Torn Down

Since the earliest days of humanity, people have either worshipped their Creator, or they have worshipped other gods. Altars were built to both.

The altars and worship dedicated to other gods have opened the wrong doors for those who have invoked them; and have unleashed the wrong influences over our cities and our nations as a result.

This is why Christians are now in a position of having to take back the "mountains" or "spheres" of human culture.

The Bible is clear that there will be a time of great apostasy before the return of Jesus.

> ### 2 Thessalonians 2:3-4 (NASB)
> *[3] Let no one in any way deceive you,*
> *for it will not come unless the apostasy comes first,*
> *and the man of lawlessness is revealed, the son of destruction,*
> *[4] who opposes and exalts himself above*
> *every so-called god or object of worship,*
> *so that he takes his seat*
> *in the temple of God,*
> *displaying himself as being God.*

The apostasy is not only the falling away from Christianity of those who once believed.

The Greek word *apostasia*, from which the English word apostasy is derived, also means "defection" or "revolt." [8] The revolt manifests through the rising up through the worldly systems of those who do not believe, and an open rebellion against the ways of the LORD.

The root of this is the false worship of the enemy of the Creator, and all the associated principalities that masquerade as "gods" by taking over and attempting to legislate within the spheres of influence that should be ruled by God and His laws, through His people.

Psalm 94:20-23 (AMP)
*²⁰ Can a throne of destruction be allied with You,
one which frames and devises mischief by decree
[under the sacred name of law]?*

*²¹ They band themselves together against the life
of the righteous and condemn the innocent to death.*

*²² But the Lord has become my high tower and defense,
and my God the rock of my refuge.*

*²³ He has turned back their own wickedness upon them
and will destroy them by means of their own evil;
the LORD our God will wipe them out.*

Within many houses of parliament all over the world, ungodly laws are being passed in an attempt to enshrine in law the very things that undermine the values of the Kingdom of God. They are devising *"mischief by decree under the sacred name of law"* **(Verse 20)**.

The Psalmist prophetically saw the slaughter of innocent unborn children, the proliferation of unjust wars, and the acceleration of Christian persecution and martyrdom in our time.

"They band themselves together against the life of the righteous and condemn the innocent to death." **(Psalm 94:21).**

The Altar that Needs to be Raised Up

As stated in Chapter 09, I believe that the essential foundation for not just slowing, but completely uprooting and utterly destroying the principalities and powers behind such evil, is by aligning ourselves with the plans of the Almighty, and of the hosts of heaven under His command, through strategic, specifically targeted 24/7 intercession and worship. These are the God-ordained activities that release His Glory.

Day and night, night and day, our role and our privilege is to fill the golden bowls with incense that releases the mercy and justice of the Most High.

As Christ lives to continually intercede for us **(Hebrews 7:25)**, so must we build the fire upon our altars of meeting until they burn continually before Him.

> **Hebrews 7:25 (NASB)**
> *Therefore He is able also to save forever*
> *those who draw near to God through Him,*
> *since He always lives to make intercession for them.*

The Old Testament altars built to God were symbolic of the spiritual fire that becomes available to us as we present ourselves as a living sacrifice to the LORD, just as the altars built to false gods were symbolic of all that needs to be uprooted and demolished by God's people in the realm of the Spirit to clear the way for the restoration of all things.

To raise up an altar of sacrifice that will be pleasing to God, we must be willing to bow very low before Him, and to lay everything down at the foot of the Cross and present ourselves as living sacrifices to Him. This is true, *"latreia"* worship; our lives poured out in sacrificial service, for the Glory of God **(Romans 12:2)**.

There is a holy fire with which He wants to ignite His bride to make her glorious; a cleansing fire that will purify us as individuals and as an ekklesia.

For us to reach that point, we must understand and acknowledge our nakedness, our wretchedness, our blindness, and our poverty. There is always a deeper level of surrender that God is requiring from His people; and there is gold that is only available from the midst of the holy, purifying burning.

> **Zechariah 13:9 (AMP)**
> *"And I will bring the third part through the fire,*
> *Refine them as silver is refined,*
> *And test them as gold is tested.*
> *They will call on My name,*
> *and I will listen and answer them;*
> *I will say, 'They are My people,'*
> *And they will say, 'The Lord is my God.'"*

1 Peter 1:6-7(NASB)
⁶ In this you greatly rejoice,
even though now for a little while, if necessary,
you have been distressed by various trials,
⁷ so that the proof of your faith,
being more precious than gold which is perishable,
even though tested by fire, may be found to result
in praise and glory and honor
at the revelation of Jesus Christ.

Revelation 3:17-18 (NASB)
¹⁷ Because you say, "I am rich, and have become wealthy,
and have need of nothing," and you do not know that you
are wretched and miserable and poor and blind and naked,

¹⁸ I advise you to buy from Me gold refined by fire so that
you may become rich, and white garments so that you may
clothe yourself, and that the shame of your nakedness
will not be revealed; and eye salve to anoint your eyes
so that you may see."

1 Corinthians 3:11-13 (NASB)
¹¹ For no man can lay a foundation other than the one
which is laid, which is Jesus Christ.

¹² Now if any man builds on the foundation with gold,
silver, precious stones, wood, hay, straw, ¹³ each man's work
will become evident; for the day will show it because it is
to be revealed with fire, and the fire itself will test the quality
of each man's work.

Revelation 1:5b-6 (NKJV)
⁵ᵇ To Him who loved us and washed us from our sins
in His own blood, ⁶ and has made us kings and priests
to His God and Father, to Him be glory and dominion
forever and ever.

Amen.

Is your heart ready to receive
the holy, cleansing, burning, purifying
Fire of God ?

He is waiting for you,
at the altar of your sacrificial
prayer, praise, and worship.

Run to meet Him there.

"Sanctuary"

Behold a door
standing open in Heaven
We see the King of Glory there
LORD, I'm on my way
And when I meet You there

I will worship You
in Spirit and Truth
In the sanctuary
of Your holiness

At the cross
my Saviour is waiting
His grace and mercy draw me there
LORD, You paid the price
You gave Your life

So I present myself
A living sacrifice
And I will praise
and glorify You with my life

Jesus, my Saviour
You're my Oil of Joy, my King
You are my Everything [9]

Chapter 11

Restoring and Maintaining Spiritual Foundations

Psalm 11:1-4 (AMP) - The Lord a Refuge and Defense
¹ In the Lord I take refuge [and put my trust];
How can you say to me,
"Flee like a bird to your mountain;

² For look, the wicked are bending the bow;
They take aim with their arrow on the string
To shoot [by stealth] in darkness at the upright in heart.

³ "If the foundations [of a godly society] are destroyed,
what can the righteous do?"

⁴ The Lord is in His holy temple;
the Lord's throne is in heaven.
His eyes see, His eyelids test the children of men.

It is instructive to briefly review the rise and fall of the kingdoms of Israel and Judah, to help us understand the need to rebuild, restore, and maintain spiritual foundations in our time, so that our nations can be reclaimed for the Glory of God.

The Promised Land

God led the Israelites, through Joshua, to conquer the land of Canaan, which He had earlier promised to Abraham's descendants **(Genesis 15:18-21).** [10]

With the priests leading the way and carrying the Ark of the Covenant, God miraculously stopped the flow of the River Jordan, and the people crossed over into the Promised Land. **(Joshua 3:17).**

While the land was given to them unconditionally **(Genesis 15:16-18),** the promise of God's continued blessing upon them depended on their continued obedience to Him **(Deut. 6:10-19; 8:1-20; 28:1-26).**[11]

The conquest of Canaan over a seven-year period cleared the way for the twelve tribes of Israel to settle in the Promised Land. Joshua divided the land between the tribes and designated cities to the Levites.

Incomplete Conquest

However, the conquest was incomplete. God had told Joshua that He would cast out *"seven nations greater and mightier than you,"* and that when He did so, the Israelites were to *"conquer them and utterly destroy them; make no covenant with them, nor show mercy to them."*

Nor were they to intermarry with them.

> ### Deuteronomy 7:1-3 (NKJV)
> [1] *"When the Lord your God brings you into the land which you go to possess, and has cast out many nations before you, the Hittites and the Girgashites and the Amorites and the Canaanites and the Perizzites and the Hivites and the Jebusites, seven nations greater and mightier than you, [2] and when the Lord your God delivers them over to you, you shall conquer them and utterly destroy them. You shall make no covenant with them nor show mercy to them. [3] Nor shall you make marriages with them. You shall not give your daughter to their son, nor take their daughter for your son."*

Each of the nations listed in **Deuteronomy 7** represented not just physical people groups, but also spiritual principalities that God required His people to remove from the land that He had promised to them.

Next came the era of the judges. This was an unsettled time, and led to the people's desire to have their own king to rule over them "like all the nations" **(1 Samuel 8:4-5)**. Reluctantly, God gave them what they wanted and Saul was appointed king of Israel.

Saul was disobedient to God early on in his reign, and the prophet Samuel told him that his kingdom would not continue.

> **1 Samuel 13:14 (NKJV)**
> *"But now your kingdom shall not continue.*
> *The Lord has sought for Himself a man after His own heart,*
> *and the Lord has commanded him to be commander*
> *over His people, because you have not kept what*
> *the Lord commanded you."*

Jerusalem

While many cities were taken over (and sometimes destroyed) as part of the conquest of Canaan, the city of Jerusalem was never fully wrested from Jebusite control.

Judges 1:8 recounts that the lower city of Jerusalem was *"taken, struck with the edge of the sword, and set on fire."* But **Judges 1:21** and **Judges 15:63** show that neither the children of Benjamin nor the children of Judah were able to remove the Jebusites from Jerusalem.

The upper city, the citadel or fortress of Zion, remained in Jebusite hands for over 400 years, until the time of King David. Interestingly, the Hebrew root of the name "Jebusite" means "to tread down or trample, desecrate, subjugate, cause ruin or downfall." [12]

> **Judges 1:21 (NKJV)**
> *But the children of Benjamin did not drive out*
> *the Jebusites who inhabited Jerusalem; so the Jebusites*
> *dwell with the children of Benjamin in Jerusalem to this day.*

Joshua 15:63 (NKJV)
As for the Jebusites, the inhabitants of Jerusalem,
the children of Judah could not drive them out;
but the Jebusites dwell with the children of Judah
at Jerusalem to this day.

One of David's first acts as king was to conquer the entire city of Jerusalem. After the conquest, the city's defenses were fortified by King David and Joab, his commander, and it became known as "The City of David" **(2 Samuel 5:9; 1 Chronicles 11:7)**.

Jerusalem became the political capital of Israel. But King David knew that physical conquest was not enough to build and establish a kingdom.

He had been a worshipper of God since his youth, and in his heart, he knew that the new political capital needed to also become the spiritual heart of the nation.

The large hill to the north of the newly captured Jerusalem was none other than Mount Moriah, where Abraham had offered Isaac as a sacrifice to the LORD; and where God had shown Abraham that his descendants would become a mighty nation **(Genesis 22:1-18)**.

The future spiritual heart of the kingdom was established by the declarations of the Almighty in that place, and by the worshipful obedience of His servant Abraham.

However, at the time of King David, it was being used as a threshing floor by Aranuah the Jebusite **(2 Samuel 24:24; 1 Chronicles 21:25)**.

David purchased it from him.

This is the most likely place where he set up the tabernacle that housed the Ark of the Covenant **(1 Chronicles 15:3)**. Mount Moriah later became the site of the temple that King Solomon built.

Establishing the Kingdom

After conquering the city of Jerusalem, fortifying it, securing the land that was the spiritual heart of the nation, and bringing back the Ark of the Covenant – the holiest of holy furnishings from the Tabernacle of Moses where the Presence of the LORD dwelled between the cherubim **(Psalm 80:1)** – David wasted no time in implementing continuous 24/7 praise and worship in the nation's capital.

During the next ten years he subdued the Philistines to the west, the Moabites to the east, the Syrians to the northeast, the Edomites to the south, and the Ammonites. **(2 Samuel 8:1-3, 23:20, 8:14, 10ff., 12:26-31).**

While King David was by no means perfect, God's own testimony of him was that he was a man after God's own heart **(Acts 13:22)**. He certainly did understand how to establish and maintain spiritual foundations, and the people enjoyed the peace, success, prosperity, and stability that this brought to the nation while it was under his leadership **(2 Samuel 8 ff.)**.

The Fall and Division of Israel

After the death of King Solomon, and due in large part to his disobedience to God, particularly in the area of re-introducing idol worship, Israel became a kingdom divided both physically (into Israel and Judah), and also from within **(1 Kings 9: 6-7; 1 Kings 11:7-13; 1 Kings 12:16-33).**

During the time of the two kingdoms, we read over and over in Scripture that a king of Israel or Judah rose to power but they did not address the issue of idol worship, or worse still, promoted it or engaged in it themselves **(1 Kings 14:23-24; 1 Kings 15:26; 1 Kings 16:30-33; 2 Kings 8:18,27, 11:18; 2 Kings 21:2-16; 2 Chronicles 33:2-10).**

In other words, the kingdom (little "k") may have been founded in name, but the demonic principalities were never completely defeated, and so the earthly kingdom could never be properly established or maintained according to Kingdom principles.

Eventually, Israel and Judah fell because of persistent disobedience and participation in idol worship, and the people were taken into captivity for 70 years. **(2 Kings 17ff., 2 Kings 24ff.)**

Restoration

Ezra 1:1-4 records a remarkable event. God stirred up the spirit (heart in some translations) of Cyrus King of Persia, to commence the restoration of the house of God in Jerusalem. Cyrus even directed the non-Jewish people to assist with the restoration.

> **Ezra 1:1-4 (AMP) - Proclamation of Cyrus**
> *[1] Now in the first year of Cyrus king of Persia*
> *[that is, the first year he ruled Babylon], in order to fulfil*
> *the word of the Lord by the mouth of Jeremiah [the prophet],*
> *the Lord stirred up (put in motion) the spirit of Cyrus*
> *king of Persia, so that he sent a proclamation throughout*
> *all his kingdom, and also put it in writing, saying:*
>
> *[2] "Thus says Cyrus king of Persia, 'The Lord, the God*
> *of heaven, has given me all the kingdoms of the earth*
> *and He has appointed me to build Him a house at Jerusalem,*
> *which is in Judah. [3] Whoever there is among you of all*
> *His people, may his God be with him!*
>
> *Let him go up to Jerusalem, which is in Judah and rebuild*
> *the house of the Lord, the God of Israel; He is God who*
> *is in Jerusalem. [4] In any place where a survivor (Jewish exile)*
> *may live, let the men (Gentiles) of that place support him*
> *with silver and gold, with goods and cattle, together*
> *with freewill offerings for the house of God in Jerusalem.'"*

Ezra the scribe and Nehemiah, mighty men of God with hearts burning for the restoration of their people, oversaw the entire rebuilding process.

Their priorities were firstly to restore the place and the practice of worship, then to rebuild the city of Jerusalem, and finally, to restore and rebuild the people **(Ezra ff,; Nehemiah ff.).**

21st Century Application

As we have seen, in Old Testament times, the kings were given spiritual and governmental authority by God to rule and reign over His people. God also raised up prophets to assist the kings in the spiritual co-governance of God's people. David's prophetic contemporary, and the one who anointed him as king, was Samuel (and later in his life the prophet Nathan spoke the words of the LORD to him when he needed correction).

The kings who listened to, and were obedient to the LORD and to His prophets, were used mightily of the LORD as instruments of revival and restoration.

In our day, fivefold ministers who are hearing clearly from the LORD have a vital and strategic role to play in the spiritual co-governance of our nations, by speaking into the lives of our nation's leaders.

We are living in a time where most of the nations of the world are subject to governments that are morally, ethically, spiritually, and economically compromised, with national foundations that either require repair or in some cases, complete rebuilding.

In that sense, prophetically, our time is similar to the time of Ezra and Nehemiah, and Kingdom reformers are urgently needed to step up with blueprints for spiritual, governmental, economic, educational, and social transformation.

There are nations where the leaders are openly hostile to Christianity, and persecution of Christians is on the rise. However, in many others, God is installing presidents and prime ministers who are either believers or at least open to Christianity.

Within those nations, God is often installing His leaders in pairs, for example President and Vice President; or Prime Minister and Deputy Prime Minister.

The appointment of one, or even better, two God-fearing individuals to the two top political positions within any nation in modern times signals a Divine intention and a Divine opportunity for Kingdom transformation and Heavenly alignment within that nation, and with obvious opportunities and open doors for the nation's ekklesia to work in harmony with like-minded, like-hearted, and like-spirited political leaders.

However, it is one thing to have God-fearing people elected to the highest political offices in the land, but quite another for them to be able to function with their intended effectiveness.

Every Godly leader will want to overturn the liberal agendas that oppose the Presence and precepts, the will and Word of God. And they will be passionate to work towards removing long-standing issues such as generationally entrenched poverty and corruption; but they cannot work or stand alone.

On the one hand, the leaders need the apostles, prophets, and teachers/reformers to arise and stand with them to help them establish the spiritual and practical foundations for reformation. Part of this process should involve government leaders being mentored into a full understanding of their spiritual roles and then set apart for increase just as Paul and Barnabas were in **Acts 13:1-2**, so that their supernatural mantles for national governance are fully activated.

And on the other, God's appointed leaders need the ekklesia to strategically partner with them in spiritual co-governance through 24/7, Holy Spirit directed, specifically targeted intercession and spiritual warfare.

Maintaining the Victory

Many mighty servants of God have applied spiritual solutions within their nations that have been successful in removing the "heads and tails" of persistent demonic influences for a time.

Yet the same problems continue to exist and continue to arise in many of those nations, and in some cases even to worsen. A **"Judges 1:8 victory"** has been achieved where the "city" has been partly captured, but the influences that cause serious issues within the nation remain firmly entrenched and protected within the "upper citadel".

Until the heart of the matter is uncovered and permanently addressed in the Spirit, the "heads and tails" will continue to grow back and to exert unholy influence.

The key word is "permanently". King David understood that after his initial military victories, he needed to establish 24/7 prayer and worship to ensure that his nation remained aligned with the plans and purposes of God, and also protected by Him.

The ancient demonic principalities that have taken hold in many nations since ancient times must be permanently disarmed and restrained; and every tie to them must be severed.

Otherwise, whatever we build at a governmental level within a nation will continue to be torn down even during the current term of Godly leadership, at the next election, or by the next generation.

Wrong spiritual foundations in every sphere of influence within a nation will continue to be established and will continue to wield their corrupt influence.

I know of nations and provinces where the entire parliamentary complexes have been dedicated as "chambers of sorcery" rather than as chambers of democracy; so that demonic influences would control decisions made by the government, rather than the prayers of God's people expressed and outworked through the election of Godly leaders, and the implementation of Godly, fair, and just governmental systems and processes.

Within those nations, this has allowed corruption of every kind to become firmly and insidiously entrenched within every sphere of society. Officials who are the channels of corruption and every other evil influence continue to be elected, re-elected, and re-elected.

This is real – and this in turn has allowed relational, spiritual, material, and motivational poverty to proliferate. [13]

As It Is In Heaven

Everything that happens in the earthly realm is a reflection of the prevailing conditions in the spiritual realm over and within a nation.

And it is our responsibility as ambassadors of Christ to ensure that the prevailing spiritual atmosphere over our nation is influenced by the incense of our prayers overflowing from the golden bowls of incense that are continually being presented to the King of Kings **(Revelation 5:8)**.

As stated in the previous chapter, I believe that continuous night and day prayer is one of the major keys that will lay the foundations for spiritual reformation and national transformation of a nation from grassroots to government.

In response to day and night prayer, God will permanently uproot and break down, overthrow and utterly destroy the usurping principalities of darkness. He will release the justice and righteousness of Christ throughout a nation, as the continuous, day and night incense arises from His unified, clothed-in-white, anointed bride.

> **Luke 18:7 (BSB)**
> *Will not God bring about justice for His elect*
> *who cry out to Him day and night?*
> *Will He continue to defer their help?*

As a result, those usurping principalities will be not only destroyed in the present, but also restrained from exerting influence in the future.

We must become a people who are *always* clothed in white - continually activating the righteousness of Christ in love within our spheres of influence through day and night prayer and acts of humility, mercy, and justice - and *always* accessing the fresh anointing oil of Heaven through continual prayer and worship.

> **Ecclesiastes 9:8 (NIV)**
> *Always be clothed in white,*
> *and always anoint your head with oil.*

Micah 6:8 (AMPC)
He has showed you, O man, what is good.
And what does the Lord require of you
but to do justly,
and to love kindness and mercy,
and to humble yourself
and walk humbly with your God?

Our prayerful sacrifices and pursuit of Biblical mercy and justice must be consistent and continual if we are to silence a relentless enemy who is intent on derailing the destinies of entire nations and destroying the individual futures of God's children.

Luke 18:2 (AMP)
Now Jesus was telling the disciples a parable
to make the point that at all times they ought
to pray and not give up and lose heart ...

The Increase of Glory

We know that Bible predicts both the rise of evil, but also the increase of Glory in the last days **(2 Timothy 3:1-4; Habakkuk 2:14)**.

The increase of Glory is where our primary focus should be.

At the time of writing, 24/7 prayer has been on the rise globally for about twenty five years, to the point where it is rising from almost every time zone. We are beginning to see the fruit of this, with stirrings of revival, and the large numbers of Christian leaders being placed into positions of leadership within the nations of the world.

If Godly leaders have been given positions of authority within our nation, the ekklesia needs to understand the nature of the opportunity that has been presented to it, and act upon that opportunity.

If they haven't been appointed yet, let's stand in the gap in fervent intercession until they are.

May we embrace the strategy of heaven to carry and release the greater Glory, through our dedicated intercession and worship, and then the restoration of our nations according to Kingdom principles for the benefit of all, until the LORD returns.

Now is the time for the global ekklesia to arise in unity, until 24/7 prayer is restored so that the golden bowls around the Throne of God are continually filled to overflowing with the fragrant incense of our prayers.

As we do so, the foundations for God's Kingdom to come and His will to be done on Earth as it is in Heaven will be established and maintained for His Glory.

> **Leviticus 6:13 (NLT)** *(emphasis mine)*
> ***Remember,*** *the fire must be kept burning on the altar at all times. It must **never** go out.*

> **Leviticus 6:13 (EXB)**
> *The fire must be kept burning on the altar · all the time [perpetually]; it must not ·go out [be extinguished].*

Chapter 12

The Role of the Ekklesia

I remember sitting on an international flight, cruising at about thirty thousand feet above the surface of the earth. I had just completed six weeks of extraordinarily fruitful ministry, with thousands saved and healed, hundreds delivered, hundreds commissioned and sent out into the fields of God's choosing. I was sitting there giving thanks and praise to the Almighty, and I remember the LORD saying to me,

> *"Son, you have done well – but there is much,*
> *much more for you to understand."*

He was saying to me that while of course the fruit of souls and healing, deliverance, and commissioning were wonderfully pleasing to Him, there was much more that He needed me to understand about the Gospel, and specifically, the Gospel of the Kingdom.

Working with the local teams, we had already been involved in the funding and construction of wells to assist with the provision of safe, clean drinking water and to limit the spread of water-borne diseases.

We had constructed computer schools and sewing schools to help lift people out of generationally entrenched poverty.

We sponsored children through school, and built safe houses for women and children at risk, as well as homes for pastors who had previously been living on railway station platforms, or simply drifting from one place to another with no stable roof over their heads.

This is what some would call a partial outworking of the "Social Gospel" or "the Mercy Gospel." But God was telling me that there was much, much more to understand.

The "more" He referred to was not just an increase in magnitude of the same kind of fruit. – He was talking about developing a much deeper understanding of what the Gospel of the Kingdom was all about.

And He was wanting to release a much broader implementation and effectiveness of the Gospel of the Kingdom through His ekklesia as a result of that deeper understanding.

What is the Ekklesia ?

I am deeply devoted to Jesus, the Creator of the Universe and Saviour of mankind, and to His Bride, the ekklesia, so it is only after much prayer and with reverential awe that I respectfully write about her.

> **Matthew 16:18 (NASB)**
> *I also say to you that you are Peter,*
> *and upon this rock I will build My church;*
> *and the gates of Hades will not overpower it.*

The Greek word in **Matthew 16:18** that we translate as "church" is *ekklesia*.

The word "ekklesia" occurs 115 times in the New Testament and was also widely used in the Greek translation of the Old Testament (Septuagint; abbreviated as LXX).

Ekklesia also had a daily usage that was well known to the Jews and other citizens living at the time of Christ.

Therefore, when Jesus declared in **Matthew 16:18** that God would build **His** *ekklesia*, He was using terminology that would have been very familiar to His audience. He was teaching the people, using words that they had heard before, and by way of illustration, using parables about events from everyday life.

But Jesus was also living in their midst, performing miracle after miracle. And He was continually astounding His listeners with the authority and demonstration of Divine power that accompanied His messages, which they had never witnessed before.

They would have begun to think through the powerful implications of an ekklesia founded by God Himself that the gates of Sheol could not overpower.

They would have realized that although the terminology He used may have been familiar, what Jesus was intending to build was going to be anything but familiar. It was going to be above and beyond imagination, and it was going to be supernatural, just as He was.

I can only imagine the anointing that was released during that profound moment in human history, when the Creator of the Universe – the same One who spoke the words "let there be light" and suddenly there was light - spoke the words "I will build my ekklesia" with the same creative power and authority that brought the sun, moon, and stars into existence.

"Ekklesia" in the Septuagint and in Daily Life

It's important to briefly look at how the word "ekklesia" was used in the Septuagint and in daily life at the time of Christ because this was the context in which the Jews would have understood the statement of Jesus.

(i) In the Septuagint

The Greek Old Testament, known as the *Septuagint* (abbreviated LXX), was widely read among Greek-speaking Jews in the years leading up to Christ, and by Christians for generations after the first century.

Inspired writers reflect this fact in their frequent quotations from the LXX in the New Testament. The Holy Spirit utilized this familiarity in the word choices and use of words that New Testament writers employed to reveal the Gospel in the pages of Scripture.

As a result, much can be learned about the meaning of words and phrases in the New Testament by considering the background of their use as illustrated in the LXX. [14]

It is evident from the frequent use of the word *"ekklesia"* in the LXX that the word held a deep significance for Greek-speaking Jews.

The *"ekklesia* of the LORD" was the covenantal assembly of Israel **(Deuteronomy 4:10)**.[15]

> **Deuteronomy 4:10 (NASB)**
> *Remember the day you stood before the Lord*
> *your God at Horeb, when the Lord said to me,*
> *'Assemble the people to Me, that I may let them*
> *hear My words so they may learn to fear Me*
> *all the days they live on the earth,*
> *and that they may teach their children.'*

Moses was instructed by God to gather the entire nation around His Person and Presence.

It was on this occasion that God made His covenant with Israel **(Deuteronomy 5:2)**.

The Law would reference this important day by simply saying "on the day of the *ekklesia*" **(Deuteronomy 9:10; 18:16)**. [16]

The Hebrew word is **qahal,** which is translated "to assemble or gather for religious or political purposes." Other conjugations of the verb confer the meaning "to assemble for the spiritual purposes, war, or judgement." [17]

This body, when assembled :-

- worshipped God **(II Chronicles 29:28, 31-32)**,
- appealed to God **(II Chronicles 20:5)**,
- repented before God **(Joel 2:16)**, and
- made choices for the nation as a whole
  (I Chronicles 13:2, 4; Ezra 10:12). [18]

1 Chronicles 13:2-4 (NASB) *(emphasis and notations mine)*
*² David said **to all the assembly***
(LXX ekklesia/Hebrew "qahal") of Israel,
"If it seems good to you, and if it is from the Lord our God,
let us send everywhere to our kinsmen who remain in all
the land of Israel, also to the priests and Levites who are
with them in their cities with pasture lands, that they may meet
with us; ³ and let us bring back the ark of our God
to us, for we did not seek it in the days of Saul."
⁴ Then all the assembly said that they would do so,
for the thing was right in the eyes of all the people.

David spoke to the qahal/ekklesia/assembly and said :-

"Gather the nation"
  and
"Let us bring back the ark of our God to us."

The Ark of the Covenant was the resting place of God's Presence.

King David was saying to the ekklesia :-

"Let us gather all the nation together, and once it is gathered, let us restore the centrality of the Presence of God to our gatherings.

Let us restore God to His rightful, pre-eminent place in our nation, as the previous generation neglected to do; and let us reform our entire nation by restoring the priority of the Presence of the LORD in our midst."

I believe this is a prophetic rallying cry and trumpet call from Heaven for the 21st century ekklesia.

Ezra 10:1 (NASB)
- Reconciliation with God (notations mine)
Now while Ezra was praying and making confession,
weeping and prostrating himself before the house of God,
a very large assembly (LXX ekklesia/Hebrew "qahal"),
men, women and children, gathered to him from Israel;
for the people wept bitterly.

The national ekklesia gathered in response to the prayers and weeping repentance of one man.

The result was legislation created with kingly authority (the King of Heaven with Ezra the scribe acting as His ambassador) on behalf of the nation that brought spiritual and social reform. The ekklesia agreed as one and enacted the national reforms that were initiated by earnest intercession and repentance in God's Presence.

> **Ezra 10:12 (NASB)** (notations mine)
> *² Then all the assembly (LXX ekklesia/Hebrew "qahal")*
> *replied with a loud voice,*
> *"That's right! As you have said, so it is our duty to do."*

Israel had become a fallen theocracy that had gone its separate ways from the path laid out for it by the LORD. God raised up worshipping prophet-warrior kings and intercessory teacher-reformers to lead Israel back towards its destiny in God. The chosen vehicle to enact the reforms initiated by the leaders was the ekklesia.

This is prophetic and a Divine pattern for the 21st century ekklesia. By and large our nations are not walking in the ways of the LORD, and the ekklesia is called to reform human culture by realigning it with Kingdom culture.

There are numerous occurrences of the word "ekklesia" in the Septuagint and it is used to signify other types of gatherings.

The occurrences mentioned above are of significance to help us understand the context in which Jesus used the word when describing the called-out assembly of the redeemed that He founded and announced He would build. From them, we can see that the ekklesia is more than a local gathering.

We tend to think of the ekklesia as a local expression meeting in a specific place, or self-contained within artificial boundaries such as districts or denominations. And while some expressions of it are indeed local, the Old Testament ekklesia from which we can draw a Divine pattern for today, was national.

In our time, in fact, it is global - one body with Christ as the head. This is the view from Heaven. It is a covenantal assembly. And, the Risen LORD and His limitless Presence are the central elements in the midst of His global body.

From our basic examination of the Hebrew word "qahal," we can see that the purpose of the qahal/assembly/ekklesia was not only to gather the nation into His Presence, but to re-establish the priority of His Presence with every sphere of the nation.

The ekklesia is called to legislate the decrees of Heaven on behalf of the nations of the earth. The ekklesia should have relational connections with the leaders of the nation in every sphere, including the political sphere, because the ekklesia is engaged in spiritual governance.

The politics of the land are not to be in the ekklesia; the ekklesia is to be a Divine guiding influence to the politics of the land. Hallelujah !

The ekklesia is called to war. As Christians, this means warring in the Spirit to restore and then maintain the spiritual foundations for reformation as outlined in previous chapters (09, 10, and 11).

(ii) In Daily Life

Thayer's Greek Lexicon defines ἐκκλησία (ekklesia) as meaning "called out or forth; a gathering of citizens called out from their homes into some public place; an assembly of the people convened at the public place for the purpose of deliberating." The word was used in this context in **Acts 19:39-41.**

> **Acts 19:39-41 (NASB)** *(bracketed reference mine)*
> *39 But if you want anything beyond this,*
> *It shall be settled in the lawful assembly (ekklesia).*
> *40 For indeed we are in danger of being accused*
> *of a riot in connection with today's events, since*
> *there is no real cause for it, and in this connection*
> *we will be unable to account for this disorderly gathering. "*
> *41 After saying this he dismissed the assembly.*

The deliberations of this assembly would be guided, decided, and then enacted according to the law of the land.

The Called Out Legislative Assembly of the LORD

But what about the ekklesia, the called out legislative assembly of the LORD ? The people He was addressing knew what He meant.

His ekklesia would guide, decide, and act according to the full power and legislative authority of Heaven.

Oh, if we could only grasp what it really means to have Christ the Hope of Glory – the Creator and Sustainer of all things – living inside of us and moving through us.

I wonder if it is even possible for a finite human mind to understand what it means to have "the mind of Christ" **(1 Corinthians 2:16)** or to comprehend what Jesus meant when He said, *"For **all things** that I have heard from My Father I have made known to you."*

> **John 15:15 (NKJV)**
> *"No longer do I call you servants, for a servant does not know what his master is doing; but I have called you friends, for **all things** that I heard from My Father I have made known to you."*

What does Jesus mean when He says "all things" ?

He created "all things" and He sustains "all things" – absolutely everything in Heaven, on Earth, and throughout the entire universe, by the power of His mighty word **(Hebrews 1:3)**. I'm feeling very small as I write these words. Could the length, breadth, and height of the "all things" that He had heard from His Father be fully comprehended by a human being ? How can we grasp this ?

All that we can hope to grasp is that we have inherited Heavenly wealth and Divine legislative authority that is simply beyond our comprehension.

A lifetime is not enough time to unpack the tiniest portion of God's "all things," God's riches, or God's authority.

> **Romans 11:33 (NASB)**
> *Oh, the depth of the riches both of the wisdom*
> *and knowledge of God! How unsearchable*
> *are His judgments and unfathomable His ways!*

Yet, all of His unsearchable, merciful judgements and His unfathomable ways are intended to be fully expressed through His ekklesia – the global body of Christ.

It is no longer necessary to retrieve the Ark and bring it into our midst to create a resting place for God. We are His ark, His temple; and we are His resting place **(Isaiah 66:1-2)**, made of living stones **(1 Peter 2:5)**. His desire is that we would bring His living, breathing ekklesia to the world.

(Matthew 28:19) This is the privilege of the called out legislative assembly of the LORD.

The Ekklesia Is Not a Building

Todays' dictionary definitions of the word "church" show what the "ekklesia" has become in the eyes of many, both inside and outside of the Body of Christ. "A building for public Christian worship" is one such definition from the *Merriam-Webster's Collegiate Dictionary.* [19]

But, although it may at times meet in a building, the ekklesia itself is *not* a building, or a network of buildings.

God does not dwell in a constructed building that is made by human hands.

> **Acts 7:48a (AMP)**
> *However, the Most High [the One infinitely exalted above*
> *humanity] does not dwell in houses made by human hands.*

We, the ekklesia, are "God's field" and "God's Building" – and He is the perfectly qualified, undisputed Builder **(1 Corinthians 3:7-9)**.

Anything built by God is indeed something to look forward to **(Hebrews 11:10)**. But while Abraham was looking forward to a heavenly, eternal city, the fully functioning, glorious ekklesia will be a foretaste and type of the eternal city that is to come.

1 Corinthians 3:7-9 (NIV)

⁷ So neither the one who plants nor the one who waters
is anything, but only God, who makes things grow.
⁸ The one who plants and the one who waters
have one purpose, and they will each be rewarded
according to their own labor. ⁹ For we are co-workers
in God's service; you are God's field, God's building.

Hebrews 11:10 (AMP)

For he was [waiting expectantly and confidently] looking
forward to the city which has foundations, [an eternal,
heavenly city] whose architect and builder is God.

The Great Co-Mission

The Great Commission is not our mission; it is God's Co-Mission that He chooses to share with us. And His ekklesia, which includes you and me, is His chosen vehicle to complete His Co-Mission.

The Great Co-Mission involves not just discipling individuals, but discipling entire nations; not just the people within them, but also to bring "all things" into subjection to Him.

Hebrews 2:7-9 (NKJV)

⁷ You have made him a little lower than the angels;
You have crowned him with glory and honour,
And set him over the works of Your hands.
⁸ You have put all things in subjection under his feet. "
For in that He put all in subjection under him,
He left nothing that is not put under him.
But now we do not yet see all things put under him.
⁹ But we see Jesus, who was made a little lower
than the angels, for the suffering of death
crowned with glory and honor, that He,
by the grace of God, might taste death for everyone.

"But now we do not yet see." Indeed, when we look with our natural eyes at the state of our fallen governments, economies, educational systems, and so on, we do not yet see all things in subjection to Him.

But - by faith, the evidence of things not "yet" seen is the privilege of the ekklesia, as His chosen and beloved ambassadors, to outwork in love and obedience across every sphere of society. More than that, it is the banner and the standard of the mature ekklesia lifted high above every nation for the Glory of God and the benefit of all. Amen.

Ed Silvoso, in his brilliant book, *Ekklesia: Rediscovering God's Instrument for Global Transformation,*" explains the dual nature of the Great Commission as follows :-

Jesus spelled out the Great Commission twice.

*In **Mark 16:15**, He sent us to "preach the Gospel to all creation." This is the individual mandate. But in **Matthew 28:19–20**, He commanded us to "make disciples of all the nations." (Notice that Jesus did not say that we should make disciples in all the nations, but rather, of all the nations.)*

This is the corporate mandate. These two are complementary yet different dimensions of the Great Commission. Historically, and more so in the last two centuries, the Church has done a great job leading individuals to faith in Jesus.

Yet in spite of the large numbers of new believers, very few nations are being discipled, if any at all. Apparently, leading people to Christ does not necessarily result in a nation being discipled, no matter how large the number of new disciples turns out to be.

Integrating these two dimensions of the Great Commission is the missing key ... while joyfully celebrating its efforts in preaching to every creature, the Church (ekklesia) must now discover and embrace the other side of the Great Commission - to disciple all nations. [20]

Ed Silvoso also writes about the authority that Jesus has been given to recover *everything* that was lost :-

> *Jesus prefaced His specific reference to discipling nations with the assertion that He has absolute authority both in heaven and on earth. Authority in heaven was something He already possessed as the Word by whom and through whom all things were created (see **Matthew 28:18; John 1:1–3**).*
>
> *But He subsequently established His authority on earth when He gave Himself in ransom for all, as **1 Timothy 2:6** says, which touches on the salvation of individuals.*
>
> ***Luke 19:10** expands on that by stating that He came "to seek and to save that which was lost." In other words, everything that was lost - not just lost individuals, but **that** which was lost.* [21]

What a glorious and all-embracing Co-Mission we have been given, and how gracious, powerful, and perfect is the One who stands in our midst to help us to see it through until the end.

Christ is head over all things, and He has been given, as head over all things, to the ekklesia.

Ephesians 1:22-23 (NASB)
[22] *And He put all things in subjection under His feet, and gave Him as head over all things to the church,*
[23] *which is His body, the fullness of Him who fills all in all.*

We must recognize and begin to move in the fullness of the authority that has been made available to us.

The nations are His inheritance **(Psalm 2:8)**, and by extension the ekklesia's, because He lives within us.

I believe that Jesus was encompassing all of the above when He chose the word "ekklesia" to define for His chosen people the multiple and far-reaching roles of the worldwide body of believers that He had just founded.

Revolutionary, and Revelatory

Over the centuries since the time of Christ, though, the true meaning has become lost. The ekklesia, or church, has become many things, some of them good, and some of them reflecting more of the desires of their human founders than the intentions of the original Divine patterns given to us by the Almighty.

It is of the utmost importance to understand what the Founder meant when He said "I will build My ekklesia." It is equally important to note that He said that **He** would build it.

When the followers of Christ begin to rediscover what the "ekklesia" really is and begin to partner with the LORD as He builds it, and as we begin to live the fullness of Christ's vision for His ekklesia in Spirit and in truth, then a spiritual revolution will occur that will touch and change and transform every family, every tribe, every people group, every community, every city, and every sphere of human influence.

The first believers in the Book of Acts grasped this. The Holy Spirit fell upon them and they immediately went out and *"turned the world upside down."*

> **Acts 17:6b (NKJV)**
> *"These who have turned the world upside down have come here too."*

The role of the ekklesia was always intended to be revolutionary, and also revelatory. The rock upon which Jesus said that He would build His ekklesia was the revelation given to Peter that Jesus was none other than the promised Messiah.

The revelation of the majestic fullness of Christ is intended to continually unfold and expand, firstly for His disciples, and then through them, for the world. The revelatory vehicle is the glorious ekklesia.

Matthew 16:13-18 (NKJV)
- Peter Confesses Jesus as the Christ

*13 When Jesus came into the region of Caesarea Philippi,
He asked His disciples, saying,
"Who do men say that I, the Son of Man, am?"*

*14 So they said, "Some say John the Baptist,
some Elijah, and others Jeremiah or one of the prophets."*

15 He said to them, "But who do you say that I am?"

*16 Simon Peter answered and said,
"You are the Christ, the Son of the living God."*

*17 Jesus answered and said to him, "Blessed are you, Simon
Bar-Jonah, for flesh and blood has not revealed this to you,
but My Father who is in heaven. 18 And I also say to you
that you are Peter, and on this rock I will build My church,
and the gates of Hades shall not prevail against it."*

As the ekklesia embraces the fullness of her Divine partnership with the Son of the Living God, the ekklesia will also embrace the nation-transforming purpose and power that is her Divine Co-Mission.

The Ekklesia Is the Glorious Bride of Christ

The limitless dimensions of the love that Jesus has for His bride cannot even begin to be expressed in human language. And He longs for His bride to be all that He has created and called her to be in all her glorious victory. He draws her with His ever-increasing Presence, and the promise of even greater fruitfulness and manifestations of His Glory as the end of days approaches.

We have mentioned that we are living in the end times, when the Bible foretells that both evil and good will be on the rise. It is the role of the ekklesia to build upon the rock of the revelation of the Risen Christ and to display the dimensions of His Glory and the depths of His love for humanity to the ends of the earth.

When the revelation of Who He is, who we are in Him, and Who He is in us is clear, bright, strong, and continually flowing into us and overflowing out of us into the world around us, it won't matter which end time storms come our way. They simply will not be able to shake or deter us.

I am glad that I have had the privilege of spending precious time amongst believers who are persecuted for their faith. The fire of pure, burning, holy love that burns within them for Jesus is "all-or-nothing" and leaves me awestruck. The willingness to give all for Him is like a deep and uninhibited bridal passion for her betrothed. The threats of the persecutors do not lessen the flame – if anything, they cause it to increase.

When **Hebrews 2:9** states that *"we do not yet see all things put under Him"* an honest examination of ourselves would reveal that this is true of the 21st century ekklesia in terms of submission to the fullness of His will.

Yet, in spite of all of our imperfections, faults, and failings, and even in spite of our misunderstanding of the great breadth and width and height of the influence that His ekklesia is called to wield, our Beloved says this to His beloved, His ekklesia, His Bride :-

> **Song of Songs 4:9 (TPT)**
> *For you reach into my heart.*
> *With one flash of your eyes*
> *I am undone by your love,*
> *My beloved, My equal, My bride.*
> *You leave Me breathless—*
> *I am overcome by merely a glance*
> *from your worshiping eyes,*
> *for you have stolen My heart.*
> *I am held hostage by your love*
> *and by the graces of righteousness*
> *shining upon you.*

The bridal veil is the last piece of bridal clothing and signifies that the bride is prepared and ready to meet the Bridegroom.

The Glory of the LORD that He declared would cover the earth **(Numbers 14:21)** is prophetically like the bridal veil of the gloriously and completely prepared Bride of Christ, as she rises victoriously out of the wilderness of a fallen and rebellious world, which has turned away from their Saviour.

But the heart of God is that this same Bride will lovingly and thoroughly search the "highways and byways" so that none will miss out on the Wedding Feast of the Lamb. He does not want to have any empty places at His table.

Selah.

Luke 14:23 (TPT)
"So the master told him, 'All right. Go out again,
and this time bring them all back with you.
Persuade the beggars on the streets, the outcasts,
even the homeless. Urgently insist that they come in
and enjoy the feast so that my house will be full.'"

Ephesians 5:25-27 (NKJV)
[25] Husbands, love your wives, just as Christ also loved
the church and gave Himself for her, [26] that He might sanctify
and cleanse her with the washing of water by the word,
[27] that He might present her to Himself a glorious church,
not having spot or wrinkle or any such thing,
but that she should be holy and without blemish.

2 Corinthians 11:2 (NKJV)
For I am jealous over you with godly jealousy:
for I have espoused you to one husband,
that I may present [you as] a chaste virgin to Christ.

Revelation 19:7 (NKJV)
Let us be glad and rejoice and give Him glory,
for the marriage of the Lamb has come,
and His wife has made herself ready.

Christ in the Midst of His Ekklesia

The ekklesia is all of Heaven's love, all of Heaven's legislative authority, all of Heaven's power, and all of Heaven's Glory operating in us and through us, as the Risen Christ stands in all the fullness of His Glory in our midst !

It just takes two or more believers together in agreement with Jesus in their midst, to initiate this.

> **Matthew 18:20 (AMP)** *(enphasis & notation mine)*
> *"For where two or three are gathered in My name*
> *[meeting together as My followers],*
> ***I am (εἰμί (I am, I have come, I am present))***
> *there among them."*

"2 or 3 + Jesus = Ekklesia" is an extremely powerful equation for supernatural change.

It's not "the 2 or 3" that give the ekklesia its power and authority; it's the One Who stands in the midst of the 2 or 3 who are in agreement *with* the One Who has all the Divine power and Heavenly legislative authority. It's the strength and depth of the relationship of the 2 or 3 with their Creator that provides a conduit for His power and glory to cover and fill the earth through the outpoured lives of His Kingdom ambassadors.

Jesus said He would stand in the midst of the assembly – the ekklesia – giving praise to His Father. **Psalm 22:22** and **Hebrews 2:12** describe something so wonderful; the Risen Christ standing in our midst.

If you have experienced this – an encounter with the Risen, Living Christ - even once in your lifetime, you know that you can never be the same as you were before such an encounter.

But the LORD desires His permanently overflowing habitation to be in our midst – because this is what the God-glorifying, miracle-working, nation-changing ekklesia is - two or three disciples (or more) plus the risen LORD right there with us !

This should be our expectation every time that we meet together, and every time that we are placed strategically by the LORD within a sphere of human influence that needs His transformative Presence and love.

Psalm 22:22 (NKJV)
I will declare Your name to My brethren;
In the midst of the assembly I will praise You.

Hebrews 2:11-12 (NKJV)
[11] For both He who sanctifies and those
who are being sanctified are all of one,
for which reason He is not ashamed to call them brethren,

[12] saying: "I will declare Your name to My brethren;
In the midst of the assembly I will sing praise to You."

The ultimate goal of the ekklesia is to reveal Jesus in all His fullness to the world, with the full expression of His love, power, and authority operating in and through His sons and daughters. This is the Gospel of the Kingdom, His word confirmed with mighty demonstrations of His miracle working power from personal to national level.

Matthew 28:18-20 (TLV)
[18] And Yeshua came up to them and spoke to them, saying,
"All authority in heaven and on earth has been given to Me.

[19] Go therefore and make disciples of all nations,
immersing them in the name of the Father and the Son
and the Ruach ha-Kodesh (Holy Spirit),
[20] teaching them to observe all I have commanded you.

And remember!
I am with you always, even to the end of the age."

Matthew 24:14 (NKJV)
*"And **this Gospel of the Kingdom** will be preached*
in all the world as a witness to all the nations,
and then the end will come."

We need to understand what the ekklesia looks like in our nation, operating from grassroots to Government level. The ekklesia is not limited to our Sunday gatherings and our midweek prayer meetings.

They are a very important, vital, necessary, and beautiful expression of it, but they are only part of the full expression.

The 21st century ekklesia will exist in the schools, in the hospitals, in the streets, in the houses of Parliament, in the cities and in the fields, and in the board rooms where ultimately billions of dollars will be transferred and transacted to fund Kingdom projects.

The ekklesia, with Christ as the head, will author government policies; the national school curriculum; blueprints for social and economic reforms; and so on.

The ekklesia will be everywhere, because God's people moving in the fullness of God's love, power, authority, and Glory, and wielding Kingdom influence and authority in His love and resurrection power, will be there.

This is why we need to understand our role as kings (see Chapter 16).

We need the life of Christ pouring into us and overflowing through us to give full, Divine expression to the ekklesia that He founded.

The Journey

The journey towards the glorious fullness and Christlike functioning of the ekklesia will start with a complete, internal surrender of ourselves to God and His Divine leading, in every area of our lives. The internal Christlike character will be demonstrated externally with supernatural, Christlike function.

There can be no fulfilment of the "outward" call without first submitting ourselves to the dealings of Christ so that we can attain an inward transformation.

God's heart's desire is to raise up end time leaders and disciples of Jesus, who are passionate to know him, to access the Throne Room of Heaven, and to take the treasures received there into the darkest corners of the world - with eternal and supernatural fruit resulting.

This is why Part 1 of this book is so important - it lays the internal, personal foundations that will empower and equip individuals to become part of the restored ekklesia. Otherwise there is always the danger that the influence of the ekklesia will be limited by our ideas of what it is or could be, rather than exponentially expanding those ideas through the correct understanding and application of the Divine templates and patterns at both individual and corporate levels.

The Bridegroom is waiting for His ekklesia to arise. He is returning for a Glorious Bride, and He will wait until her glorious veil covers the earth as the alert, prepared Bride of Christ rises up in the transformative Kingdom fullness that He always intended for her to display to the world.

Ephesians 3:20-21 (TLV)
20 Now to Him who is able to do
far beyond all that we ask or imagine,
by means of His power that works in us,

21 to Him be the glory in the community
of believers and in Messiah Yeshua
throughout all generations
forever and ever! Amen.

Revelation 21:9 (NKJV)
Then one of the seven angels
who had the seven bowls filled
with the seven last plagues
came to me and talked with me, saying,

"Come, I will show you the bride, the Lamb's wife."

Chapter 13

Seven Mountains, Seven Spheres, and the Gospel of the Kingdom

Isaiah 2:2 (NKJV)
*Now it shall come to pass in the latter days
that the mountain of the Lord's house
shall be established on the top of the mountains,
and shall be exalted above the hills;
and all nations shall flow to it.*

Matthew 6:10 (NKJV)
*"Your Kingdom come,
Your will be done on earth as it is in Heaven."*

Denali – The Great One

When measured from base to top, the Alaskan mountain known as "Denali" is the tallest mountain in the world. Mount Everest, and a few others, register a greater height above sea level, but their bases are already at a greatly elevated height. Denali rises up as a single mountain peak almost all the way from sea level.

It is a massive mountain - so immense that on a rare clear day in Alaska it can be seen from 600 kilometers away.

A few years ago, I had the great privilege of taking a trip through Alaska with my youngest son. It is an extraordinarily beautiful place. The highlight of our trip was a visit to Denali. We'd glimpsed it many times from afar on the journey towards it. I had such anticipation in my spirit about standing in front of this mighty mountain that had been created by the hands of our Creator God. When the day came to travel to it, the Presence of God became overwhelming, and I began shaking under the power of the Spirit when we were still one hour away.

It was early spring and the snow was still blocking many of the roads, so the closest that we could approach the mountain was a distance of about fifty kilometers. Even from that distance, Denali was huge, and simply awe inspiring – natural pristine beauty and splendor beyond anything I'd ever experienced in my life.

I wanted to pray, I wanted to speak, but I was so overwhelmed and surrounded with the majestic Holiness of God that all I could do was just stand there weeping and speechless. Almighty God was there with me in that place that He had created. I beheld His Glory on and all around the mountain, and out of the midst of His Presence He imparted many life-changing truths to me that day.

Rain had been predicted for that day and the previous day. Instead, we had a clear day with full sun. The National Parks Service said only five per cent of visitors to the park ever get to see what we had seen on that day - Denali uncovered, in all of its stunning beauty.

On another day, we flew over Denali and the mountain ranges surrounding it. I could not stop weeping. The Presence of God was in that tiny eight-seater plane, and He seemed to be saturating the majestic mountains that we were flying over with His Presence.

The plane was no more than a speck against the mighty flanks of the mountains and the enormous, u-shaped, glacier-carved valleys below.

The name "Denali" is the indigenous name for this beautiful mountain.

It means "Great One" or "Mighty One."

It is a very appropriate name.

Ever since encountering God in that wonderful place and beholding the sheer scale and indescribable beauty of it with my own heart and my own eyes, my concept of what a mountain is has changed forever.

And every time I read the word "mountain" in Scripture, I am filled with trembling wonder at the awesome creative power of the Almighty.

I have also become even more aware of how His Presence can transform any place on earth into a holy meeting place, and a place of powerful and life-changing Divine encounter with Him.

> **Psalm 65:6 (TPT)**
> *What jaw-dropping, astounding power is yours!*
> *You are the mountain maker who sets them all in place.*

Holy Mountains of Meeting and Instruction

Many significant supernatural meetings between God and man have occurred on mountain tops or mountain sides. Covenants have been made, instructions have been given, and great demonstrations of God's power have occurred.

God established His awesome Presence at the top of Mount Sinai with lightning, thunder, the sound of trumpets, mighty shaking, and a thick cloud of smoke **(Exodus 19:16-19; see also Revelation 5:8-14)**.

God then invited Moses to meet Him on the mountain on numerous occasions. **Exodus 34:28** records that Moses spent forty days and nights becoming saturated in the Presence and Glory of the LORD, and speaking with Him. Precepts to guide the people of God were given to Moses on the mountain top, and also spoken by God from the mountain top to the people, as recorded in **Exodus 20:1-21**.

The mountain top was the place where Moses was given the detailed Divine patterns that were needed to construct the tabernacle – another place where God's people would meet with Him.

> **Exodus 25:40 (AMPC)**
> *And see to it that you copy [exactly] their pattern*
> *which was shown you on the mountain.*

As the name implies, the Sermon on the Mount was delivered from a mountain **(Matthew 5:12)**.

Jesus was transfigured on a mountain in the sight of Peter, James, and John who were with Him.

Matthew 17:1-2 (AMP) - The Transfiguration
*[1]Six days later Jesus took with Him Peter and James
and John the brother of James, and led them up
on a high mountain by themselves.*

*[2] And His appearance changed dramatically
in their presence; and His face shone
[with heavenly glory, clear and bright] like the sun,
and His clothing became as white as light.*

Moses, and seventy three others went up on to the mountain, saw God, and ate and drank in His Presence.

Exodus 24:9-11 (NKJV) - On the Mountain with God
*[9] Then Moses went up, also Aaron, Nadab, and Abihu,
and seventy of the elders of Israel, [10] and they saw
the God of Israel. And there was under His feet
as it were a paved work of sapphire stone,
and it was like the very heavens in its clarity.
[11] But on the nobles of the children of Israel
He did not lay His hand.*

So they saw God, and they ate and drank.

The mountain is symbolic of the place where we meet with God in all His Glory. We are always profoundly changed by such encounters.

Jesus calls all who are hungry and thirsty and serious about following Him to meet Him on the mountain.

Mark 3:13 (NKJV)
*And He went up on the mountain and called to Him
those He Himself wanted. And they came to Him.*

Mount Zion – symbolically the abode of worshippers and intercessors – will be covered with the Glory of the Almighty.

> **Isaiah 4:5 (NASB)**
> *Then the Lord will create over the whole area*
> *of Mount Zion and over her assemblies a cloud by day,*
> *even smoke, and the brightness of a flaming fire by night;*
> *for over all the glory will be a canopy.*

Holy Foundations

> **Psalm 87:1 (NKJV)**
> *His foundation is in the holy mountains.*

The above Scripture is powerful.

What is it that makes a mountain holy ? It is because God is there.

If God is inhabiting the foundations of a mountain, I would love to set foot on such a mountain, because from the moment I did, I know that I would encounter Him, and His holy Presence would fill me and change me.

When God's Presence abides in a place, it changes. It becomes holy.

People become like their God by abiding in His Holy Presence. Not only do we become like Him, but our world also becomes like His in atmosphere and character, when we live and work out of His holy Presence and according to His precepts.

Holy Ground

Moses was tending his father-in-law's flock when he encountered a burning bush.

The bush was burning because the LORD was there. God spoke to Moses out of the middle of the bush and said, "Take off your sandals, for the place where you are standing is holy ground." The ground was holy, because God was there.

Exodus 3:1-6 (NIV) - Moses and the Burning Bush

¹ Now Moses was tending the flock of Jethro his father-in-law, the priest of Midian, and he led the flock to the far side of the wilderness and came to Horeb, the mountain of God.

² There the angel of the Lord appeared to him in flames of fire from within a bush. Moses saw that though the bush was on fire it did not burn up.

³ So Moses thought, "I will go over and see this strange sight - why the bush does not burn up."

⁴ When the Lord saw that he had gone over to look, God called to him from within the bush, "Moses! Moses!"

And Moses said, "Here I am."

⁵ "Do not come any closer," God said. "Take off your sandals, for the place where you are standing is holy ground." ⁶ Then he said, "I am the God of your father, the God of Abraham, the God of Isaac and the God of Jacob." At this, Moses hid his face, because he was afraid to look at God.

Seven Mountains

In 1975, two Christian leaders, Dr. Bill Bright and Loren Cunningham, got together to give each other a message from God. To their amazement, each had the same message, independently given to them by God, to give to the other.

Bill Bright was the founder of the world's largest ministry, Campus Crusade for Christ, a worldwide ministry with 26,000 full-time employees and missionaries in 191 countries. Loren Cunningham was the founder of Youth With a Mission (YWAM), a ministry with 20,000 full-time staff of more than 150 nationalities. Both of these individuals brought the Gospel to millions around the world.

> *However, God showed both of them that many areas*
> *of modern culture still needed the Gospel.*
>
> *The Lord showed them seven major areas of society,*
> *or "mountains" as they called them, which needed Godly*
> *people to influence them, thereby influencing untold millions*
> *who were engaged in those seven mountains of society.*
>
> *These seven mountains are business, government, media,*
> *arts and entertainment, education, family and religion.*
> *God was showing them, in 1975, that His Kingdom would*
> *win back our culture through these fronts. God wanted*
> *these men to equip people to go into these seven mountains*
> *of culture and to change them: to begin reconciling culture*
> *back to God. [22]*

The spirituality mountain (or sphere) does not have nearly the influence that it used to have over any of the other spheres of human influence; in many nations, the influence is non-existent.

Many laws that are out of alignment with Godly precepts have been passed in our time. Most would not have even been considered in past times when Christians were leaders and major influencers of the decision-making processes within every sphere of society. The current low representation (or in some cases, complete absence) of Christians in positions of authority within the majority of nations has led to a subsequent absence of Kingdom influence.

The lack of understanding and applying of the "making disciples of nations" aspect of the Great Commission has created a vacuum that has been effectively filled by other influences that have flourished. Also, every time that a Christian refuses or abdicates their position within a sphere that they are called to influence, they are in effect issuing an invitation to counterfeit spiritual authorities to come in and take their place.

The direct consequence of this is that the very fabric of society is under threat. Endemic corruption, generationally entrenched poverty, drug and alcohol addictions, and sharp increases in the number of family breakdowns are some examples of this.

I think it's very significant that God spoke to two of the world's most successful and well known global evangelists of the day, to broaden their vision of the Great Commission beyond the Gospel of Salvation, and to include the Gospel of the Kingdom. He did not in any way tell them to stop winning souls, but rather to include the transformation of nations as part of their vision – the second tier of the Great Commission as discussed in the previous chapter.

Other Kings

It is difficult to imagine the state of blindness, arrogance, and apostasy that caused the Pharisees to respond, when Jesus was presented to them by Pilate as their King, "We have no king but Caesar."

> **John 19:15 (NKJV)**
> *But they cried out,*
> *"Away with Him, away with Him! Crucify Him!"*
> *Pilate said to them, "Shall I crucify your King?"*
> *The chief priests answered, "We have no king but Caesar!"*

Yet we too have allowed many kings to take over thrones within our nations, and within our own hearts, which were intended for God alone to inhabit, and then ourselves as His children.

This could not have happened if the ekklesia had been positioned and fully functioning in its role as God's Legislative Assembly on earth.

Historically, it may be that we may have not always understood our authority as Kingdom ambassadors or our role as the stewards of Kingdom righteousness and justice.

We must recognize the time in which we live, and understand that now is the time to take up our rightful roles and exercise our Divine governmental authority, standing in the gap for the nations and ushering in the greatest move of God that the world will ever know.

God wants His children to glorify Him from within the spheres of government, economy, education, family, arts and entertainment, and media and communication, just as much as we do through our ecclesiastical gatherings.

This is so that those who do not yet know Him may have the opportunity to encounter Him through every expression of culture.

Joshua and the Seven Nations "Stronger and Mightier Than He"

We learned in Chapter 11 that the conquest of Canaan, led by Joshua, was intended to displace *"seven nations greater and mightier"* than the Israelites. The Israelites were to *"conquer them and utterly destroy them; make no covenant with them, nor show mercy to them"* **(Deuteronomy 7:1-3)**.

The Israelites did not complete the conquest of Canaan. Because of this, the influence of the principalities that ruled those seven nations retained a measure of authority over the nation that became Israel.

The Connection Between God's Command to Joshua and the Completion of the Great Commission

Taking back the seven mountains or spheres of human culture is evidence of the full release of the Gospel of the Kingdom that Scripture says will occur before the return of the LORD Jesus Christ.

Social reformer, speaker, and author Johnny Enlow wrote a powerful book titled *The Seven Mountains Prophecy.*[23] He correlated each mountain / sphere with one of the seven attributes of God as outlined in **Revelation 5:12**, and called them the pillars of every nation's society. [24]

When God's people are releasing Kingdom influence within each sphere, then the following attributes of God will be evident : government will reflect His power; economy, His riches; spirituality, His honour; arts and entertainment, His glory; families, His strength; media, His blessing; and education, His wisdom. Glory to God.

He also correlated each mountain/sphere of society with each of the seven nations, and specifically with the spiritual influences controlling them, which God had commanded Joshua and his armies to conquer.

These correlations are highly worthy of our consideration as we wait upon the LORD for His Divine patterns, templates, and strategies that will equip us to release God's Kingdom fullness within our spheres of influence. Using this information, we can begin to develop some targeted and highly effective strategies in the spiritual realm and also on a practical level. The tables below are adapted from Mr. Enlow's extremely valuable, revelatory, and spiritually insightful work. [25]

Mountain *(Attribute of God from Revelation. 5:12 in brackets)*	Indicators of Godly Leadership, Purpose, and Direction *(God's Presence and Precepts)*
Government *(Power)*	Lead the nation with integrity and Godly wisdom based upon Godly righteousness and justice
Economy *(Riches)*	Prosper the nation with Kingdom resources and implementation of Kingdom strategies
Spirituality *(Honor)*	Impact the entire nation with Christian values and spiritual life
Education *(Wisdom)*	Restore educational values that glorify God in every respect
Family *(Strength)*	Strengthen social systems so that the family unit is prioritized and protected
Arts and Entertainment *(Glory)*	Create and release art, music, entertainment, and sports that glorify God in every way
Media & Communications *(Blessing)*	Fill the airwaves with the Good News of the Gospel and wholesome programming

A culture that is reflecting Kingdom values will reflect the indicators listed in the above table. For this to occur, Christians will need to take hold of their callings within spheres other than spirituality and become trained, equipped, and activated as influential ambassadors of Christ within their spheres.

Psalm 30:7 (NASB)
O LORD, by Your favor You have made my mountain to stand strong; You hid Your face, I was dismayed.

The above verse shows us that the favor of God causes our mountains to stand strong. By contrast, when God hides His face, we become dismayed, because His favor is removed.

We have observed that when Christians abdicate the seven spheres of influence, the door is opened for ungodly, counterfeit authorities and principalities to exert their influence. The counterfeit authorities always seek to "hide the face of God" on their mountain, by removing His influence from society, or worse, by portraying the influence of God and/or His people as a bad thing for society.

Remember that mountains are intended by the Almighty to be meeting places between God and man. When a nation chooses to pursue its own pathway that is devoid of Godly wisdom, guidance, and Presence, the effect upon each mountain of society is devastating.

Mountain (Counterfeit authority/usurping principality in brackets	When Godly Purpose, Leadership, and Direction is Lacking
Government (*Girgashites : Corruption / Lucifer : manipulation*)	Corruption, pride, manipulation, poor decision making, astronomical debt, bankruptcy
Economy (*Canaanites : Love of money / Mammon : greed*)	Greed, bribery, debt, short-sighted economic strategy, giving away Divine birthright (e.g., relinquishing natural resources)
Spirituality (*Perrizites : idolatry / Religious spirit : false worship*)	Idolatry, false worship, witchcraft, and the destructive fruits thereof
Education (*Amorites : humanism / Beelzebub : lies*)	Humanism, lies, propagation of godlessness and false religions through schools
Family (*Jebusites : rejection / Baal : perversion*)	Rejection, perversion, family breakdown
Arts and Entertainment (*Hivites : compromise / Jezebel : seduction*)	Compromise, seduction, promotion of sinful values, corruption of emerging generations of youth
Media & Communications (*Hittites : bad news / Apollyon : destroyer*)	Bad news, destruction, deception, fake news, generate fear and confusion

Sadly, the above table paints a very accurate picture of what we see in many, if not most, of the nations of the world. For our nations to reach their full potential as Kingdom nations, then the ungodly, counterfeit power bases must be eliminated from each of the seven mountains or spheres of society.

Specific strategies will vary from district to district and from nation to nation; but the Divine patterns and strategies will be accessed in the place of deep, travailing prayer and through revelatory study of the Word of God.

One major key to the success of any Divine strategy that is revealed is for the ekklesia to proactively identify, pray for, and support in any way possible those who are called to stand and lead within those spheres to take them back for the Kingdom of God.

The Gospel of the Kingdom

The 21st century ekklesia is called to transform nations from grassroots to government according to the principles of the Gospel of the Kingdom – specifically "**this** Gospel of the Kingdom" spoken of by Jesus in **Matthew 24:14**.

> **Matthew 24:14 (NKJV)** *(emphasis mine)*
> *And **this** Gospel of the Kingdom will be preached*
> *in all the world as a witness to all the nations,*
> *and then the end will come.*

Jesus focused on the Gospel of the Kingdom, and He taught that the Kingdom of God was here and present in our midst.

What does the Gospel of the Kingdom embrace ?

It is more than the Gospel of salvation.

Of course our primary mission is to lead people to repentance and then salvation. But as we saw in the previous chapter, the Great Commission is dual in nature, being addressed to individuals, and also to nations.

The Gospel of the Kingdom is the fullness of the Gospel; and it has everything to do with transforming nations from grassroots to government, according to Kingdom principles.

> **Matthew 24:45-47 (NKJV)**
> **- The Faithful Servant and the Evil Servant**
> ⁴⁵ *"Who then is a faithful and wise servant,*
> *whom his master made ruler over his household,*
> *to give them food in due season?*
> ⁴⁶ *Blessed is that servant whom his master,*
> *when he comes, will find so doing.*
> ⁴⁷ *Assuredly, I say to you that he will make him*
> *ruler over all his goods.*

The above verses speak of the great need during these days when evil is on the increase **for God's servants to be the ones** "ruling over households" and ensuring that there is "food in due season."

Households represent mountains/spheres of influence; and food in due season represents the Presence and precepts of the Kingdom.

This *is* the Gospel of the Kingdom.

God's servants governing nations – ruling the "households" through Godly governance and Kingdom economy, and bringing stability and peace in the midst of turbulent times through Kingdom administration, is what the reclaiming the seven mountains is all about.

Isaiah 33:6 is a key verse for our current age.

> **Isaiah 33:6 (NKJV)**
> *Wisdom and knowledge*
> *will be the stability of your times,*
> *And the strength of salvation;*
> *The fear of the Lord is His treasure.*

The wisdom and knowledge of God, dispensed through His servants whom He has placed strategically in positions of influence during the end times, will provide great guidance and stability to an unstable world being buffeted by the schemes of the enemy.

Imagine if each one of the mountains of society was established on holy foundations and therefore became holy ground, and a place of holy instruction and Divine encounter. Imagine if billions of dollars were exchanged around board room tables to further the advancement of Kingdom purposes. Imagine if the governments of every nation were passing laws based upon Kingdom righteousness and justice that protected families and ensured a fair, Godly, and equitable society for all.

Let's believe for a full release of the Gospel of the Kingdom in our day and in our time.

The Year of the LORD's Favor

The message that Jesus shared to mark the beginning of His public ministry is recorded in **Luke 4:19-22.** He was quoting from **Isaiah 61:1-2**. He finished that foundational message by proclaiming that the Spirit of the LORD – the *"Ruach Adonai"* - had anointed Him to proclaim *"the Year of the LORD's Favor."*

> **Luke 4:18-19 (TLV)**
> *18 "The Ruach Adonai is on me,*
> *because He has anointed me*
> *to proclaim Good News to the poor.*
> *He has sent me to proclaim release to the captives*
> *and recovery of sight to the blind,*
> *to set free the oppressed,*
> *19 and to proclaim the year of Adonai's favor."*

Jesus' reminder of the Year of the LORD's Favor had multiple levels of meaning. There was the once-and-for-all-time cancellation of mankind's debt of sin, and our freedom from slavery to sin, through His shed blood on the Cross of Calvary.

But "The Year of the LORD's Favour" also signifies much more.

When Jesus declared that He had come to restore *"The Year of the LORD's Favor,"* He was also referring to the Jubilee program that had been outlined in the Book of Leviticus.

After seven consecutive seven-year cycles of Shemitah years, Jubilee – the Year of the LORD's Favour - was celebrated during the fiftieth year.

At this time, the ram's horn would sound, all slaves would go free, and all debts would be cancelled.

> **Leviticus 25:8-10 (NASB)**
> [8] *'You are also to count off seven sabbaths of years*
> *for yourself, seven times seven years, so that you*
> *have the time of the seven sabbaths of years, namely,*
> *forty-nine years.* [9] *You shall then sound a ram's horn abroad*
> *on the tenth day of the seventh month; on the Day*
> *of Atonement you shall sound a horn all through your land.*
> [10] *You shall thus consecrate the fiftieth year and proclaim*
> *a release through the land to all its inhabitants. It shall be*
> *a jubilee for you, and each of you shall return to his*
> *own property, and each of you shall return to his family.*

Dr. Kim Tan has written a wonderful volume titled *The Jubilee Gospel* of which the following is a paraphrase :-

The Jubilee programs were God's mechanism for restoring
the socio-economic order He had originally intended for His people
to follow. God was seeking to create "social Holiness" :-

> *- a society that was holistic in its approach to holiness;*
> *- a society that reflected His nature and character*
> *by caring for the poor, the oppressed, the defenseless,*
> *and the disadvantaged;*
> *and*
> *- a society that ensured rest for everyone.*

Stewardship was a central aspect of Jubilee.

The Jubilee programmes taught the nation about stewardship
of the land and each other. God was the ultimate owner of everyone
and everything, but they also had a duty of care towards his creation.
Chosen People, Promised Land; Family; The Division of the Land; the
People and the Land; and Lending; all of these were covered
by the Jubilee. [27]

If the precepts of Jubilee can be embraced and applied to our times in practical ways, then entire nations have the potential to become "blessed in the city and blessed in the field" in ways that are currently unprecedented. These precepts represent much of the societal outworking of the Gospel of the Kingdom.

However, none of these precepts can be addressed by the ekklesia working separately from the rest of society. This is why the ekklesia must re-establish its influence and connections within every sphere of society, by reclaiming the seven mountains.

Know your Sphere

To transform a nation, believers will need to know their God-ordained spheres of influence, and then become :-

- true disciples **(Luke 6:40; Isaiah 50:4-5)**;
- true priests **(2 Chronicles 29:11; 1 Peter 2:9)**;
- true ambassadors **(2 Corinthians 5:20)**; and
- true kings **(Revelation 1:5b-6; Proverbs 21:1; Proverbs 8:14-16; Genesis 17:6; Genesis 35:11)**

within their spheres of influence.

The ekklesia will need to become **the ekklesia against which the gates of hell cannot stand.** This is because we are taking the battle right to the gates, just as David did when he took *all* of Jerusalem.

Rather than focus on bringing people out of the mountains to integrate them into "church" culture, our vision must broaden so that we are focused on influencing every sphere of influence within the nation.

Having a nation full of strong and healthy ekklesias is an essential foundation; but building the Kingdom of God goes far beyond this. We must know which spheres that we are called to influence, and then wait upon the LORD until we receive His strategies to reclaim them.

Sphere Leaders and Sphere Partners

The success of the 21st century ekklesia will be measured, not only by the harvest of souls, but also by the level of Kingdom transformation that it achieves. What is your metron, your sphere of influence and authority, that has been assigned to you, your ekklesia and/or your network by the LORD ? What is the Divine pattern that has been given to you that will enable you to align your sphere of influence to its Kingdom purposes ?

Sphere leaders will need to be recognized, trained, and set apart for increase. Sphere leaders are people who are called to high-level leadership positions, strongly connected with God, and interconnected with other people and organizations of influence. They are continually engaged in laying the foundations and implementing the strategies for the transformation of nations from grassroots to government.

Sphere leaders will engage with sphere partners. Sphere partners are also highly motivated individuals called to leadership. A sphere partner will belong to a different organization, and may be called to a different sphere, or different areas of influence within the same spheres as the sphere leader that they are called to partner with.

Sphere leaders and sphere partners may be apostles, prophets, pastors, teachers, or evangelists actively working within one or more of the seven spheres of society.

They may also be Kingdom entrepreneurs, Kingdom economists, worshippers or intercessors, or a combination of the above. The world may see them as politicians, business leaders or administrators– but they will carry one of the mantles listed here, as they will need the breakthrough anointing of the LORD associated with that mantle in order to succeed in taking back their sphere of influence for the LORD. They will also need strong partnerships with apostles and prophets and their networks.

Through their connection and active Kingdom partnership with each other, diverse spheres of influence become connected and transformed.

Holy Encounters for National Transformation

God desires all people everywhere to know Him, and to encounter Him in life-changing ways. He has a desire for face-to-face encounter with every single man, woman, and child whom He has created. This will not happen if the only place that He can be encountered is during a Sunday gathering that is separate from the world.

At the moment of salvation, we became the temples of the Holy Spirit. We became carriers of His Presence, carriers of His Glory, and potentially, carriers of revival and national transformation and reformation. Jesus did not save us to remove us from the world, but rather to be in it as His ambassadors, and to be influencers of culture, rather than to be influenced by it.

There is a huge difference between the two.

God desires His foundations of righteousness and justice to be firmly established within every sphere of human culture, and for His glory to cover and permeate those spheres. Government, arts and entertainment, education, economics, media, family, and spirituality - all were designed to glorify Him !

He desires every mountain of culture, every sphere of influence, to be reformed by His Presence and precepts and to reflect His holiness.

The restored ekklesia is His chosen vehicle to release the reformation.

The role of the 21st century ekklesia is to influence every mountain, or sphere, of human culture, through Christ's delegated legislative authority, establishing the foundations of His throne within every sphere of society until Kingdom culture reigns.

The worshippers and intercessors have a crucial role to play in releasing the Glory of the LORD until it covers every mountain as per the covering over Mount Zion in **Isaiah 5:5**. Where the worshippers and intercessors continually abide in God's Presence, the covering of Glory will manifest and increase.

Mankind was originally given dominion over all things; and through Christ, the nations are the inheritance of His followers **(Psalm 2:8, Genesis 1:26 -28)**. The role of the ekklesia is all embracing, leading nations to redemption by reclaiming all that was lost **(Luke 19:10)**, as well as leading individuals to redemption through salvation.

When the mountains/spheres of society are filled with His holy Presence and His holy precepts through the restored ekklesia, then the mountain of the LORD (the mountain or sphere of spirituality) will take its place of pre-eminence as prophesied in **Isaiah 2:2.**

LORD, may Your Kingdom come, in all its fullness, and may the Divine foundations for every mountain and sphere of society be re-established In Your Name, and for Your Glory.

Amen.

Genesis 1:26-28 (NASB)
[26] Then God said,
"Let Us make man in Our image, according to Our likeness;
and let them rule over the fish of the sea and over the birds
of the sky and over the cattle and over all the earth,
and over every creeping thing that creeps on the earth."
[27] God created man in His own image, in the image of God
He created him; male and female He created them.

[28] God blessed them; and God said to them,
"Be fruitful and multiply, and fill the earth, and subdue it; and
rule over the fish of the sea and over the birds of the sky and
over every living thing that moves on the earth."

Psalm 2:8 (NASB)
"Ask of Me, and I will surely give
the nations as Your inheritance,
And the very ends of the earth
as Your possession."

Luke 19:10 (NASB)
"For the Son of Man has come
to seek and to save that which was lost."

Chapter 14

Ideal Conditions for Revival

Acts 4:13 (NIV)
When they saw the courage of Peter and John
and realized that they were unschooled,
ordinary men, they were astonished and they
took note that these men had been with Jesus.

When we have frequently *"been with Jesus,"* and particularly when we have developed a lifestyle of continually being with Him and communing with Him, I believe that what we call "revival" will become our natural state of being.

Focused, Hungry Individuals

In part 01 of this book, we discussed personal revival as preceding corporate revival, and that there is always "more" of God for us to discover. We looked at the importance of seeking the deeper encounters with God, of walking as kings, of becoming the "greater things Christians" of **John 14:12**, and of keeping the gates of our hearts and minds.

We looked at habitations and visitations of the LORD, permanent abiding, and the risen Christ standing in our midst as we worship. We saw that consecration, repentance, humility, forgiveness, and unity are foundational to our effectiveness as servants of the Most High God.

A Committed, Unified Ekklesia

In Part 02, we have discussed the Heavenly and Earthly patterns of 24/7 prayer; altars, living sacrifices, and God's response to all the above; the importance of establishing and maintaining spiritual foundations; the establishment of the Kingdom of God; maintaining the spiritual victories that are won; and the increase of Glory.

We looked at the revolutionary, revelatory role of the ekklesia as the called-out legislative assembly of the LORD, and also as the glorious Bride of Christ; mountains as places of holy encounter with the Living God; and the mountains or spheres of society that we are called to transform through the presence and precepts of the Gospel of the Kingdom working in and through us.

When individuals and ekklesias are focused and unified as above, then we will have an ekklesia that God can use to bring revival and reformation to the nations of the earth.

Preparedness

I have heard people say, "Revival will bring these things. None of those things will happen until revival comes." But the fact is, when Jesus brings revival to our midst, it will magnify and enlarge what we already have in Him, and who we are in Him. And revival will also put the spotlight upon that which we do not yet have.

If we look at the Book of Acts, Chapters 1 and 2, we see 120 people who were gathered in the Upper Room - continually praying, focused, and unified **(Acts 1:12-14; Acts 2:1-4)**.

It was upon this group that the Holy Spirit fell. He came in response to their waiting and their unity of purpose. It was this group that caught fire for the LORD, brought countless thousands to faith in Him, and turned the world upside down.

I think it's very possible that initially there could have been many more than 120 people crowded into that upper room. If that was the case, then it would seem that one by one, those whose focus was elsewhere decided that there were more important things to do than wait upon the LORD.

One thing is certain – the 120 who remained for forty days were intently focused on the purposes of the Almighty. They were surrendered, obedient, and unified in their passion for a Divine encounter such as they had never experienced before.

Most importantly, they were prepared to wait upon the LORD until He came.

> **Luke 24:49 (NASB)**
> *"And behold, I am sending forth the promise*
> *of My Father upon you; but you are to stay in the city*
> *until you are clothed with power from on high."*

Their instructions were simply to wait until they had been *"clothed with power from on high."* They had no idea what was going to happen or what form that power from on high was going to take – they just knew that Jesus had effectively told them to not do anything except wait, until they had received this gift. They knew they were going to meet with God, and nothing was going to stand in their way.

God always wants to pour out His Spirit, and He is seeking out those who are ready. If the Holy Spirit falls upon unprepared vessels, they may not recognize or receive the day of their visitation. In this scenario, little benefit will result, either to the vessel or to those around them.

God sends revival to the individuals and communities who are already engaged with Him and already committed to His Divine purposes. Through revival, He brings further unity, further increase, further restoration, and further reformation.

In preparation for the dedication of the Temple of Solomon, the priests had consecrated themselves. The singers and musicians were so well prepared that 120 trumpeters and all the singers and musicians sounded "as one."

Because of their preparedness, God poured out His Spirit in such powerful measure that no one could stand because the cloud of His Glory absolutely filled the temple.

2 Chronicles 5:11-14 (TLV) - God's Glory Fills the Temple
*¹¹ And it came to pass, when the kohanim
came out of the Holy Place - for all the kohanim
that were present had consecrated themselves,
without regard to divisions - ¹² all the Levite singers
- Asaph, Heman, Jeduthun, their sons and their relatives
- dressed in fine linen with cymbals, harps and lyres,
were standing at the east end of the altar and with them
were 120 kohanim blowing trumpets.*

*¹³ Then it came to pass that when the trumpeters and singers
joined as one to extol and praise Adonai, and when the sound
of the trumpets, cymbals and musical instruments and the
praise of Adonai -*

"For He is good, for His mercy endures forever"

*- grew louder, the Temple, the House of Adonai,
was filled with a cloud. ¹⁴ The kohanim could not stand
to minister because of the cloud, for the glory of Adonai
filled the House of God.*

Having said that, we need to be clear that revival is not just about wonderful meetings, although revival meetings will be gloriously wonderful ! The precious gift of revival will only be given to us to steward if we understand that we are not its "end point."

We are designed to be channels of the blessing of God. His river - His life-giving, overflowing Spirit - is intended to flow through us to the ends of the earth **(Acts 1:8)**.

Acts 1:8 (NIV)
*"But you will receive power when the Holy Spirit
comes on you; and you will be My witnesses in Jerusalem,
and in all Judea and Samaria, and to the ends of the earth."*

Where the river of God's Spirit flows, everything shall live.

All kinds of life will be sustained by it, and it will yield a great harvest.

Where the river of God's Spirit does not flow, it stagnates because it has no outlet. It becomes a swamp and eventually dries up; it becomes a place where there "used to be a flow," but at the present time due to the lack of flow, nothing can live there. If something tries to grow there, it will die.

> **Ezekiel 47:9-11 (NIV)**
> [9] *Swarms of living creatures will live wherever the river flows.*
>
> *There will be large numbers of fish, because this water flows there and makes the salt water fresh; so where the river flows everything will live.*
>
> [10] *Fishermen will stand along the shore; from En Gedi to En Eglaim there will be places for spreading nets. The fish will be of many kinds—like the fish of the Mediterranean Sea.* [11] *But the swamps and marshes will not become fresh; they will be left for salt.*

In the parable of the sower **(Matthew 13:1-9; 18-23)** Jesus speaks of the seed that fell on good ground and yielded a crop 30-, 60-, and 100-fold. Those who heard and understood were the ones who became fruitful. To fully understand the words and ways of the LORD, we must be in a state of continual preparedness and consecration.

In **verse 12**, Jesus made the statement *"For whoever has, to him more will be given, and he will have abundance; but whoever does not have, even what he has will be taken away from him."* The context of this statement is understanding the mysteries of the Kingdom of Heaven.

Upon those who have made themselves ready and had their ears opened to the words and ways of the Spirit **(Isaiah 50:4-5)**, God will pour out His spirit, and they will become carriers of His Presence, carriers of His Glory, and carriers of revival. For those who have not availed themselves of the abundance of the spiritual riches in Christ, there is a danger of being left behind when revival comes.

Again, revival will both magnify what we have in Christ, and also underscore what we do not yet have.

Foundational Aspects of Revival

There is no such thing as a mono-cultural, mono-generational, or mono-denominational revival. Revival, renewal, and restoration are for all people.

Any and every sustained revival will demonstrate at least these four foundational aspects :-

(i) **Unity – Human choice leading to Divine commanded blessing**

   (Acts 2:1-4; Psalm 133:1-3; Chapter 7 "Repentance, Forgiveness, Humility, and Unity")

(ii) **Strategic, Spirit-led intercession**

   (Leviticus 6:13; Revelation 5:8; Chapter 9 "Day and Night, Night and Day")

(iii) **Strategic, Spirit-led worship**

   (John 4:24; Leviticus 6:13; Revelation 5:8; Chapter 20 "Kingdom Worship Centers and Kingdom Resource Centers")

(iv) **Strong agape fellowship that extends across communities and cities; generations and cultures, denominations, and spheres of influence.**

   (Acts 2:42-27; 1 John 1:3; John 13:34; Romans 12:13; Hebrews 10:24-25; Romans 1:12; 1 Corinthians 10:24; Ephesians 4:1-3; Joel 1:3; Psalm 145:4; Chapter 7)

There is a responsibility that comes with revival to steward it well. It is a weighty responsibility, but in the *Kabod* sense (i.e., glorious).

Revival seed is excellent seed. May our hearts be found by the LORD to be excellent, fertile ground **(Matthew 13:3-13).**

Generational Aspects of Revival

Calling All Generations, Nations, and Denominations

When Jesus comes into our midst, in all of His miraculous, wondrous majesty and power, all of the generations will be drawn to Him, and will be powerfully touched and radically changed.

Revival has at least three generational aspects to it. The first is that revival will touch everyone from infants to great-great-grandparents, and all the generations in between.

The second is that wherever generational seeds of the Word have been sown, there will eventually, and suddenly, come a generation where God will send the Holy Spirit to take the sown word and ignite it with the holy flames of revival and a supernatural outpouring accompanied by signs and wonders. Old and familiar meets new and fresh **(Matthew 13:52-53)**.

The third is that if genuine, generational agape relationships have been established, they will serve as conduits for the manifest blessing of the LORD to flow out from the center of the revival into a much wider community.

1 - Multiple Generations

In terms of revival touching multiple generations, cultures, and denominations, I remember visiting a beautiful mountainside town that was inhabited by hill tribe people as well as refugees. The local people were really lovely folk, mostly farmers.

There were believers from every denomination, and many people of faiths other than Christianity who attended the meetings. The LORD was in our midst, manifesting His Holy Fire, Glory, and miracle working power.

During the first meeting, two women with seizures – referred to as epilepsy by the local people - came for prayer. Demons were cast out of both of them, the seizures stopped, and they both received Christ.

The freeing of the first woman involved a fairly intense spiritual battle. There were many onlookers to her deliverance and as a result quite a few gave their hearts to Jesus at the conclusion of the meeting. Scores of people were baptized in the Holy Spirit as well.

Between the "official" meetings, quite a few people came for prayer. The woman with the most severe case of seizures, who had been delivered and saved the night before, brought her entire extended family to receive Jesus the next day. This included her children and grandchildren, her parents and grandparents, and also their friends – five generations in all, sitting on the floor, overwhelmed, weeping, and receiving Jesus.

After becoming born again, everyone who was present – from small children to the very elderly - was baptized in the Holy Spirit, including the pastor.

Later during our stay in that remote area, God used the team to help restore many broken marriage relationships. Also, couples who were unable to conceive were prayed for. God answered every prayer, and their babies were dedicated to God the following year, each conceived through the miraculous intervention of the LORD on behalf of both the present and as-yet-unborn generations.

On another day, a tattoo-covered heroin addict came to one of the meetings, and gave his heart to Christ. His best friend had come to Christ in one of the previous meetings.

Many people had come to the meetings from other towns and villages in the hill tribes areas, and some had come from surrounding nations.

We sensed that those few days of encounter had generated a sustained hunger for the deeper things of God that would have an impact across a broad spectrum of communities and cultures. This was confirmed over the next few years as the fires of revival spread.

In another meeting in a rural location, a nine-year-old boy, born mute, was instantly & miraculously healed. His eyes were full of wonder and gratitude to God, as he began to speak and his first words were in a language unknown to him – English. "Hallelujah – Praise the LORD!"

God gave him three languages that day – English, his local language, and the spiritual language of tongues. His mother, grandmother, uncles, and sister all gave their lives to Jesus. The next day, as the people in their village saw what God had done, scores of people, from the youngest to the most senior, gave their hearts to Jesus in right there in the home village, because of the miraculous testimony.

This is just a taste of what the beginnings of revival can be like, and about the generational impact that it can have.

2 - Generational Seeds

In terms of generational seeds being sown, what we are witnessing at our main ministry hub in Central Province of Papua New Guinea and the surrounding villages and districts is a good example of this.

The seeds of the Word of God have been sown by faithful believers for generations, since the first missionaries arrived about 100 years ago. They were strong in the Word of God and laid wonderful foundations for the coming move of God.

The early government of Papua New Guinea in the 1960s contained many members who were strong Christians who worked together with the church to achieve strong outcomes within the nation. Many movements rose up that were interested in the wellbeing of society as a whole.

However, Papua New Guinea also had to deal with the "upper citadel" scenario as discussed in Chapters 8 and 11. Other influences also arose, and while much of the early legacy may not have borne the expected long term fruit, the strong, solid foundations of the Word of God remained, ready to be watered by a future outpouring of the Holy Spirit.

This is occurring with the current generation. God is adding His outpoured Spirit and Glory to the foundations of Scripture that have been laid over many generations, with many souls saved, signs and wonders, and an Open Heaven being established in the region.

The Holy Spirit is releasing the revelation of the Gospel of the Kingdom, and confirming it with demonstrations of Divine power.

A genuine hunger to restore the entire nation has arisen, and the concept of the role of the ekklesia as an influencer of every sphere of society is being embraced from grassroots to government.

Some youth who had hands laid upon them in prayer during previous meetings are now regularly being taken up to Heaven as they pray. They meet three times a week on a mountain overlooking their village at 5:30 a.m. for prayer.

The prayer mountain has been set up according to Divine patterns shown to them by the Holy Spirit. Six months earlier, I had prophesied over the leader of this prayer team that God would use her powerfully in revival. That is exactly what is happening right now.

Their Heavenly testimonies are extraordinary. The children and youth have testified about their experiences in detail, and they align exactly with descriptions of Heaven, Heavenly beings, and the Throne Room of God as described in the Bible by the prophets Isaiah and Ezekiel, and the apostle John.

It is also wonderful to greet people over whom it had been prophesied that they would enter government. They have now been elected and are sharing the principles of the Gospel of the Kingdom on the government mountain for the Glory to God.

3 - Generational Agape

Another key factor here is that Thomas and Barana Abe, the couple who lead our center in Central Province, have tirelessly visited outlying villages for the past thirty years, praying and sharing the Word of God, with wonderful eternal fruit resulting. In some villages where there were no gathering places, they constructed buildings where local believers could meet together.

Because the relationships and mutual respect are well established, news of what God is doing moves quickly throughout the region, and there is a complete openness to the new things that God is doing in the midst of the people.

Everyone who is invited comes to the gatherings at the apostolic center, regardless of their denominational affiliation. People come from many different villages all over the district and also from much further afield.

We invite people from as many different villages as we can so that as many people as possible can be influenced by the outpouring of God's Spirit and the teaching of the Gospel of the Kingdom - the Presence and precepts of God. The key point is this : God loves to pour out His commanded blessing upon the unity that this generational agape has engendered within the region.

True revival will ultimately influence every sphere of human culture.

Revival is for all people to the ends of the earth – we are simply the channels or vessels designed and predestined to carry it.

Global Conditions that Prepare the Way for Revival

1 – Adversity and Persecution

Adversity will be used by God to bring His people, individually and collectively, to their knees in prayer. For those who are not yet Christians, adversity will often lead to an openness to the existence of God that is just not there when everything is going well.

Adversity in the form of persecution of the ekklesia will often cause it to flourish. Persecution leads us to an Upper Room, all-or-nothing preparedness to follow Jesus regardless of the steepness of the cost.

We must never neglect to pray for and support our brothers and sisters who live under continual threat of persecution, and sometimes torture or death, because of their confession of Jesus Christ as Lord of all within an environment that is hostile to Him and also to them.

2-God-Given Opportunity in the Midst of the Storm

Genesis 50:20 (NIV)
You intended to harm me, but God intended it
for good to accomplish what is now being done,
the saving of many lives.

2020 will be remembered as the year that the COVID-19 pandemic swept the world, affecting virtually every nation with sickness and death; locking down local, national, and international communities and travel; and bringing previously booming economies crashing to a halt.

I lost a friend and someone who had great influence on my life during the early stages of the pandemic; and I know many other people who lost loved ones. The virus and its effects are clearly very real, and it may take years for some nations, and the world economy, to recover from the effects.

Without meaning in any way to minimize the losses of loved ones and livelihoods, the changes to what we could and could not do that were the result of the pandemic-related lockdowns meant that we were all given the precious gift of time.

God presented a once-in- a-generation opportunity to the world wide ekklesia, to press in to the Throne Room as never before; to pray for the nations of the world as one; and to refocus and realign ourselves with God's Divine patterns, priorities, and passions for every family, every ekklesia, every government, and every people group.

So, what did believers choose to do with that precious gift of time ?

3 – The Rest That Remains

With physical gatherings not permitted for a time as a result of the pandemic, God almost enforced a season of rest for His people, and a season of seeking Him on a deeper personal level. This is something that we had seen prophetically, pre-pandemic, in late 2019 - the necessity at the beginning of the new decade for all of us to enter into the *"rest that remains for the people of God"* **(Hebrews 4:9-10)**.

We saw that this would be a vital key to the release of unprecedented levels of His Glory throughout the coming decade.

> **Hebrews 4:8-10 (NKJV)**
> *⁸ Now if this promise of "rest" was fulfilled*
> *when Joshua brought the people into the land,*
> *God wouldn't have spoken later of another*
> *"rest" yet to come.*
>
> *⁹ So we conclude that there is still a full and*
> *complete "rest" waiting for believers to experience.*
> *¹⁰ As we enter into God's faith-rest life we cease*
> *from our own works, just as God celebrates*
> *His finished works and rests in them.*

There are dimensions of God's rest that are so deep that most of us have very little idea about them ... hence *"we conclude that there is still a full and complete "rest" waiting for (all) believers to experience."*

Our God is infinite, and His riches are unfathomable !

> **Ephesians 3:8 (NASB)**
> *To me, the very least of all saints, this grace was given,*
> *to preach to the Gentiles the unfathomable riches of Christ ...*

God used the pandemic of 2020 to give His people the opportunity to learn to trust Him implicitly at deeper levels than they'd perhaps had to in the past. Many also learned, again, at a much deeper level, how to live in the midst of His Shalom regardless of circumstances.

God also used His people - as much as we allowed him to - to declare to a hurting world that was desperately seeking answers that the Creator God continued to sit upon His Throne, and that He was continuing to work in glorious ways in every nation of the world.

He always desires to use His people to help the world find the calm in the midst of the storm. The world has no answers to global crises. Christ and His Kingdom are the answers.

4 - Unified Prayer and Worship

One thing that God raised up during this time was an increasing number of globally connected prayer networks, who are coming together regularly to repent on behalf of the nations of the world.

God will honor this global unity and repentance; He will pour out His Spirit - the latter and former rain together - as prophesied in the Book of Joel.

> **Joel 2:23 (AMPC)**
> *Be glad then, you children of Zion,*
> *and rejoice in the Lord, your God;*
> *for He gives you the former or early rain*
> *in just measure and in righteousness,*
> *and He causes to come down for you the rain,*
> *the former rain and the latter rain, as before.*

What an opportunity was given to the ekklesia, in the midst of adversity, to reconsecrate ourselves, our families, our communities, our cities, and our nations to the LORD. It wasn't about finding the "next big thing" – it was about rediscovering out first love with "the One who is all and is in all" **(Colossians 3:11)** and watering the foundational roots of our faith through deepening intimacy with the Lover of our souls.

There are times when we all need to be reminded that, truly, everything we need and everything we desire is found in Him.

> **Isaiah 12:2-3 (AMP)**
> *[2] Behold, God, my salvation!*
> *I will trust and not be afraid,*
> *for the Lord God is my strength and song;*
> *yes, He has become my salvation.*
>
> *[3] Therefore with joy*
> *will you draw water*
> *from the wells of salvation.*

John 7:37-38 (AMPC)

[37] Now on the final and most important day
of the Feast, Jesus stood, and He cried in a loud voice,
"If any man is thirsty, let him come to Me and drink!

[38] He who believes in Me
[who cleaves to and trusts in and relies on Me]
as the Scripture has said, from his innermost being
shall flow [continuously] springs and rivers
of living water."

I pray that we will recognize the uniqueness of every season of God, and that we will allow and even invite His spotlight to examine us, and to examine our motivations and our ministries. From the eye of every storm, the Lamb of God will speak profoundly, one on one, to each and every one of His precious children.

The next time that you encounter a storm that rocks your boat, press in until you receive your glorious treasure and your Divine instructions.

Ask God to show you not only how to survive the storm season, but also how to maximize your fruitfulness during the storm, and how to prepare as effectively as possible for the coming season of revival.

5 – The Obstacles of Misunderstanding and Distraction

When a major shift of circumstances occurs, such as the sweeping global changes caused by the 2020 pandemic, we can always choose to continue to do what we have always done, perhaps with a minor alteration to format or location, but without an understanding of the Divine purpose for allowing the change to impact us.

If we do not recognize the purpose of seasons of change, there is a very real danger that we may also miss the deeper things that God is wanting to do in us and through us that will prepare us to be used mightily for His Glory.

During the 2020 pandemic, many became caught up in
"The Great Whodunnit."

Conspiracy theories abounded, and they were used by the enemy to distract God's people from the deeper truths that God wanted to reveal.

During these times of intense global testing and trial, mainstream media pumped up the hysteria, and in general did not report on the good that God continued to work through His people.

The reality is that there is nothing happening in the world today that was not predicted thousands of years ago in the Bible. The Word of God has the following to say about where our focus should and should not be, and about what really matters at the end of the day.

Isaiah 8:11-13 (AMP)
[11] For in this way the Lord spoke to me with His strong hand [upon me] and instructed me not to walk in the way of this people [behaving as they do], saying,[12] "You are not to say, 'It is a conspiracy!' In regard to all that this people call a conspiracy, And you are not to fear what they fear nor be in dread of it. [13] "It is the Lord of hosts whom you are to regard as holy and awesome. He shall be your [source of] fear, He shall be your [source of] dread [not man]."

The spiritual cause of disasters that affect humanity is known.

What matters during times of disaster is how God's people respond.

Deuteronomy 8:2 (NASB)
You shall remember all the way which the Lord your God has led you in the wilderness these forty years, that He might humble you, testing you, to know what was in your heart, whether you would keep His commandments or not.

The testing in the wilderness was all about God's people getting to know what was inside their own hearts. God already knew what was in their hearts – and He surely knows what is inside ours, even more than we do.

He needs *us* to see how we will respond to Him, when our world radically changes due to circumstances beyond our control, and when life becomes a little bit tough, unusual, and inconvenient. Will we lose focus, or will we rise up on eagle's wings ?

We are called to be the hands, feet, heart, and voice of Jesus to the people of this world. When the world is in crisis, and fear and confusion are being force fed to everyone who lives in it by the media (including social media), Then the people of God have been given an ideal opportunity to love those who are scared and confused into the truth.

> **Galatians 5:6b (NIV)**
> *The only thing that counts is faith*
> *expressing itself through love.*

6 - Shaking

Speaking about the times in which we are living,
God said, as recorded in **Hebrews 12:26-29 :-**

> **Hebrews 12:26-29 (NKJV)**
> ... *^{26} whose voice then shook the earth;*
> *but now He has promised, saying,*
> *"Yet once more I shake not only the earth, but also heaven."*
>
> *^{27} Now this, "Yet once more," indicates the removal*
> *of those things that are being shaken, as of things that are*
> *made, that the things which cannot be shaken may remain.*
>
> *^{28} Therefore, since we are receiving a kingdom*
> *which cannot be shaken, let us have grace,*
> *by which we may serve God acceptably with reverence*
> *and godly fear. ^{29} For our God is a consuming fire.*

God allows the shaking because He loves us, and He loves our communities and our nations. He wants the attention of those within the ekklesia and those who are not yet believers. Divine shaking grants us a Divine opportunity to examine everything that we have become accustomed to doing, and to readjust our lives as necessary to ensure that we are aligned with God's end time purposes.

Through the shaking, through the testing, through the seeking, and through the resting, everything is being put into place for an unprecedented outpouring of the Spirit of God.

We are living in a time where the conditions are becoming ideal for revival.

Are we ready, as individuals and as the unified ekklesia, to become overflowing carriers of God's Presence and Glory, and carriers of revival ?

No One Knows the Day or Hour

Matthew 24:36 (NKJV) - No One Knows the Day or Hour
"But of that day and hour no one knows,
not even the angels of heaven, but My Father only."

Regardless of what the world may look like, Jesus said that no-one knows the day and the hour when Christ will return - not even the angels – but only God the Father.

What we do know is that He is returning for a *glorious* Bride, one who is fully engaged with her Bridegroom, and also fully engaged in her mission **(Revelation 19:7-9)**.

As in the parable of the ten virgins, we want to be found with the oil of the Holy Spirit already burning brightly and continuously within us when Jesus visits us with revival **(Matthew 25:1-13)**. That parable speaks clearly into the times in which we live, of the absolutely crucial need to be spiritually prepared for the visitations of the LORD.

Matthew 25:6-10 (NKJV)
⁶ "And at midnight a cry was heard:
'Behold, the bridegroom is coming; go out to meet him!'
⁷ Then all those virgins arose and trimmed their lamps.

⁸ And the foolish said to the wise, 'Give us some of your oil, for our lamps are going out.' ⁹ But the wise answered, saying, 'No, lest there should not be enough for us and you;
but go rather to those who sell, and buy for yourselves.'

¹⁰ And while they went to buy, the bridegroom came,
and those who were ready went in with him to the wedding;
and the door was shut."

The Gospel of The Kingdom is all about the transformation of our nations from grassroots to government. There is much to do, particularly in the spiritual, governmental, and economic spheres so that God's heart's desire – to see every man, woman, and child born again and also transformed from Glory to Glory - can be fulfilled.

> **1 Timothy 2:3-4 (NIV)**
> *³ This is good, and pleases God our Saviour,*
> *⁴ who wants all people to be saved*
> *and to come to a knowledge of the truth.*

Jesus also said that He came to proclaim the year of the LORD's favor – Jubilee. This means freedom from every kind of captivity; not just from personal sin, but also from every effect of poverty, through the socioeconomic and spiritual transformation of every nation according to Kingdom principles.

> **Matthew 6:10 (NKJV)**
> *Your Kingdom come,*
> *your will be done on Earth as it is in Heaven.*

> **Luke 4:18-19 (NIV)**
> *¹⁸ "The Spirit of the Lord is on me,*
> *because he has anointed me*
> *to proclaim good news to the poor.*
>
> *He has sent me to proclaim*
> *freedom for the prisoners*
> *and recovery of sight for the blind,*
> *to set the oppressed free,*
> *¹⁹ to proclaim the year*
> *of the Lord's favour."*

So, let's proclaim Him and His Kingdom Gospel until He comes, and maximise the harvest through the release of Kingdom influence in every sphere of society. Let us become the carriers of the revival that the world so desperately needs. Creation is groaning, shaking, and desperately waiting for Christ and His followers to arise.

Romans 8:19-23 (NASB)
[19] For the anxious longing of the creation
waits eagerly for the revealing of the sons of God.

[20] For the creation was subjected to futility,
not willingly, but because of Him who subjected it,
in hope [21] that the creation itself also will be set free
from its slavery to corruption into the freedom
of the glory of the children of God.

[22] For we know that the whole creation groans
and suffers the pains of childbirth together until now.
[23] And not only this, but also we ourselves, having the first
fruits of the Spirit, even we ourselves groan within ourselves,
waiting eagerly for our adoption as sons, the redemption
of our body.

The Ideal Vehicle for Revival and Reformation

The Bride of Christ, His glorious ekklesia, and specifically an ekklesia that is focused on the restoration of all spheres of society, as well as the salvation of individuals, is God's chosen vehicle to spread revival.

In Part 03 we will examine some Divine patterns for the end times ekklesia that can maximise our local, national, and global effectiveness.

Part 03

Transformation

Ancient Paths and 21st Century Paradigms

Jeremiah 6:16a (AMP)
Thus says the Lord,
"Stand by the roads and look;
ask for the ancient paths,
Where the good way is; then walk in it,
And you will find rest for your souls."

Ephesians 2:19-21 (AMP)
[19] So then you are no longer strangers and aliens
[outsiders without rights of citizenship],
but you are fellow citizens with the saints (God's people),
and are [members] of God's household,
[20] having been built on the foundation
of the apostles and prophets,
with Christ Jesus Himself as the [chief] Cornerstone,
[21] in whom the whole structure is joined together,
and it continues [to increase] growing into
a holy temple in the Lord
[a sanctuary dedicated, set apart,
and sacred to the presence of the Lord].

Chapter 15

Ancient Paths
and
21st Century Paradigms

When we speak of 21st century paradigms, what we are really looking at is the rediscovery of the ancient paths laid out for us by the LORD, and applying them with the revelatory understanding of the Holy Spirit that is needed to become effective Kingdom ambassadors in our time.

Part 03 explores ancient paths revealed to us by the Ancient of Days, and how best to apply them in the 21st century for the Glory of God, the maturing of the ekklesia and the transforming of nations.

After I experienced the "One Net, Many Boats" encounter (documented in Chapter 2), over the next few weeks I had a series of other powerful encounters in the Spirit that were all focused on the same theme; a worldwide network of ekklesias, with each part connected to and supporting every other part, and ever-increasing Presence and Glory and supernatural fruitfulness at the focal points that would overflow into the entire network.

Networks of Holy Fire and Glory

The following encounter occurred as I was leading worship in a First Australians and Pacific Islanders fellowship here in Australia. It was a revelatory glimpse into the shape of the revived, unified Body of Christ of the 21st century and beyond.

I was taken up and found myself looking down at a multitude of small groups meeting all over the world and covering the earth with the Presence and Glory of God. Each group appeared as a powerful flame of Holy Fire. The fires were burning in the midst of darkness and displacing it.

Each group was interconnected in many directions to many other groups, by something in the form of a dynamic, moving, changing, glowing, powerful net – like a planet Earth-sized fishing net – a supernatural power grid encircling the globe !

A second vision overlaid on top of this one. There were liquid streams of fire, running out along the grid lines that had been established by the "supernatural power grid."

The streams of Holy Fire were being poured out from Heaven; and they were running along preformed paths that had been formed by the Holy Spirit connections.

The grid touched every single nation on the earth. There were no countries where there was greater or lesser fire, and the fire remained molten, bright, dynamic, and flexible. There were no regions where the Fire of God was not present.

All the groups were interconnected by the Spirit of the Living God (the supernatural power grid) - and they possessed unity and great spiritual power because of that. If the fire or power ever seemed to be waning in one group, it could be instantly supplied by the "backup power" from all the interconnected fires, so there was never any noticeable "power drop" anywhere on the grid. This is because the groups were connected relationally to each other and praying for each other.

The effectiveness of each group was not determined by the number who were meeting under one roof, but rather by the multitude who were meeting all over the world. All the small groups were part of one single body of believers, consisting of billions of individuals.

I believe that this is a view from the Heavenly perspective of God's desire to raise up vibrant, powerful, and apostolically aligned end time networks. They will be filled with Holy Fire, Glory, and Kingdom purpose, and they will connect and unify diverse groups, encircle the planet, and be very effective across all seven mountains of human culture.

Selah and Amen.

Isaiah 40:5 (NKJV)
"The glory of the LORD shall be revealed,
and all flesh shall see it together;
for the mouth of the LORD has spoken."

(also see Isaiah 4:5)

Ephesians 4:1-6 (NKJV) - Walk in Unity
[1] I, therefore, the prisoner of the Lord, beseech you
to walk worthy of the calling with which you were called,
[2] with all lowliness and gentleness, with longsuffering,
bearing with one another in love, [3] endeavoring to
keep the unity of the Spirit in the bond of peace.

[4] There is one body and one Spirit, just as
you were called in one hope of your calling;
[5] one Lord, one faith, one baptism;
[6] one God and Father of all, who is
above all, and through all, and in you all.

Angels Over Movements

Revelation 4:1 (NKJV) - The Throne Room of Heaven
After these things I looked, and behold,
a door standing open in heaven.
And the first voice which I heard
was like a trumpet speaking with me, saying,
"Come up here, and I will show you things
which must take place after this."

I was praying and presenting myself to the LORD as a priest and also as a king. I told Him that I would pursue Him – His Face rather than His hand, and also that I would pursue my Kingly inheritance as well as my priestly inheritance.

Then, I saw hundreds of people gathering as part of a local apostolic center, and represented amongst them were hundreds of ministries – that is to say, that everyone who was a part of the local apostolic center was bearing very abundant kingdom fruit.

Then God spoke and said "you think you know what fruitfulness looks like. You think you know what My Presence looks like. But I have things in store for My people that are simply unimaginable for them – even in spite of all of My wonders that they have experienced up until now."

Then I was shown a massive tree with unbelievably ripe, juicy, tasty fruit – like nothing that is found on the earth – it had every color and every flavor. I believe this signifies the multicultural convergence and also the divine abundance that God has in store for the coming revival.

This does not just mean people of different backgrounds being at the same gathering – it signifies a respectful and meaningful spiritual exchange between cultures.

Then, I saw the angel that was over that particular movement. At that stage, I had never seen anything like that in the Spirit before and it startled me. The angel over the movement was sounding a very loud trumpet.

The angel was blowing its trumpet and a very loud voice from the Heavens declared, **"It Is Time. It Is Time. It Is Time."**

The trumpet also sounded a warning; but the warning was to the enemy that God's people were arising as a mighty army. They were strategically positioning themselves to pursue and recover all, and would no longer be subject to his intimidation or the derailment of their destinies.

> **Revelation 14:6 (NKJV)**
> *"Then I saw another angel flying in mid-air,*
> *and he had the eternal gospel to proclaim*
> *to those who live on the earth – to every nation,*
> *tribe, language and people."*

> **Revelation 2:1, 2:8, 2:12, 2:18, 3:1, 3:7, 3:14 (NKJV)**
> *"...to the angel of the church of ..." "write..."*

> **Exodus 19:13b (NKJV)**
> *"When the trumpet sounds long,*
> *they shall come near the mountain [of the LORD]."*

Ancient Wells Uncovered

In another brief but powerful Divine encounter, I saw ancient wells being uncovered by the LORD for the people who were pressing in for revival through worship and intercession.

I saw row upon row of very large angels, a myriad of them, encircling the wells, watching and listening, and waiting to be activated by the LORD in response to the revival prayers of the saints.

We know that it is God who activates the angels. They are under His command, not ours. But as a result of our hunger and thirst and our commitment to pray and to worship, they are activated on our behalf through His commands to them.

Hallelujah.

Isaiah 12:2-5 (AMP)
*² Behold, God, my salvation! I will trust and not be afraid,
for the LORD God is my strength and song; yes, He has
become my salvation. ³ Therefore with joy will you draw water
from the wells of salvation.*

*⁴ And in that day you will say, Give thanks to the Lord,
call upon His name and by means of His name [in solemn
entreaty]; declare and make known His deeds among
the peoples of the earth, proclaim that His name is exalted!*

*⁵ Sing praises to the Lord, for He has done excellent things
[gloriously]; let this be made known to all the earth.*

Isaiah 51:9 (NKJV)
*Awake, awake, put on strength, O arm of the Lord!
Awake as in the ancient days, In the generations of old.*

Jeremiah 6:16a (NIV)
*This is what the LORD says:
"Stand at the crossroads and look;
ask for the ancient paths, ask where the good way is,
and walk in it, and you will find rest for your souls."*

Connected to the Source, and to Each Other

During another time of prayer, I had a further vision of an underground water system with vertical tunnels, which prompted some research, because I wanted to know what I was being shown by the Holy Spirit.

I discovered that there is an ancient system of underground water resourcing that is thought to have originated in Iran about 2,500 years ago, but is found in various forms throughout Central Asia, North Africa, and South America. In its place of origin it is known as the "qanat" system.

The qanat system is a subterranean infrastructure that gave access to ancient and hidden water sources, which are located at the foot of mountain ranges. Qanat systems allow human habitation in areas that otherwise would not support it - notably, deserts.

The structure consists of vertical shafts of successively increasing depth, which are connected by a horizontal underground tunnel that directs the water from subterranean water sources down a slight slope to gardens, farms, and settlements.

The vertical shafts are not themselves used for accessing water. They are used for calculating the right direction and proper angle of slope for the horizontal tunnel. Later, during excavation, they are used for faster removal of dug materials, as well as for regulating pressure and oxygen for workers. Finally, after the completion of construction, these shafts are used for maintenance, providing workers an easier way to get at the underground horizontal tunnels for repair. [28]

Qanats are constructed by a class of ancient diggers. The role was inherited from people who worked for the Persian kings 2,500 years ago. This specialist community of workers travels from place to place to strengthen the qanat networks as the need arises.

The tools that they use are simple : a pick, a shovel, and an oil lamp.

The work is often dangerous; the men are lowered down the access shafts by a rope into the subterranean water channels that require maintenance.

Water flows around them as they work. The ventilation is sufficient to aerate the water, but not for humans to breathe for long periods. The tunnels are known to occasionally collapse during construction and maintenance.

The importance of the qanat system is in the way it organizes territory through the process of revealing water to the surface and thereby providing the possibility of habitation. [29] The "point of revelation" of underground water to the surface would affect the placement, size, and character of towns, cities, farms, and gardens.

The qanat system shaped the landscape, organized the territory, and was the basis for habitation, construction, and prosperity.[30] Sharing the resource, as well as sharing the maintenance of the source and supply, helped form close social relationships within a neighborhood. [31]

Prophetic Significance

I was so excited when I researched what I had seen, as the qanat system is fully laden with prophetic significance for those who are entrusted with building the Body of Christ.

The ancient water source was hidden at the base of the mountains. The Bible says that God's foundation is in the holy mountains **(Psalm 87:1)** and as we discussed in Chapter 13 it is the Presence of the LORD that causes the mountain to be holy.

Where He is, there is life **(John 10:10)**. How important it is to remain spiritually connected to the Ancient of Days, to find the ancient paths and walk in them **(Jeremiah 6:16)** and to ensure that our spiritual supply of living water remains new and fresh **(John 7:37)**.

> **Psalm 87:1 (NASB)**
> *His foundation is in the holy mountains.*
>
> **Proverbs 25:2 (NASB)**
> *It is the glory of God to conceal a matter,*
> *But the glory of kings is to search out a matter.*
>
> **Proverbs 25:2 (TPT)**
> *God conceals the revelation of his word*
> *in the hiding place of his glory.*
> *But the honour of kings is revealed*
> *by how they thoroughly search out*
> *the deeper meaning of all that God says.*
>
> **Colossians 2:2b-3 (NASB)**
> *...* [2b] *resulting in a true knowledge of God's mystery,*
> *that is, Christ Himself,* [3] *in whom are hidden*
> *all the treasures of wisdom and knowledge.*

The water source is ancient. The system is old and familiar, almost taken for granted by the desert residents. Yet if the water ceases to flow through a failure to maintain the qanat system, nothing and no one could live there. The network of wells, when connected together, provides more than enough water to sustain tens of thousands of people who otherwise would not be able to live. Where the river flows ... everything *shall* live.

Ezekiel 47:9 (NASB)
It will come about that every living creature which swarms
in every place where the river goes, will live. And there will be
very many fish, for these waters go there and the others become
fresh; so everything will live where the river goes.

The vertical shafts of the qanat system ensured the health of the horizontal, outwards flow of life-giving water by allowing fresh air to mix with the water, and to allow easy maintenance when required.

It is vital to maintain and to continually strengthen our "upwards" connection to God and our "outwards" relationships with others. We need continual and fresh Holy Spirit infilling, fresh revelation and fresh encounters to sustain and invigorate our life in Christ; and we need to ensure the channels to receive from Him and to give to others remain clean and unblocked **(Luke 12:35; Acts 13:52; Ephesians 5:18b)**.

Acts 13:52 (NASB)
And the disciples were continually filled
with joy and with the Holy Spirit.

The work of constructing the system is pioneering. The work of maintaining the system can be dangerous, but it is absolutely essential if the life-giving water is going to continue to flow to everyone. Their tools were simple and functional; digging tools, and an oil lamp to illuminate the path.

This is like the roles of the apostles and prophets who are charged with laying correct foundations and pioneering in areas where the Gospel of the Kingdom is yet to be established **(Ephesians 2:20)**. It can often be dangerous work, as we will see in Chapter 18 (Apostolos).

An abundant supply of fresh anointing oil is essential, as is the knowledge of how to build and maintain a strong foundation, and how to tap into the Heavenly Source of love, revelation knowledge, and power.

Luke 12:35 (NASB) - Be in Readiness
"Be dressed in readiness, and keep your lamps lit.

The point of revelation of the water source organized the territory.

The foundational revelation that apostles and prophets are entrusted with receiving from the Throne Room is intended to organize the spiritual territory within their given spheres of influence **(Revelation 4:1; Hebrews 8:5b)**.

The elders – those of the generations that have gone before us, and who know the ancient paths - are entrusted with passing on what they know to the emerging generations **(2 Timothy 2:2)**. It is old and familiar to them, but because of what they know, the foundation is laid for the entire community to receive sustenance that is always new and fresh **(Matthew 13:52-53)**.

A single well, on its own, could not sustain even a single community. So it is with the ekklesia. Communities of God's people that have strong connections to others through the Living Waters of the LORD will sustain and grow in ways that they simply could not on their own. Nor is it ever God's intention to have just a single, isolated network, business, denomination, or nation in revival.

The coming move and habitation of the Spirit are for the entire globe and every sphere of human influence. Nations will know that God is in their midst when they experience His love and His Glory, and when they see the great and mighty exploits of His people **(Numbers 14:21; Daniel 11:32b)**.

This revelation was the fourth time within a month that God had shown me that the coming revival would be far too "weighty" [*with Kabod Glory, Divine attributes and design, and generational responsibility*] to be carried by a single Christian community.

As we connect our wells together through prayer, worship, relationship, and sharing of resources (anointing, human, teaching, financial, and agape), and each other's visions and burdens for the lost and for our nations, Divine visitation will become habitation, and the Living Waters of the LORD will flow and bring life into every nation on the face of the earth.

Habakkuk 2:14 (NKJV)
For the earth will be filled
with the knowledge of the glory of the Lord,
as the waters cover the sea.

Zechariah 14:8-9 (NKJV)
8 And in that day it shall be that living waters
shall flow from Jerusalem, half of them toward
the eastern sea and half of them toward the western sea;
in both summer and winter it shall occur.

9 And the LORD shall be King over all the earth.
In that day it shall be - "The LORD is one,"
and His name one.

Ephesians 4:14-16 (NKJV)
... 14 that we should no longer be children,
tossed to and fro and carried about with
every wind of doctrine, by the trickery of men,
in the cunning craftiness of deceitful plotting,
15 but, speaking the truth in love, may grow up
in all things into Him who is the head - Christ -
16 from whom the whole body, joined and knit together
by what every joint supplies, according to the effective
working by which every part does its share, causes
growth of the body for the edifying of itself in love.

Chapter 16

Convergence, Emergence, and Walking as Kings

Obadiah 1:15a (NIV)
"The day of the Lord is near for all nations."

Proverbs 1:5 (AMP)
The wise will hear and increase their learning,
And the person of understanding will acquire
wise counsel and the skill [to steer his course
wisely and lead others to the truth].

Proverbs 11:14b (AMP)
But in the abundance of [wise and godly]
counsellors there is victory.

There is a convergence and emergence of so many things at this time; old and new paradigms, strategies, ministries, networks, spheres of influence and mantles.

The convergence, through the sharing of revelatory knowledge and transference and multiplication of anointing, will increase unity, release the commanded blessing of Heaven, and lead to a supernatural explosion of fruitfulness.

There is a very intentional drawing together by the LORD and a convergence of apostles and prophets; pastors, teachers and evangelists; Kingdom economists and entrepreneurs; and prophetic worshippers and intercessors at this time that will be followed by their re-emergence with new levels of authority.

This is occurring in our day and our time, because now is the time for the ancient Divine patterns to be activated and implemented with an understanding that can only occur through the Divine convergence of the different streams mentioned above.

This is in contrast to the previous era where the fivefold and other ministry streams as listed above, as well as ekklesias, networks, and denominations, have been relatively isolated in terms of their function and operation, and only communicating with each other in a limited way.

God is also converging different streams from within the Body of Christ to connect with those outside of it. God's people are converging, and then being equipped to emerge into the spheres of government, economics, education, and more.

One of the major paradigm shifts that still needs to be understood and enacted by many followers of Jesus is the understanding that we are to be the planting of the LORD - *in the world.*

> **Matthew 13:38a (NASB)**
> *"...and the field is the world;*
> *and as for the good seed,*
> *these are the sons of the kingdom."*

The sons (and daughters) of the Kingdom realm are His good seeds !

Hallelujah. Good seeds grow into strong plants that produce abundant crops of every kind. Note that those good seeds are planted by the LORD into the field of the world, with the intention that they flourish there. God never intended for us to receive of His fullness and then be hidden away from the world, or to be uprooted from within our spheres and networks of influence.

On the contrary, He always intended for us to be firmly established in those places - a visible witness in and to the world, and transforming it from within according to Kingdom principles, while not partaking of it.

This means we should be converging and cross-communicating with others in different spheres of influence and from diverse revelatory streams, and emerging as a powerful and unified ekklesia, with each member powerfully equipped as a Divine change agent to realign culture until it reflects the Kingdom of God in every aspect.

Hubs of Divine Convergence and Emergence

Converging means a drawing together in purpose and unity - not a drawing out of the world but an intentional going into and establishment in the world of Kingdom strategies that will literally shake and transform nations in Kingdom unity and purpose – a powerful Divine convergence so that there can be an equally powerful Divine emergence.

God is bringing this all to pass in our day and in our time. There is such a Divine intentionality about what God is doing, particularly through apostolic hubs and networks because of the convergence and the diverse expressions of Christ that are manifested there.

These "hubs of Divine convergence and Divine emergence" are designed by God to train people to operate at an "enhanced discipleship level" - which is a powerful level. This is the level of the "Greater Things Christians" – those whom Jesus declared in **John 14:12** would do even greater things than the things that He did.

> **John 14:12 (NASB)**
> *Truly, truly, I say to you,*
> *He who believes in Me,*
> *the works that I do, he will do also;*
> *and greater works than these he will do;*
> *because I go to the Father.*

Walking as Kings

But also, the hubs of Divine convergence and emergence will train and equip people to be further released into the level of operating as Kings.

At the level of kings, Divine wisdom is released that will solve otherwise unsolvable problems and issues facing the world.

There will also be a powerful release, at a governmental level, of the commanded blessing of unity, through the unified convergence, and emergence of the kings of the Risen Christ.

> **Proverbs 25:2-3 (NKJV)**
> *² It is the glory of God to conceal a matter,*
> *But the glory of kings is to search out a matter.*
>
> *³ As the heavens for height and the earth for depth,*
> *so the heart of kings is unsearchable.*

> **Matthew 16:19 (AMP)**
> *"I will give you the keys (authority)*
> *of the kingdom of heaven; and whatever you bind*
> *[forbid, declare to be improper and unlawful] on earth*
> *will have [already] been bound in heaven,*
> *and whatever you loose [permit, declare lawful] on earth*
> *will have [already] been loosed in heaven."*

The kingly anointing will enhance the power of the speech of God's servants. Less words and less actions, wielded with much greater Divine authority, will bear supernaturally multiplied fruit due to the kingly authority released through them.

The era that He is drawing us into is an era where there is an accelerated Divine convergence between what is done and spoken in Heaven, and the reflection of that upon the earth through the lives of His submitted servants. This convergence will produce a powerful, end times expression of the glorified Lord within us and flowing through us, with an accompanying emergence into the fullness of all that we are called to be, and the extension of the Kingdom of God as a result.

Matthew 6:10 (NKJV)
"Your kingdom come,
Your will be done on earth as it is in Heaven."

This is going to occur in and through submitted, poured-out lives who understand the Glory realm and who understand that this Divine convergence and emergence are empowerment for us to share amongst those who need God and His Kingdom the most, across all seven mountains of human culture.

Proverbs 21:1 (AMP)
The king's heart is like channels of water
in the hand of the Lord;
He turns it whichever way He wishes.

When we master the art of speech and song in the realm of kings, then the words that we speak and sing out of our mouths will cause a change - a shift - in the heavenly realm.

This in turn will cause a resonance and reflection of the Heavenly realms on the earth that will transform nations.

Job 22:28 (AMP)
"You will also decide and decree a thing,
and it will be established for you;
And the light [of God's favor] will shine upon your ways."

John 15:15-16 (AMP)
15 I do not call you servants any longer,
for the servant does not know what his master is doing;
but I have called you [My] friends, because I have revealed
to you everything that I have heard from My Father.

16 You have not chosen Me, but I have chosen you
and I have appointed and placed and purposefully
planted you, so that you would go and bear fruit
and keep on bearing, and that your fruit will remain
and be lasting, so that whatever you ask of the Father
in My name [as My representative] He may give to you.

The further that we progress into the end times prophesied throughout the Word of God, we will see that it is not hit-and-miss proposition to walk as kings. There is a graduating from priests to kings, retaining all the attributes of priests and adding to that the attributes and authority of kings.

Some believe that only the fivefold ministers can walk in kingly authority. I believe as the end times progress there will be more and more believers, not just the fivefold, who will learn to access and exercise their kingly authority, which is their birthright as sons and daughters and ambassadors of Christ. The King of Kings lives within us.

He is the Hope of Glory **(Colossians 1:27)**.

He is the One Who changes us from Glory to Glory in direct proportion to the quality time that we spend with Him **(2 Corinthians 3:18)**.

Convergence has a time component to it. Time flows completely differently in Heaven than it does on the Earth **(2 Peter 3:8)**. However, the Divine acceleration that is occurring denotes less delay between the issuing of decrees in Heaven and their follow through by God's servants here on the Earth.

Intimacy is the key. End times acceleration requires a deepening relationship with our Creator so that we can understand, through daily revelation, the rapidly changing times in which we live from Heaven's perspective.

Intimacy is also the key that releases the Glory of God in greater measure in and through His servants. The Glory of God *will* cover the earth as God's servants become overflowing carriers of His Presence and of His Glory. The little "k" kings of the LORD will overflow with the glorious essence of the King of Kings and carry and release His Glory wherever they go.

I want to decree and declare in Jesus Name that each person who is reading this will be filled with the hunger, the longing, and the ever-deepening discipline and focus to graduate from operating at the level of disciple and priest to the level of a king – and to *emerge* with greater Divine authority and greater Divine influence, to proclaim and release the Gospel of the Kingdom to the uttermost ends of the Earth.

Amen.

Genesis 17:6 (NASB)
I will make you exceedingly fruitful;
and I will make nations of you,
and kings will come forth from you.

Psalm 72:1 (AMP)
Give the king [knowledge of]
Your judgments, O God,
And [the spirit of] Your righteousness
to the king's son [to guide all his ways].

Psalm 119:45-47 (NKJV)
⁴⁵ And I will walk at liberty,
For I seek Your precepts.

⁴⁶ I will speak of Your testimonies
also before kings,
And will not be ashamed.

⁴⁷ And I will delight myself
in Your commandments, which I love.

Psalm 138:4-5 (NKJV)
⁴ All the kings of the earth
shall praise You, O Lord,
When they hear the words of Your mouth.

⁵ Yes, they shall sing of the ways of the Lord,
for great is the glory of the Lord.

Proverbs 8:14-16 (TPT)
¹⁴ "You will find true success
when you find me,
For I have insight into wise plans
that are designed just for you.
I hold in my hands living-understanding,
courage, and strength.
¹⁵ I empower kings to reign
and rulers to make laws that are just.
¹⁶ I empower princes
to rise and take dominion,
and generous ones
to govern the earth."

Isaiah 60:21 (NASB)
"Then all your people will be righteous;
They will possess the land forever,
The branch of My planting,
The work of My hands,
That I may be glorified.

Chapter 17

Domata

One of the deep desires of the Father's heart is to raise up end-time leaders and disciples of His Son Jesus, who are passionate to know Him and to live according to every beat of His heart.

His end-time leaders must be passionate to access the Throne Room of Heaven, and to take the treasures received there into the darkest corners of the world – demonstrating His love through the resulting spiritual breakthroughs and abundance of supernatural and eternal fruit. The end-time leaders will eagerly develop their "upward and inward call" - the relational part of our calling that is not visible or obvious to anyone except the LORD - through an understanding of, and a desire to, develop a lifestyle where the disciplines that are involved to form Christlike character are the central focus.

This is vital for the success of our "outward call" - the part of our call that is visible to others - which will fail without consistent, upwards devotion, and inward surrender. When those areas of our walk are strong and consistent, then the outward call will reflect the supernatural nature of the Almighty.

So, what is the meaning of domata ?

In *Renewal Theology (Volume 2)* J. Rodman Wilson writes :-

> *The primary New Testament delineation*
> *of the gifts of the Holy Spirit is in*
>
> > **1 Corinthians 12:8–10**
> > [8] *For to one is given the word of wisdom*
> > *through the Spirit, and to another*
> > *the word of knowledge according to the same Spirit;*
> > [9] *to another faith by the same Spirit,*
> > *and to another gifts of healing by the one Spirit,*
> > [10] *and to another the effecting of miracles,*
> > *and to another prophecy, and to another*
> > *the distinguishing of spirits,*
> > *to another various kinds of tongues,*
> > *and to another the interpretation of tongues.* **(NASB)**

A few verses earlier Paul wrote :-

> > *"Now there are varieties of gifts, but the same Spirit"*
> > **(1 Corinthians 12:4)**.

*The Greek word for "gifts" in this text is "**charismata**"*
("a gift of grace, a free gift" (Strong's Concordance)).

After listing these nine gifts Paul adds,

> > *"But one and the same Spirit works all these things,*
> > *distributing to each one individually just as He wills"*
> > **(1 Corinthians 12:11)**.

The spiritual gifts as described here, therefore, are
distributions of the Holy Spirit.

*"**Gifts**" are also described in **Ephesians 4**; but here they are*
*not called **charismata** but **domata**. Shortly after quoting **Psalm**
68:18 "he gave **gifts** [**domata**] to men" [**Ephesians 4: 8**], Paul*
*listed five such gifts [**Ephesians 4:11**]. It is clearly stated*
*that the source of the gifts is Christ [**Ephesians 4:7**].* [32]

Ephesians 4:8 is an extremely important verse of Scripture.

> **Ephesians 4:8 (BIB)** *(emphasis mine)*
> διὸ *(Therefore)* λέγει *(it says):*
> "Ἀναβὰς *(Having ascended)* εἰς *(on)* ὕψος *(high),*
> χμαλώτευσεν *(He led captive)* αἰχμαλωσίαν *(captivity),*
> *(καὶ) (and)* ἔδωκεν *(gave)* **δόματα *(domata = gifts)***
> τοῖς *(-)* ἀνθρώποις *(to men).* "

The Greek word used here for "gifts" is "δόματα" (domata), an entirely different word from the word "charis" used elsewhere.

Charis are spiritual gifts that can be distributed freely to all. Domata has a completely different meaning. The domata referred to in **Ephesians 4** are not activities or things, but specific individuals; i.e., the people themselves are the gifts, and they have been granted specific functions by God.

Paul explains further in **Galatians 1:1 (NLT)** *(emphasis mine)* :-

> *"This letter is from Paul, an apostle. I was not appointed*
> *by any group of people or any human authority,*
> *but by Jesus Christ himself and by God the Father,*
> *who raised Jesus from the dead."*

The implication here is that God the Father and God the Son had a conversation (and doubtless more than one) regarding Paul, agreeing between themselves to select him to become a Kingdom ambassador, specifically functioning as an apostle. They were (obviously) in total agreement about this. At a later time, they had the conversation with Paul, in effect inviting him to covenant with them as a domata.

Why do I say "covenant" ?

Because a covenant is essentially an agreement between God and man. Because Christ is involved, if we say "yes" to our domata call, even if we stumble – and we are bound to because we are human - we will still be successful to fulfill our mission, because of God's involvement and His choosing of us.

God will always honor His part of any agreement between Himself and man; it is up to us to simply trust and obey, to will and to act, according to the utmost of our ability to do so.

Francis Frangipane in his brilliant book *The Power of Covenant Prayer* says the following about the nature of a covenant :-

> *A covenant relationship is a lifelong pledge,*
> *an unbreakable oath,* **which God Himself initiates**
> **and promises to sustain.** [33]

When God calls/invites someone to enter into a domata calling, He will supply everything that is needed to fulfil it.

Will there be trials ? Of course !

But God will strengthen and sustain His servants, because it is He Who has asked them to fulfil these specific, lifelong, and very challenging functions.

> *Contained within His promise is His unalterable*
> *commitment not only to fulfil His highest plan*
> *of redemption but also* **to supply grace and faith**
> *to His human counterparts along the way. Together,*
> *the all-sufficient God and a believing man accomplish*
> *the impossible through their covenant relationship.* [34]

In **Ephesians 4:11,** Paul lists apostles, prophets, evangelists, pastors, and teachers as Christ's gifts *[domata]* to His body. These domata have been invited to enter into a sacred and holy calling; a lifetime of service to their King for which they have been specifically chosen. The purpose is for the *equipping* and the *unifying* and *maturing* of the saints and *edifying* of the body of Christ in *love*, for the *work of ministry*.

(διακονία – diakonia : Spirit- empowered service guided by faith. Service and faith (service rendered through total dependence upon the Sender) – are often closely related in Scripture). [35]

Ephesians 4:11-16 (NKJV)
*[11] And He Himself gave some to be apostles, some prophets,
some evangelists, and some pastors and teachers,*

*[12] for the equipping of the saints for the work of ministry,
for the edifying of the body of Christ, [13] till we all come
to the unity of the faith and of the knowledge of the Son
of God, to a perfect man, to the measure of the stature
of the fullness of Christ; [14] that we should no longer
be children, tossed to and fro and carried about
with every wind of doctrine, by the trickery of men,
in the cunning craftiness of deceitful plotting,*

*[15] but, speaking the truth in love, may grow up
in all things into Him who is the head
– Christ - [16] from whom the whole body,
joined and knit together by what every joint supplies,
according to the effective working by which every part
does its share, causes growth of the body
for the edifying of itself in love.*

It is just so vitally important that those who are called into these five equipping functions have truly allowed themselves to be tested, refined, crushed, emptied, and finally - commissioned by the LORD Himself.

Many drop out during these carefully designed "choosing processes" (which could also be called "the crushing processes") of the LORD, often blaming the devil for what was in fact the Divine processing of God working to form Godly character in them, so that they could withstand the often crucible-like pressures of fivefold leadership.

There are so many tests that occur during the time of ministry preparation, and often they are not understood as tests. That is why Jesus said that *"many are called (invited and summoned), but few are chosen"* **Matthew 22:14 (AMPC).**

The cost is great, and for many, it is simply too great.

The domata have been chosen to daily lay down their lives upon the altar of living sacrifice to their Beloved **(Romans 12:1-2; 1 Corinthians 15:31)**, to be entirely poured out for Him, and for those whom He chooses for us to serve and live amongst, in selfless love and like a drink offering, until nothing is left **(Philippians 2:17)**.

God intends for His domata to be willing to be broken like a communion meal and fed to the poor, and all for the sake of the redemption of the lost and for the Glory of God, never for the furtherance of their own reputation **(Philippians 2:5-9)**.

For God's domata, self must decrease until it has died, so that Christ in us, the Hope of Glory **(Colossians 1:27)**, can increase to His fullest possible expression in and through us.

The purpose of these fivefold "domata" gifts is

> *"to equip the saints for the work of ministry,*
> *for building up the Body of Christ"*
> **(Ephesians 4:12).**

From all of the above, we can see that being chosen by God to fulfil a domata function is not an occasion to lead us to become puffed up with pride, or to expect others to serve us or see us as somehow better than themselves – God forbid.

No - being chosen by God to fulfill a domata function is an occasion to fall on our knees in reverent awe, acknowledging our weaknesses and our reliance upon God every step of the way. If we are genuinely called, and if we persevere through the choosing process, then the full power, authority, anointing, and love of the LORD will be lovingly released through us, by Him, as we minister.

Jesus functioned in each of the fivefold functions of apostle, prophet, evangelist, pastor, and teacher; and He is our wonderful and perfect example of how the domata can function when completely surrendered to Him.

Set Apart for Increase

An important affirmation of the domata call of the LORD is that it will be recognized by other fivefold ministers. Remember though, that we are speaking of a *function*, and not a title.

A person cannot simply decide that they want to be a pastor, teacher, evangelist, prophet, or apostle. This is a decision that is made by the Godhead and the anointing is released by them to the person that they have chosen. But the anointing and fruitfulness will be seen and the nature of that anointing will be recognized by others.

And, there will be a measurable increase in anointing and fruitfulness that comes through the process of being set apart for increase in God's way and in His perfect timing.

> **Acts 13:1-3 (AMP)**
> *¹ Now in the church at Antioch there were prophets*
> *[who spoke a new message of God to the people]*
> *and teachers: Barnabas, Simeon who was called Niger, Lucius*
> *of Cyrene, Manaen who had been brought up with Herod*
> *[Antipas] the tetrarch, and Saul.*
>
> *² While they were serving the Lord and fasting,*
> *the Holy Spirit said, "Set apart for Me Barnabas*
> *and Saul (Paul) for the work to which I have called them."*
>
> *³ Then after fasting and praying,*
> *they laid their hands on them [in approval and dedication] and*
> *sent them away [on their first journey].*

In the above passage of Scripture, we see prophets, teachers, and apostles (Paul and Barnabas are specifically mentioned) fasting, praying, and serving together.

In verse 2, the Holy Spirit directs the gathering to "set apart" Barnabas and Saul for the work that they were called to do.

There are a few things that are of significance here.

(i) Being set apart for increase has specific place and time components attached to it.

Place : The word translated into English as "set apart" is the word ἀφορίζω (aphorízō) that means "to appoint, set apart for some purpose" and "to mark off from others by boundaries, to limit, to separate."

It would seem that being set apart for increase and being limited or marked off from others by boundaries would seem to be a cross purposes to each other – but that is not the case. Each person with a domata call on their lives has a metron – a sphere of influence - within which they are called to increase. Paul expands on this in **2 Corinthians 10:13-16**.

> **2 Corinthians 10:13-16 (NASB)**
> *13 But we will not boast beyond our measure,*
> *but within the measure of the sphere which God*
> *apportioned to us as a measure, to reach even as far as you.*
>
> *14 For we are not overextending ourselves,*
> *as if we did not reach to you, for we were the first*
> *to come even as far as you in the gospel of Christ;*
>
> *15 not boasting beyond our measure, that is,*
> *in other men's labors, but with the hope that*
> *as your faith grows, we will be, within our sphere,*
> *enlarged even more by you,*
>
> *16 so as to preach the Gospel even to the regions*
> *beyond you, and not to boast in what*
> *has been accomplished in the sphere of another.*

The word translated "sphere" comes from the Greek word μέτρον (metron). This word is translated in various ways by Bible translators, including *"limits of the sphere," "area of ministry," "measure of the sphere," "area of authority,"* and *"area of influence."* A metron is all of these. It is important for everyone with a domata call to understand the full extent of their sphere of influence, and also the limits of it.

Time : I always share with my spiritual sons and daughters that :-

- The wrong thing will always be the wrong thing no matter when and where we attempt to achieve it;

- The right thing, done at the wrong time and/or in the wrong place, equates to doing the wrong thing;

- The right thing done at the right time and in the right place is the only right thing;

- The timing of God is crucial in all that we do.

"In the fullness of time, God sent His son" **(Galatians 4:4)**.

If you have a domata call on your life, God has sent you into the world in the exact fullness of time for you to fulfil it. The good news is that God is a great father; and He even allows for our mistakes and builds them into the overall timing when He calls us.

So then, the domata release defines the nature and function of a person's calling, and being set apart for increase will mark off the boundaries of it, i.e., the place and the timing of the fivefold call. Note that "place" could include a people group, subculture, or sphere of society.

Both releases originate from the Godhead. The second requires obedience from both the one who is called, and from other fivefold ministers.

(ii) They were already functioning as apostles prior to being set apart for increase.

Paul and Barnabas did not become domata because of the setting apart. They had already been chosen by God to operate in the function of apostle; and they were already functioning in their callings **(Acts 4:36, Acts 9, Acts 11)**. They had demonstrated their call, anointing, and function through the abundant, supernatural fruit that was already manifesting in and through their lives.

But – after they had been set apart, there was a tremendous increase in their fruitfulness, and also an enlargement of the territory that they were called to minister within. Paul, the tent-making apostle, had his cords lengthened, his pegs strengthened, and the place of his tent enlarged.

(iii) Obedience is important
(not just for those who were called to be set apart).

The fruit of the call was already in evidence prior to Paul and Barnabas being set apart for increase. It was God Who called and equipped Paul and Barnabas. But, the ekklesia were shown the apostolic anointing that was upon them and the function to which they were called.

And it was the ekklesia who were called to set them apart for an increase of the anointing that they already carried.

"Serving the LORD and fasting" (**Acts 13:2**) involved prayer, worship, teaching, and prophesying. The command from the Holy Spirit to lay hands upon Paul and Barnabas was to those who were gathered.

In other words, the fulfilment of Paul and Barnabas's calling was not just conditional upon their obedience but also on the obedience of those who were called to set them apart for increase.

(iv) Impartation Through the Laying on of Hands

There is tremendous impartation that occurs when we obey the LORD and lay hands upon those whom He chooses, in His way, and at His appointed time. This is particularly true in terms of increase, when the domata lay hands upon someone. The impartation is at another level when it is an apostle who is called by God to lay hands upon someone.

I remember a time of very fruitful ministry on the island of Borneo in 2007. There had been a tremendous number of people born again, a multitude of healing miracles, and during the worship, the Heavens were literally opened.

During one particular evening meeting, the majority of the few hundred people who were present became aware that there was a cloud of thick Glory hovering above our heads; and many were aware of the thick presence of angels in the midst of the Glory.

On the way to the airport, the senior minister of the fellowship, himself an apostle, and his assistant who was a prophetic worshipper, evangelist, and emerging apostle, took me out for a meal and asked me, "Steve, are you aware of the gift and calling that you are functioning in ?"

I replied, "Yes, but I would like to hear it from you."

They went on to say that they could see a clear apostolic function and call, and that the Holy Spirit had spoken to them to set me apart for increase. They took me to the **Acts 13:1-3**, and after reading it, right there in the restaurant, they anointed me with oil, laid their hands upon my head, and set me apart for increase as an apostle.

From that moment onwards, there was a tangible increase of fruitfulness, anointing, Heavenly encounters, and Open Heaven experiences; and also, doors began to open into many other nations of the world.

There were other factors that contribute to this that have been discussed in earlier chapters, but the setting apart for increase by these two humble, mighty Men of God was a marker stone and a turning point in my life and ministry. I'm forever grateful to them for their obedience to the LORD in this matter.

Apostolic Function

For the remainder of Part 03 of this book, we are going to focus primarily on what the call, character, and outworking of one of the domata functions looks like.

We are referring to apostles. They have a crucial role to play in terms of bringing the rest of the Body of Christ into alignment with the end times purposes of the LORD.

Chapter 18

Apostolos

Ephesians 4:11-12 (NASB)
*[11] And He gave some as apostles, and some as prophets,
and some as evangelists, and some as pastors and teachers,
[12] for the equipping of the saints for the work of service,
to the building up of the body of Christ.*

The domata :-

> *... are sovereign grants from the ascended and reigning Christ for the equipping of His church. They are not the result of individual choices but come about through divine action.*
>
> *The gifts are persons - apostles, prophets, etc., (not activities) who are given by Christ to the church for the equipping of the body of believers.*
>
> *The personal, exalted Christ provides persons for this critical task. And, these equipping ministries are necessary to the continuing life of the church.*
>
> *The fact that Christ "gave" cannot refer only to the past, because the gifts are for the ongoing work of equipping the saints of all times and places for their work of ministry.* [36]

Like the other domata fivefold functions, but in a broader sense due to the nature of the apostolic function, the apostle is called to imitate Christ **(1 Corinthians 11:1)** and to radiate every aspect of who He is to the Ekklesia, and to the world.

Ephesians 2:19-22 (NASB)
[19] So then you are no longer strangers and aliens,
but you are fellow citizens with the saints,
and are of God's household, [20] having been built
on the foundation of the apostles and prophets,
Christ Jesus Himself being the corner stone,
[21] in whom the whole building, being fitted together,
is growing into a holy temple in the Lord,
[22] in whom you also are being built together
into a dwelling of God in the Spirit.

"Apostolos" is the New Testament Greek word that is translated "apostle" in English. "Apostolos" denotes an envoy, ambassador, or messenger commissioned to carry out the instructions of the commissioning agent. [37]

In the Septuagint, the word *"apostello" (or "exapostello")* is used around seven hundred times to translate the Hebrew word *"salah" (to stretch out, to send)*. "Apostello" denotes the authorization of an individual to fulfill a particular function, *with the emphasis being on the one who sends, not on the one who is sent.* [38]

This is an important definition. It aligns with **Ephesians 4:8,** which emphasizes the domata as being gifts of Christ that He gave to men.

They are ambassadors and representatives of God, not of themselves.

Ephesians 4:7-8 (NASB)
[7] But to each one of us grace was given
according to the measure of Christ's gift.
[8] Therefore it says,
"When He ascended on high,
He led captive a host of captives,
And He gave gifts to men."

The First and Foremost Apostle

> **Hebrews 3:1 (NASB)**
> *Therefore, holy brethren, partakers of a heavenly calling, consider Jesus, the Apostle and High Priest of our confession.*

Jesus Christ is the first and foremost apostle, the original "Sent One," sent from the Father to redeem the world. He is the cornerstone.

"Christ is all and is in all" **(Colossians 3:11)**.I could meditate upon that one profound statement in **Colossians 3:11** for the next twenty years.

Can we even begin comprehend what the word "all" means, when it is connected to the Name above all Names ? I can imagine the apostle Paul, having spent another day lost in the love, wonder, and Presence of the LORD, encountering Him face to face and trying to express in words what he was seeing, hearing, and feeling.

"Christ is all and is in all."

Every time I read that simple verse, I begin to weep. Can we ever truly understand just Who it is that lives inside of us and has forgiven *all* of our sins and granted us eternal life ? Not in this life time.

All apostolic authority originates in Him, and flows through Him, into and through those whom He has called to be apostles – to be like Him in love and in purpose and to implement His divine patterns and strategies in and through the ekklesia for the redemption of souls and the transformation of nations.

He has declared that as we walk in His ways, we will do greater things than even He has done **(John 14:12)**.

The Original Twelve Apostles (The Apostles of the Lamb)

> **Revelation 21:14 (NKJV)**
> *Now the wall of the city had twelve foundations, and on them were the names of the twelve apostles of the Lamb.*

Matthew 10:2-4 (NKJV)
² Now the names of the twelve apostles are these:
first, Simon, who is called Peter, and Andrew his brother;
James the son of Zebedee, and John his brother;
³ Philip and Bartholomew; Thomas and Matthew
the tax collector; James the son of Alphaeus,
and Lebbaeus, whose surname was Thaddaeus;
⁴ Simon the Cananite, and Judas Iscariot,
who also betrayed Him.

The original twelve apostles were uniquely privileged. They physically walked with Jesus and were eyewitnesses of His life, ministry, death, burial, and resurrection. They were of that privileged company who had literally *"been with Jesus,"* **(Acts 4:13)** existing within the same physical realm at the same physical time.

The Twelve were personally instructed by Him, and they were sent out by Him to preach and teach the Gospel of the Kingdom with signs and wonders following. They ate and drank with Him, travelled with Him, and stayed with Him. Do you ever wonder what that must have been like, to sit around the campfire with Jesus; to be there when He raised Lazarus from the dead; to see a multitude fed with two fish and five loaves of bread; to be in the boat with Him, and to see him walking on the water; just to be near Him; and to hear the love and beauty and authority in His voice ?

They saw Him in risen form and received instructions to wait in Jerusalem until they received power from on high **(Luke 24:49; Acts1:8; Chapter 14)**.

Once they had received the Baptism of the Holy Spirit, they were entrusted with the amazing mission of laying the foundations for the original Ekklesia. And they spread the Gospel of the Kingdom far and wide.

The Book of Revelation tells us that the New Jerusalem has twelve foundations, and that on each of them is written one of the names of the twelve apostles of the Lamb.

They are the only Christ-followers who are honored in this way by God. They were truly foundational in terms of the establishment of the ekklesia and the Kingdom of God.

Some were entrusted with writing some of the books of the New Testament.

The Apostle Paul

Galatians 1:1 (NASB)
Paul, an apostle (not commissioned and sent from men nor through the agency of man, but through Jesus Christ - the Messiah - and God the Father, who raised Him from the dead) ...

Paul was hand-picked by God to *"bear His Name before the Gentiles, kings, and the sons of Israel"* **(Acts 9:15).** The LORD testified to Ananias that it was so.

The LORD went on further to say to Ananias in **Acts 9:16** :-

... *"for I will show him how much he must suffer for My name's sake"* **(NASB).**

There were surely times when Paul felt as though his heart and his flesh were about to give way. And given the trials that he suffered because of his calling, it is not surprising that he felt that way.

Read **2 Corinthians 4:7-18, 11:23-32** and **2:7-12,** and put yourself in his shoes (or perhaps you have already walked a distance in shoes that seem as though they may have once belonged to the apostle Paul).

There were times when he must have felt as though he were losing his mind. There were times when others were sure that he had, and they told him so **(2 Corinthians 5:13; Acts 26:24-29).**

2 Corinthians 5:13 (NASB)
For if we are beside ourselves, it is for God; if we are of sound mind, it is for you.

Acts 26:24-29 (NASB)
²⁴ While Paul was saying this in his defense,
Festus said in a loud voice,
"Paul, you are out of your mind!
Your great learning is driving you mad."

²⁵ But Paul said, "I am not out of my mind,
most excellent Festus, but I utter words of sober truth.
²⁶ For the king knows about these matters,
and I speak to him also with confidence, since
I am persuaded that none of these things escape his notice;
for this has not been done in a corner.

²⁷ King Agrippa, do you believe the Prophets?
I know that you do." ²⁸ Agrippa replied to Paul,
"In a short time you will persuade me to become
a Christian." ²⁹ And Paul said, "I would wish to God,
that whether in a short or long time, not only you,
but also all who hear me this day, might become
such as I am, except for these chains."

Yet it is clear from what he wrote in the pages of Ephesians, Philippians, and Colossians just how deeply he was undone and unraveled by the depth of his revelation of God's love for him.

It is clear that his relationship with God was real, profound, continuous, and supernatural, and well beyond the level that most believers enter into. It needed to be that way to sustain the rigors of the call; but it cuts both ways.

Paul had a deep relationship with his Creator, because that is what he desired; and because of His desire, God could use him as mightily as He did.

Regardless of the trials – shipwrecks, beatings, imprisonment, ridicule, riots, floggings, sleep deprivation, hunger and thirst, extreme cold, and exposure to the elements, and his intense burden for the people of God - Paul persevered until the end. Christ sustained him and gave him the domata victory that he was born to achieve.

In between the lists of trials and persecutions listed in **2 Corinthians 11 and 12,** Paul shares the testimony of a man who was "caught up to the third heaven" and *"caught up into Paradise and heard inexpressible words, which a man is not permitted to speak."*

> **2 Corinthians 12:2-4**
> *² I know a man in Christ who fourteen years ago*
> *- whether in the body I do not know, or out of the body*
> *I do not know, God knows - such a man was caught up*
> *to the third heaven. ³ And I know how such a man*
> *– whether in the body or apart from the body I do not know,*
> *God knows - ⁴ was caught up into Paradise and heard*
> *inexpressible words, which a man is not permitted to speak.*

It is clear from the wider context of Chapter 12 that Paul is speaking of himself.

On the other side of the lists of persecutions, Paul says :-

> **2 Corinthians 12:7-10 (NASB)**
> *⁷ Because of the surpassing greatness of the revelations,*
> *for this reason, to keep me from exalting myself,*
> *there was given me a thorn in the flesh, a messenger*
> *of Satan to torment me—to keep me from exalting myself!*
> *⁸ Concerning this I implored the Lord three times*
> *that it might leave me.*
>
> *⁹ And He has said to me,*
> *"My grace is sufficient for you, for power is perfected*
> *in weakness." Most gladly, therefore, I will rather*
> *boast about my weaknesses, so that the power of Christ*
> *may dwell in me.*
>
> *¹⁰ Therefore I am well content*
> *with weaknesses, with insults, with distresses,*
> *with persecutions, with difficulties, for Christ's sake;*
> *for when I am weak, then I am strong.*

Yet the LORD was always with Paul. Scripture records that He came to him and encouraged him.

Acts 18:9-10 (NKJV)
⁹ Now the Lord spoke to Paul in the night by a vision,
"Do not be afraid, but speak, and do not keep silent;
¹⁰ for I am with you, and no one will attack you to hurt you;
for I have many people in this city."

Unimaginable trials and persecutions, glorious Heavenly encounters, thorns in the flesh - welcome to the apostolic life ! When I get to Heaven, I want to meet this great man.

Paul wrote more of the New Testament than anyone else.

After his personal encounter with Jesus on the road to Damascus, which resulted in his salvation **(Acts 9:3-6)** – and also struck him blind – **Galatians 1:11-17** indicates that he spent considerable time with the Risen Christ during the years that he spent in the desert.

That is why he was able to declare :-

Galatians 1:11-12 (NASB)
¹¹ For I would have you know, brethren, that the gospel
which was preached by me is not according to man.
¹² For I neither received it from man, nor was I taught it,
but I received it through a revelation of Jesus Christ.

Paul achieved everything that the LORD said he would - he declared His Name before the Gentiles, the Jews, and kings - and he also suffered as the LORD said that he would. He went from place to place, leading people to salvation, strengthening and encouraging gatherings of believers, establishing training, equipping and sending centers, and testifying of the greatness of the LORD.

Acts 14:21-22 (AMP)
²¹ They preached the good news to that city and made
many disciples, then they returned to Lystra and to Iconium
and to Antioch, ²² strengthening and establishing the hearts
of the disciples; encouraging them to remain firm in the faith,
saying, "It is through many tribulations and hardships
that we must enter the kingdom of God."

(also see **Acts 15:40-41; Acts 16:3-5**)

He brought the strong Presence of God with him; extraordinary miracles took place wherever he went **(Acts 19:12)**. Even handkerchiefs that touched him would be enough to heal the recipient.

Paul embarked on three major missionary journeys that impacted cities and entire regions **(Acts 13 – 19ff.)**. He took teams with him.

After this period of his life, although he was in the custody of the Roman empire, he penned the Epistles and appeared before rulers, kings, and finally the emperor of the Roman empire, testifying of the lordship of Christ. Eventually, he was martyred for his faith.

With Jesus and the Twelve, the apostle Paul is a wonderful example for us of the potential fruitfulness, influence, and cross-cultural reach of the apostolic function, and also of the genuine relationship with God and people, love, humility, perseverance, endurance, and personal sacrifice that are required to fulfil it.

Other New Testament Apostles

Many others are referred to as apostles within the New Testament; they were involved in spreading the Gospel and in establishing, strengthening, and encouraging the believers. These include Mathias **(Acts 1:26)**, Barnabas **(1 Corinthians 9:5, 6)**, Andronicus and Junia (a woman) **(Romans 16:7)**, Apollos **(1 Corinthians 4:6)**, James (the Lord's brother) **(Galatians 1:19)**, Silas and Timothy **(1Thessalonians 1:1)**, Titus **(2 Corinthians 8:23)**, and Epaphroditus **(Philippians 2:25)**.

What an exciting time to be alive ! They ran in anointed ministry and heavenly authority with the Holy Spirit, which led to explosive growth of the early ekklesia; and they also ran from the earthly authorities who pursued them with the intent to persecute and kill them.

If not for their faithful commitment and determination to complete their mission, we would not have an ekklesia at all today.

Thank God for the Twelve, for Paul, and for the rest of the New Testament apostles. Wherever they went, they *"turned the world upside down"* **(Acts 17:6)**. This is evidence that they did not just share the Gospel of salvation but also the Gospel of the Kingdom, which would have challenged every governmental, economic, spiritual, and educational paradigm of the day – just as it does in our day.

Apostles Today

We have seen above that the domata, of whom apostles are one function, are an ongoing, continual gift from the LORD that He will continue to give for as long as the household of God continues to be built.

The function of apostles today is to continue to found, establish, strengthen, and encourage the ekklesia in all its forms, in every nation and across every sphere of influence.

Their call is cross-denominational and they are called to see the Body of Christ as one and to work to unify it. *"Father, make them one as we are one"* **(John 17:22)**.

Modern day apostles are still the gifts of Christ **(Ephesians 4:8)** and chosen and sent by the Father and the Son **(Galatians 1:1)**. Modern day apostles preach and teach the Gospel of the Kingdom with signs and wonders following.

This will occur because just like the first apostles, they will have been with Jesus. They will encounter the Risen Christ through their intense relationship with Him. They will see what He is doing and hear what He is saying in the Heavenly realms, so that they can then speak His words and release His actions here on the earth.

The apostolic function will reveal the character of Christ through the fruit of the Holy Spirit and the supernatural function of Christ through the gifts of the Holy Spirit. Modern day apostles, working with prophets, will lay Divine, strategic foundations for the ekklesia, and then to train, equip, and release Christians into the fullness of their destinies.

The apostolic function is governmental in nature in the spiritual realm. Some apostles will have a specific call to influence earthly governments and to work with them, and in some cases to author or co-author policies for them, for the Glory of God and for the sake of Kingdom advancement at a national level.

The apostolic function also involves pioneering work in territory where the Gospel of the Kingdom is not yet known. This relates to both physical territory (nations and people groups) and cultural territory (spheres of influence). The ekklesia is called to take back the mountains of human culture, and the apostles are called to lead the way.

Another aspect of the modern day apostolic function is to complete the revelation where the ekklesia has only partial revelation of the Gospel of the Kingdom.

Modern day apostles will train and equip Christian disciples to become transformers of society at every level. They are called to model and impart Divine principles to the disciples of Jesus that will release powerful, effective, Spirit-fueled Kingdom strategies across all seven mountains of human culture.

The Senders, Not the Sent

Those who are sent by The Senders (see **Galatians 1:1**) are representatives in character, supernatural authority and function, and agape love of those by whom they have been sent. The sent ones are God's messengers and emissaries, sent to convey His message, to release His authority and His anointing, to demonstrate His character (love and supernatural power) and to lead people into His truth with His love. Jesus is the capital "A" Apostle. His sent ones are the small "a" apostles, called to serve those to whom He will send them.

The power and Kingdom authority and anointing are His. His decrees are final and absolute. On one particular trip to a nation where believers were persecuted for their faith, at most of the meetings, the message would often consist of just one verse.

That verse was **Luke 4:40** which says,

> *"When the sun was setting, all those who had any*
> *that were sick with various diseases brought them to Him;*
> *and He laid His hands on every one of them and healed them"*
> **(NKJV).**

At that point, I would close my Bible, and then I would say :-

"Now, we are going to invite the Author of that verse,
Jesus Christ, to come and demonstrate His Holy Word."

This was not something that I had decided to do. I was under direct instructions from the King of Kings to read one verse, close my Bible, and invite Him to come.

This set the pattern for the majority of the meetings over the next four weeks. Night after night, all but a handful of the people who were in those meetings would be healed of major, long-standing illnesses and conditions.

In one particular meeting, after we had prayed and invited Jesus to come demonstrate His Word, the Glory of God appeared as flames of fire. The flames were resting on people's heads, and they formed a diagonal line from the front to the rear of the building.

I heard the voice of the LORD saying, *"Run ! Follow the fire and lay hands on the sick."* So I ran through the crowd and did as He said.

Bodies were falling everywhere, and as they fell under the power of the Holy Spirit, blind eyes and deaf ears were opening; the lame were walking; shrivelled hands were being made whole; bad hearts were being healed; tuberculosis was vanishing; and so on.

It was an extraordinary meeting in the middle of an extraordinary month. On that night, every sick person was healed, and many people of other faiths were born again. It was all about Jesus, the Sender, using an envoy to demonstrate His love and supernatural character to people who desperately needed Him.

Jesus loves to demonstrate His Word and His character, and miracles are one of His many expressions of love to broken people. As His apostolic ambassadors, it is definitely a case of "less is more" – we must decrease, so that He may increase **(John 3:30)**.

Philippians 2:5-9 reveals the level of death to self the Lord of Glory gave as an example for His messengers to follow. *"Have this attitude in yourselves which was also in Christ Jesus"* **(v5)**. He *"... emptied Himself, taking the form of a bond-servant"* **(v7a)**. *"He humbled Himself by becoming obedient to the point of death"* **(v8)**.

Paul declared that he died daily; and that it was no longer him who lived, but Christ that lived in him. Hallelujah ! This "declaration of invisibility" is at the heart of the apostolic call.

1 Corinthians 15:31 (AMPC)
[I assure you] by the pride which I have in you in
[your fellowship and union with] Christ Jesus our Lord,
that I die daily [I face death every day and die to self].

Galatians 2:20 (NKJV)
I have been crucified with Christ; it is no longer I who live, but
Christ lives in me; and the life which I now live
in the flesh I live by faith in the Son of God,
who loved me and gave Himself for me.

Equal to and Less Than (not Greater Than) Our Family in Christ

Father, Son, and Holy Spirit are God. They are equal in authority, power, and love. Yet they are very different in function. Can you imagine the conversations that they have between themselves, and the manner in which they are conducted ? If we could glimpse into that realm of supernatural Trinitarian dialogue, we would have the perfect model for how we are to relate to each other.

They are omnipotent, omnipresent, and omniscient, yet one of the Three sent another of the Three to become as nothing, and humble Himself even unto death on a cross, for our sakes ... this is the fully surrendered love and humility of the Creator, on our behalf, on a level that is simply beyond comprehension for us.

Jesus willingly decreased Himself and sacrificed Himself so that another member of the Godhead, the Holy Spirit, could increase His involvement in the affairs of man and in the work of the Kingdom.

John 16:7 (NASB)
But I tell you the truth, it is to your advantage that I go away; for if I do not go away, the Helper will not come to you; but if I go, I will send Him to you.

"Going away" meant going to the cross and all the agony and suffering associated with that, followed by His glorious ascension.

Christ is "The" Apostle; and He is our example to understand that we are to treat one another not only as equals, but even more, that we are to pour out our very lives for the sake of one another and for the sake of the reputation of Christ and His Bride. Our service is to be such that we decrease so that others may increase.

The apostle Paul spoke more than once about his life being poured out like a drink offering for those whom he was called to serve **(Philippians 2:17; 2 Timothy 4:6)**.

We are not superior to our brothers and sisters in any way. In fact, the apostolic function requires a deep level of surrender in our service to them as well as to Him.

The ekklesia consists of people, and it seems that God willingly chooses to have a "blind spot" when it comes to our faults and failings. Look at the way that He speaks of His beloved bride (His ekklesia) in the Song of Solomon; or the way that He *"passes over our rebellious acts"* and *"casts our sins into the depths of the sea"*. **(Micah 7:18-19 (NASB))**

He loves us into the truth in such a way that our faults and failings, when revealed by the LORD, cause us to rejoice as we are set free from them by His loving and tender heart surgery. Apostles must lead the way in tender love and in demonstrating that all are equal within apostolic culture. To this end, apostles must learn and teach the art of correction in such a way that it joyfully releases people from their burdens, rather than condemning them to suffer under the weight of them.

Shoulder to Shoulder

Zephaniah 3:9 (NASB)
"For then I will give to the peoples purified lips,
That all of them may call on the name of the LORD,
To serve Him shoulder to shoulder."

Zephaniah 3:9 is another verse that was highlighted to me as a very young Christian. I'll never forget the accompanying vision of field after field, filled with joyful servants of the LORD, all with arms linked together, worshipping and bringing in a massive harvest, with Jesus standing in the midst of His people as per **Hebrews 2:12,** and singing and smiling and rejoicing at the sight of His people gathered together as one in the field of His choosing. This is apostolic culture. It builds bridges that unite generations, denominations, and nations as well as promoting unity by example, at every level.

Characteristics of Apostles

Just as the original apostles did, modern day apostles will have personal encounters with God. They will be with the Risen Christ with just as much closeness and reality as the original twelve who walked the earth with Him **(1 Corinthians 9:1; Galatians 1:11-12)**.

This is important, as it is in the place of personal encounter with the LORD that they will receive the revelation and the divine patterns **(Hebrews 8:5)** that the Body of Christ needs to fulfil both aspects of the Great Co-Mission.

1 Corinthians 9:1 (NKJV)
Am I not an apostle? Am I not free?
Have I not seen Jesus Christ our Lord?
Are you not my work in the Lord?

Apostles will act as spiritual parents **(1 Cor. 4:15; 1 Thess. 2:11)**, and be patient in suffering, **(Romans 5:3-4; 2 Corinthians 6:4-11)** and in enduring persecution **(2 Corinthians 4:12)**.

1 Thessalonians 2:11-12 (NKJV)
... [11] as you know how we exhorted, and comforted,
and charged every one of you, as a father does
his own children [12] that you would walk worthy of God
Who calls you into His own kingdom and glory.

2 Corinthians 6:4-5,8-9 (NKJV)
[4] But in all things we commend ourselves as ministers of God:
in much patience, in tribulations, in needs, in distresses,
[5] in stripes, in imprisonments, in tumults, in labours,
in sleeplessness, in fastings; ... [8] by honour and dishonour, by
evil report and good report; as deceivers, and yet true;
[9] as unknown, and yet well known; as dying, and behold
we live; as chastened, and yet not killed ...

They will be intimate with and obedient to the voice of the LORD **(Acts 16:6-10; Romans1:5; Romans 16:26)** ; demonstrate servant leadership **(Luke 22:24-27; Matthew 20:26-28; John 13:14-17)**; and walk in supernatural power **(Acts 5:12; Acts 14:3; Romans 15:18-19)** characterized by strong anointing and administered with humility and agape love **(Philippians 2:5-9)**.

Spiritual gifts will be in evidence **(1 Corinthians 2:1-5; Acts 19:11-12; Acts 20:7-12)**; and persecution will accompany the apostolic call **(1 Corinthians 4:9-13)**. Add to these characteristics, everything that was discussed in Part 01 of this book.

Apostles will develop, and teach others to develop, a prayer-filled and worshipful lifestyle of watching and waiting, and of listening and obedience; of writing down the Heavenly vision(s); of overflowing with God's fullness, and of always seeking deeper encounters and the "Greater things" of God.

They will develop and teach others to develop an ever-increasing level of engagement with the Almighty; of going beyond visitation to habitation and permanent abiding; of knowing the times and season of the LORD and what to do; of living a consecrated life, and of continually walking in repentance, forgiveness, and agape love.

Much of the apostle's teaching will be achieved by demonstration and participation. Rather than learning about the things that apostles do as an abstract principle, those who are taught will see the powerful moving of God and participate in everything of the spirit that is released within the apostolic environment.

There have been a number of times on the mission field when people have come for prayers of healing, when, in obedience to the LORD's on-the-spot instructions, I have invited the children to come up and help me to pray. Christ is the Healer and He loves to operate through the willing little ones; and He has never failed to move in the fullness of His healing power on such occasions. These have also been very useful times to teach the children, and the entire gathering, about how to pray for the sick.

Many other times, prayer teams or youth teams will be taught on the spot in the middle of a time of Holy Spirit moving how to pray for souls, healing, and deliverance. "I do, you watch; I do, you help; you do, I help; You do, I watch" is a powerful way to impart.

The Nature of the Apostolic Call

When one understands the suffering and persecution that are an inseparable part of this particular domata function, then an understanding comes that it truly must be God who calls and prepares someone to the apostolic ministry, as it can only be fulfilled through complete surrender to Him and in His strength. Heart and flesh may fail, but the "God-portion" of our lives will not ! **(Psalm 73:26)** God *must* choose you for this role.

When I was a very young Christian (a few weeks old), I bought a pocket-sized Bible that I carried everywhere with me. I would read it on the bus on the way to and from work. I would take it into the restroom with me and read. I would read it in the park at lunch time. And I would read it when I woke up in the morning and until I fell asleep at night.

I was so hungry for the Word of God that I devoured it like a starving man. In truth, I was starving – for the life contained within its holy pages. I read the entire Bible cover to cover over ten times during my first few years as a Christian.

I remember just nine months into my Christian walk, coming across **Philippians 3:10-14**; not for the first time, but on this particular occasion, the Holy Spirit illuminated the passage to me. It seemed as though the words were on fire and almost jumping out of the pages of my Bible as I read it. Something began to stir deep inside of me.

Philippians 3:10-14 (NASB)
¹⁰ ... that I may know Him and the power
of His resurrection and the fellowship of His sufferings,
being conformed to His death; ¹¹ in order that
I may attain to the resurrection from the dead.

¹² Not that I have already obtained it or have already
become perfect, but I press on so that I may lay hold
of that for which also I was laid hold of by Christ Jesus.

¹³ Brethren, I do not regard myself as having laid
hold of it yet; but one thing I do: forgetting what lies
behind and reaching forward to what lies ahead,
¹⁴ I press on toward the goal for the prize
of the upward call of God in Christ Jesus.

I remember God speaking audibly to me and saying, "Son, this is what your walk with Me is going to be like." That is the moment that He chose me. The persecution began almost immediately – but so did the fruit.

When He chose me, I was at the park, sitting under a tree, reading my pocket Bible with a hungry heart overflowing with love for him. When He spoke those words to me, I began to weep from a very deep place inside my soul.

I adored Him so much and I remember immediately replying through the weeping "LORD I love You ! I will follow wherever You lead."

Father and Son had engaged in one of those **"Galatians 1:1** conversations" on my behalf, and I had said "yes" (see Chapter 17).

In my spirit, I knew that I had just stepped into a place of no return, into something very deep and "kabod heavy" and unknown, which was completely beyond my understanding.

But I also knew in that moment that I had somehow entered into my life purpose and into something that was going to being great pleasure to my Beloved Saviour. I had no idea as such a young Christian what either "the fellowship of His sufferings" or His "resurrection power" would be like. It is fair to say that as I look back over my life, He has been exceedingly generous with both; and I would not have it any other way.

If you are called to be an apostle, let me tell you this; the only way to truly experience the fullness of His Glory is through a willingness to embrace His sufferings. While this is true in varying degrees for every Divine call, it is more so for the apostle.

When we learn to submit to the dealings of God with true humility and sweet loving surrender, then there is a corresponding fragrance and sweetness that will be released in us and through us in the midst of it all.

May God grant us the grace that is sufficient so that we may always give Him the reverential glory which is His due, in spite of and at times even because of our challenging circumstances.

There is so much depth, strength, and beauty in **Philippians 3:10-14**.

God supplies all that we need – we simply need to be willing to pay the cost of obedience.

Paul also says that as we learn to forget what is behind and press in to what lies ahead, we will receive the prize of the upward call …

… what a glorious prize, and at the same time, what an incredibly costly journey we embark upon when we say "yes" to the call of God – and particularly to the apostolic call.

Paul said that apostles had been "made as the filth of the world, the offscouring of all things."

1 Corinthians 4:10-13 (AMPC)
*[10] We are [looked upon as] fools on account of Christ
and for His sake, but you are [supposedly] so amazingly
wise and prudent in Christ! We are weak, but you are
[so very] strong! You are highly esteemed, but we are in
disrepute and contempt!*

*[11] To this hour we have gone both hungry and thirsty;
we [habitually] wear but one undergarment [and shiver
in the cold]; we are roughly knocked about and wander around
homeless.*

*[12] And we still toil unto weariness [for our living],
working hard with our own hands. When men revile
us [wound us with an accursed sting], we bless them.
When we are persecuted, we take it patiently and endure it.*

*[13] When we are slandered and defamed, we [try to] answer
softly and bring comfort. We have been made and are now
the rubbish and filth of the world [the offscouring of all things,
the scum of the earth].*

He knew only too well from personal experience about the persecution and misunderstanding that would accompany this call.

The apostolic call is not for the faint-hearted. This is why it must be God who calls and chooses the apostle; and the apostle must choose to endure the "crushing process" (see Chapter 17) that will refine his character until he has been purified to the point of reflecting Christlikeness in all that he thinks, speaks, and does.

Then he will indeed become a truly powerful and effective instrument of personal and societal transformation in the loving hands of the LORD.

Chapter 19

Apostolic Centers and Networks

Judges 5:2 (NLT)
*Israel's leaders took charge,
and the people gladly followed.*

Praise the Lord!

The Fullness of the Gospel

In Chapter 12, we looked at the fact that the Gospel of the Kingdom aspect of the Great Commission has been not completely understood, and therefore not fulfilled, by much of the modern ekklesia.

We saw that when the early believers were accused of *"turning the world upside down"* **(Acts 17:6),** this was referring to much more than the salvation of souls. It referred to the world system being challenged, and every sphere of influence having its core values shaken until they were realigned with Kingdom values.

When the apostles were in town, the Kingdom of God was undeniably present; and everyone, from the common people to the rulers, had to make a decision one way or the other about where they stood in relation to the Kingdom that was suddenly and powerfully in their midst.

The question arises for the 21st century ekklesia : How is it that a nation can be filled with born again believers and churchgoers, and yet that same nation can also suffer from chronically corrupt governance, abject, generationally entrenched poverty, and low human development across the board (as indicated by a low HDI (Human Development Index))? [39] Where is the evidence of the live-giving effect of the Gospel upon such a nation ?

There are many nations that come to mind where there is a high ratio of believers but also an extremely high ratio of the issues mentioned above. This seems incompatible with the purposes of God for mankind that He has called His ekklesia to fulfil.

The church in our day and in our time needs to heed the end times call, which is a call to embrace the absolute fullness of the Spirit, and the Heavenly mandate to release the Gospel of the Kingdom.

The 21st century ekklesia will need to be flexible enough to run with the things that God is releasing in the times in which we live. What is the vehicle that will enable this ?

The Bigger Picture

The view from the Earth and the view from Heaven regarding the ekklesia can be quite different – sometimes even opposite in nature.

From the Earthly viewpoint, a city can have many thousands of churches, hundreds of denominations; and all can be quite separated from each other, never communicating outside of denominational or parish boundaries, and sometimes not even within them. This often leads to misunderstandings, which in turn can lead to further isolation, division, and strife.

This was already happening in the earliest days of the ekklesia; things are compounded and even more complex now. Satan loves to use the strategy of "divide and conquer" within the ekklesia, by sowing seeds of discord and disunity, false doctrine, and arguments about unimportant things **(Acts 15:1-5; Romans 16:17-20; 1 Corinthians 1:10-13; 1 Corinthians 11:18; 1 John 2:19).**

This is in complete contrast to the objectives of an apostolic center.

When God looks at a city, He sees one body that is called to minister to the entire city and beyond **(Revelation 2:1, 2:8, 2:12, 2:18, 3:1, 3:7, 3:14).** *"...to the angel of the church of ... write..."*

His intention is that the citywide ekklesia shall be based upon the foundation of the apostles and prophets who will be based at the apostolic center (and/or hubs) located within their region.

They are servants of God, appointed by Him to serve the men, women, and children who live within their spheres of influence. Through Jesus, many are also servants of their nation, and the nations of the world, again, according to their God-appointed metron (sphere of influence) **(2 Corinthians 10:13-16)**.

Foundations for Transformation

Apostles are *"sent ones,"* commissioned by God the Father and Christ the Son. Amongst many other things, they are called to download and interpret the Divine patterns of the LORD **(Hebrews 8:5b)** that will establish and strengthen the correct foundations for the ekklesia **(Ephesians 2:19-22)**, and ultimately transform nations.

This transformation begins with individual lives. Every Christian is called to change culture from the inside out until the Kingdom of God is fully expressed through all facets of society. This is so that people of every tribe, nation, and tongue are given the opportunity to prosper spiritually, economically, and in every other area of human endeavour.

Apostles and prophets are called to build the ekklesia by training, equipping, activating, and releasing people to function as above **(Ephesians 4:11-16)**.

When I had the series of powerful encounters that are documented in Chapter 15 (End Times Kingdom Paradigms) it brought me to the place of prayer, a search of the Scriptures, and also to do some research on what was happening in the worldwide Body of Christ.

The Promise of the Father

In the Gospels, we find Jesus imparting to the 12 (**Matthew 10:1** (εδωκεν *"edoken"* root *didomi* = imparting, bestowing, endowing) and they were suddenly healing the sick, and casting demons out of people.

In **Luke 10:1**, he "appointed" (απεστειλεν *"apesteilen"* root *apostello* = commissioned or despatched) seventy who found themselves doing the things that they had seen Jesus do. This was an apostolic sending.

In **Luke 24:49**, Jesus said :-

> **Luke 24:49 (AMP)** *(exposition mine)*
> *Listen carefully: I am sending the Promise of My Father*
> *[the Holy Spirit] upon you; but you are to remain*
> *in the city [of Jerusalem] until you are clothed (fully equipped)*
> (ενδυσησθε *"endusesthe"* put on, clothe yourself) *with power*
> (δυναμιν *"dunamin"* power, powerful ability of God)
> *from on high."*

The word "sending" used here is once again the word (exapostello), which means the authorization of an individual to fulfill a particular function, with (as we noted above) the emphasis being on the one who sends, not on the one who is sent. Jesus was authorized by the Father to send the Holy Spirit.

This is the birthing process of the ekklesia – it begins on high and it is the work of the Godhead, outworked through willing, emptied human vessels.

In **Acts 2:1-4** everyone in the Upper Room was baptized in the Holy Spirit, and the ekklesia was born. This was the beginning of the fulfilment of the Promise of the Father, which Peter referred to again in **Acts 2:39** when he said, *"For the promise is for you and your children and for all who are far off, as many as the Lord our God will call to Himself."*

It's interesting that John the Baptist described the mission of Jesus this way in **Matthew 3:11 :-**

> **Matthew 3:11 (AMP)**
> *"As for me, I baptize you with water for repentance,*
> *but He who is coming after me is mightier than I,*
> *and I am not fit to remove His sandals;*
> *He will baptize you with the Holy Spirit and fire."*

Jesus is the baptizer in the Holy Spirit. The fullness of the Holy Spirit – the Promise of the Father - is just as much what Jesus came to impart, as salvation and the Gospel of the Kingdom are.

The Holy Spirit *fulfils* the Promise of the Father, and Jesus is the One Who *activates* His Father's Promise.

The mandate of the Gospel of the Kingdom can only be fulfilled if we have received the Promise of the Father and are walking in the fullness of all that He intends for us to receive.

That is why Jesus essentially said to His disciples (and continues to say to His disciples down through the ages) :-

"Don't try to do anything until you have received the Promise,
are clothed with power from on high, and have received the full
impartation of My supernatural abilities and authority"
(**Luke 24:49**, paraphrase).

Divine Patterns

The progression from **Matthew 10:1** to **Luke 10:1** through to **Acts 2:1-4** is amazing. It's like Jesus is saying: "Look what just a few can do with just a little bit of impartation. Here's what a few more can do with a little bit more" – until finally the fullness of the promise was multiplied to all who were in the Upper Room, and the New Testament ekklesia was born.

It's so important that we understand and embrace this fullness coming to us from the Father, Son, and Holy Spirit.

The fullness of the Holy Spirit poured out marked the beginning of the implementation of the Divine pattern for the global ekklesia.

The fullness of the Holy Spirit ensures the continuity and fulfilment of God's purposes for the ekklesia through to the end of the age. God intends for His ekklesia to be filled with His Spirit life so that the ekklesia can impart the fullness of His Spirit life to all people.

If you sit down and read the last chapter of Luke and continue through the next 28 chapters of Acts in one sitting, the incredible spiritual momentum caused by the outpouring of the Holy Spirit is evident.

The ekklesia grew rapidly and strategically; and while not perfect in every detail, it was certainly vibrant and filled with "greater things Christians" **(John 14:12)** who were used mightily by God to transform their world.

In **Luke 24** we hear of the coming Promise of the Father. In the **Book of Acts Chapters 2 to 6** we see the early ekklesia meeting from home to home, we see powerful miracles, and we also see the beginning of persecution of believers. In **Acts 7** we see the martyrdom of Stephen.

In **Chapter 8** we read of believers being scattered because of persecution, and of Philip bringing the Gospel to Africa. In **Chapter 9** we read of Saul's encounter with Jesus, and his powerful conversion. We see Peter struggling with the concept that the Gospel may be meant for more than just the Jews in **Chapter 10**.

Another Level

In **Acts Chapter 11**, we witness the birth of something new in the city of Antioch.

We read in **Acts 11:19-26** that many who had been persecuted because of their faith began to gather there; that the word of God was preached at first to the Jews, but then to others as well; that apostles and prophets visited the Antioch center from in Jerusalem; that Barnabas and Paul remained there for one year with the people, teaching them; and that many were added to their numbers through salvation.

Acts 11:19-26 (NKJV) - Barnabas and Saul at Antioch

19 Now those who were scattered after the persecution that arose over Stephen traveled as far as Phoenicia, Cyprus, and Antioch, preaching the word to no one but the Jews only.

20 But some of them were men from Cyprus and Cyrene, who, when they had come to Antioch, spoke to the Hellenists, preaching the Lord Jesus.

21 And the hand of the Lord was with them, and a great number believed and turned to the Lord.

22 Then news of these things came to the ears of the church in Jerusalem, and they sent out Barnabas to go as far as Antioch. 23 When he came and had seen the grace of God, he was glad, and encouraged them all that with purpose of heart they should continue with the Lord.

24 For he was a good man, full of the Holy Spirit and of faith. And a great many people were added to the Lord.

25 Then Barnabas departed for Tarsus to seek Saul.

26 And when he had found him, he brought him to Antioch.

So it was that for a whole year they assembled with the church and taught a great many people. And the disciples were first called Christians in Antioch.

In **Acts 13:1-3** we see that the Antioch center is the place where Paul and Barnabas were set apart for increase and sent out to share the Gospel, by prophets and teachers who were based there (and who were probably trained there).

Acts 13:1-3 (NKJV)
- Paul and Barnabas Are Sent to the Gentiles
[1] Now in the church that was at Antioch
there were certain prophets and teachers:
Barnabas, Simeon who was called Niger,
Lucius of Cyrene, Manaen who had been
brought up with Herod the tetrarch, and Saul.

[2] As they ministered to the Lord and fasted,
the Holy Spirit said, "Now separate to Me
Barnabas and Saul for the work to which I have called them."

[3] Then, having fasted and prayed,
and laid hands on them, they sent them away.

From the above Scriptures, it can be seen that Antioch was very much a gathering, training, equipping, and sending center. It is so significant that this is the place where the disciples were first called "Christians" – Christlike ones.

Indeed, it was at an apostolic center, where the disciples were being trained by the apostles and others, to become history makers, nation shakers, and world transformers.

Antioch was the prototype apostolic center; it was the first, but certainly not the last. Paul established similar centers in other locations, and some of the other apostles would have done the same.

Notice that it was not a gathering center for the sake of gathering. People gathered for the purpose of being trained, equipped, and sent. In our day, many ekklesias have developed a mindset that their success is measured by the number of people who be gathered out of the world to meet together in a building on the weekend.

But this is the opposite of the New Testament model, which is all about discipling, training, equipping, and releasing and sending as many as we can, to transform nations, people groups, and every mountain of culture.

Hallelujah.

Strategic Placement and Development

Alain Caron has written some of the very best books that are available on the subject of the development of apostolic centers, both in New Testament and modern times. He runs a thriving apostolic center and network that is based in Gatineau, Canada. In his wonderful book *Heaven's Headquarters - Apostolic Centers*, Mr. Caron summarizes the strategic placement and development of apostolic centers in the time of the Book of Acts as follows :-

> *The Birth of Apostolic Centers*
>
> *Paul stayed longer in some places, such as in Ephesus and Corinth, remaining there a few years instead of weeks. Using Antioch as an example, the first base of operations he was sent from as an apostle, he developed a different kind of church that I call an apostolic center.*
>
> *The centers were strategically located in cities that were the socio-economic centers for their region, crossroads for major commercial routes, junction points in the bustling activity of the ancient world. The Holy Spirit specifically chose those places to develop centers that would feed the churches covering the land. They were resource and training centers, sending bases for missionary troops, and places of great spiritual activity.*
>
> *Take Ephesus, for example. All the churches of Asia benefited from the influence of Ephesus, from that particular type of church.*
>
> *Paul took three years to develop this base, which had a central location in relation to the many smaller churches growing in Asia.*
>
> *The same thing happened in Corinth. The apostolic center in Corinth was a resource center for all of Greece.* [40]

It can be seen that there was a definite Holy Spirit plan to influence the maximum number of people and regions, by strategically locating the apostolic centers at the crossroads that linked different geographical regions. These cities were also centers of commerce and trade.

They were ideal locations for gathering, training, equipping, and sending people from all walks of life and from diverse nationalities; and for the convergence and emergence of teams who would take the Gospel of the Kingdom to the ends of the earth.

Purpose

Over the past twenty years or so, the terms "apostolic center" and "apostolic hub" have been used to describe what may appear to be a new type of ekklesia. It is really a 21st century restoration of the Divine pattern for the strategic growth and dunamis empowering of the ekklesia, which was implemented by the apostles as led and empowered by the Holy Spirit throughout the Book of Acts, and intended to continue throughout history until the return of Jesus.

So, the apostolic center is one of the original forms of the ekklesia as described in the Book of Acts. It is God's planting. In a sense, the terms "apostolic center" and "ekklesia" are very much interchangeable.

Everything that has been written in chapter 12, "The Role of the ekklesia," applies to apostolic centers and hubs, because they are simply an expression of the ekklesia that are led by apostles. Other ekklesias are led by other God-ordained leaders, including pastors.

It is Christ who builds His ekklesia (**Matthew 16:18** *"I will build My ekklesia"*). He will choose and send apostles to plant and water, and to lead the apostolic centres and hubs - but God alone will give the increase (**1 Corinthians 3:6-7**).

Apostles and prophets will set the foundations for the apostolic center with an emphasis on societal transformation according to the principles of the Gospel of the Kingdom. The heartbeat of an apostolic center, hub, and network is for the redemption and transformation of society as a whole, because this is what the Gospel of the Kingdom embraces.

Every believer can be trained, equipped, and released into the fullness of their destinies at an apostolic center. But there will be an emphasis on raising up the fivefold ministry functions (because they are for the equipping of the rest as per **Ephesians 4:12**). Also, prophetic worshippers and intercessors, Kingdom economists and Kingdom entrepreneurs, will be trained and released, as will apostolic, prophetic, and Zebulun companies of believers. (The concept of apostolic companies will be expanded later in this chapter).

An apostolic center or hub will be a Kingdom resource center for the wider Body of Christ (see Chapter 20). It will connect with other apostolic centers, and also to ekklesias and networks of ekklesias, both local and global.

Characteristics of Apostolic Centers

In Chapter 12 we saw that in **Deuteronomy 4:10**, the gathering of the entire nation of Israel around the Presence of God was referred to in the Septuagint as the ekklesia. This is the kind of national vision that will burn in the hearts of the leaders of apostolic centers and hubs.

Having said that, apostolic centers and hubs can and will take on many forms, and will have different emphases depending upon the God-given sphere of influence. Some may focus more on prayer and worship and others may focus more on training and equipping people for a particular mountain. But regardless of the primary focus or form, they will share some common characteristics.

The vision of an apostolic center will be a Kingdom vision. The leaders will be passionate for every local ekklesia to become stronger in the ways of the Holy Spirit, and to be unified with the wider body of Christ in terms of Kingdom vision and purpose.

You will hear the words "impart," "transform," "activate," and "commission," spoken frequently at an apostolic center. The apostolic center will train, equip, and release individuals and teams; it will be passionate about strengthening and expanding the local, national, and international Body of Christ according to its God-given sphere of influence, and to become a vehicle of national transformation.

The format of meetings will be flexible so that the Holy Spirit is free to move as He wills. The release of Glory to Glory through Holy Spirit-led worship, and a genuine invitation to the Risen Christ to come and stand in our midst as we honor Him **(Hebrews 2:12)**, are some of the reverent expectations of apostolic gatherings.

An apostolic center will led by an apostle, but the leadership team will include all, or at least most, of the fivefold functions, with a goal to include all. In the previous chapter "Apostolos," we spoke about the principle of "Equal to or Less than (not Greater Than)." This will be the guiding principle in terms of the relationships within the leadership and with the assembly at the apostolic centre.

An apostolic center's growth will not be measured simply by the number of people who attend or by the number of souls saved, but just as much by the societal influence and transformation that it brings to its metron (sphere of influence; **2 Corinthians 10:12-16**).

The Australian headquarters of my apostolic network, Global Influencers, is quite small numerically, but it has significant influence from a grassroots level to government level across many different people groups in different nations of the world.

Because the Holy Spirit is honored and God is worshipped in Spirit and in truth within the apostolic center, the members will become expectant of Divine encounters whenever they come together, be it at the center or in their homes, or in the marketplace. The culture of Divine expectancy will become an established part of their personal times with God.

The full Gospel of the Kingdom **(Matthew 24:14)** will be taught, and members will engage in "enhanced discipleship training," i.e., being taught and then teaching others to walk in the fullness of supernatural, "greater things" Christianity **(John 14:12)**.

An apostolic center should be multi-generational, multi-cultural, and multi-denominational, i.e., it should draw people of all ages, backgrounds, and denominations.

Acts 8:8 (NIV)
So there was great joy in that city.

Add to these characteristics the "Characteristics of Apostles" listed in the previous chapter, because it is apostolic culture that the apostolic center will aim to reproduce.

2 Timothy 2:1-2 (AMP) – Be Strong
So you, my son, be strong [constantly strengthened]
and empowered in the grace that is [to be found only]
in Christ Jesus. ² The things [the doctrine, the precepts,
the admonitions, the sum of my ministry] which you have heard
me teach in the presence of many witnesses,
entrust [as a treasure] to reliable and faithful men
who will also be capable and qualified to teach others.

The Centrality of Worship and the Glory of God

Worship will be central at the apostolic centre. We are talking about the kind of worship that connects with and unravels the heart of God; worship that sets people free; worship that releases miracles and draws people into the Holy of Holies. Lingering in God's Presence will be a hallmark of the worship at an apostolic center, as will spontaneous, Spirit-led worship. The atmosphere will be charged and fragrant with the Presence of God, and filled with the tangible Glory of God.

In Chapter14 ("Ideal Conditions for Revival") I shared testimonies of the visible Glory of God manifesting in the meetings at our apostolic center located in Central Province, Papua New Guinea. Many of the testimonies shared throughout this book speak of the Glory of God preceding the release of salvation, deliverance, miracles, and Holy Spirit Baptism. Jesus said that He wants to share the Glory that His Father gave Him, with us **(John 17:22-24)**.

There is a unifying purpose contained within His desire to do this. Scripture tells us that all of God's riches are in His Glory **(Philippians 4:19)**, and so it is no surprise that when the Glory of God manifests, wonderful things begin to happen as a result.

At the beginning of Chapter 8 ("Keeping Our Gates and Guarding Our Hearts"), I shared a testimony about the establishment of an Open Heaven, and the rest of that chapter dealt with the importance of maintaining it.

The Open Heaven is where a continuous release of the Glory of God occurs. Intimacy with God is the door, and worship is the key. Apostolic centers will understand the importance of the establishment of an Open Heaven **(Revelation 4:1)** and will desire everyone to experience this. There is no formulaic approach to this. It takes poured out vessels who adore the LORD of Glory and who like King David know that the dwelling places of the LORD are lovely beyond compare, and who long for His intimacy above all else. The fruit of this will ultimately be the establishment of an Open Heaven with angels ascending and descending as per **John 1:51.**

God loves worshippers, and He chooses true worshippers to be His ambassadors. If ever there was a gift that would being you before the great men of this world, it is the gift or worship, because the fragrance of worship opens the heart of God to the worshippers, and He pours out His favour and opens doors for them that no man can shut.

Throughout my life I've been so blessed to participate as both a worshipper and a minister of the Word of God in gatherings where the Glory of God has been poured out over and over again. I've seen so many things and had so many supernatural encounters, but above all, I just count it a privilege never to be taken for granted, simply to be with God in His Glorious environment. It is our honor to approach His holy Throne through worship and to adore Him here on the Earth during our lifetimes, and then forever in Heaven.

As stated earlier, I do believe that the increasing levels of Glory being released in our midst will become the "normal," as we empty ourselves of any hindrance to our intimacy with Him, and as we surrender more fully to His end time purposes. I also believe that apostolic centers will be at the very forefront of capturing the sounds and melodies of Heaven, and then of releasing them as a brand new type of worship that will arrest believers and nonbelievers alike with its beauty, abiding Glory, and Heavenly authority.

Apostolic Companies of Believers

Luke 10:1 records that "seventy others" (i.e., not the original twelve) were appointed by the Apostle Jesus to go forth - sent by Jesus just as the Father had sent Him and to do the things that He did, and even greater things.

> **Luke 10:1 (NKJV)**
> *After these things the Lord appointed seventy others also, and sent them two by two before His face into every city and place where He Himself was about to go.*

The word translated into English as the word "appointed" in this verse is απεστειλεν (apesteilen, root apostello - commissioned, despatched).

The root word makes it clear that this was an apostolic sending, i.e., those who were sent were given apostolic authority. In other words, Jesus filled them with apostolic power, His own power, and then He sent them out. Look what happened when they were "apostello-ed" by Jesus.

> **Luke 10:17-18 (NKJV)**
> *[17] Then the seventy returned with joy, saying, "Lord, even the demons are subject to us in Your name." 18 And He said to them, "I saw Satan fall like lightning from heaven."*

The seventy who were sent were amazed. After being commissioned by Jesus, they suddenly saw mighty things being worked through themselves - the same things that they had seen Jesus do. This is how Jesus responded to their amazement :-

> **Luke 10:19-20 (NKJV)** *(Parentheses mine)*
> *[19]"Behold, I give you the authority (εξουσιαν exousian (authority) to trample on serpents and scorpions, and over all the power (δυναμιν (dunamin) (power, ability)) of the enemy, and nothing shall by any means hurt you. [20]Nevertheless do not rejoice in this, that the spirits are subject to you, but rather rejoice because your names are written in heaven."*

He gave them full authority over all the spiritual power of the enemy, to the extent that nothing could harm them. This delegated authority that He had given them was His apostolic authority.

We do not know who they were as none of them were named – but they carried apostolic authority because of their appointment and sending out by "The Apostle" – the LORD.

The domata who have been set apart for increase must be the ones who lead the way for the ekklesia to step out into the fullness of her destiny, which is to implement the fullness of her legislative Heavenly authority throughout every sphere of human influence.

The spiritual power of the enemy cannot stand in the face of this authority. Jesus made this clear in **Luke 10:19**. Neither can he continue to control any territory that he may have temporarily inhabited, whether it is a geographical area or a sphere of influence.

From this we can see the Divine imperative for the ekklesia to go to the seven mountains. The enemy will not be displaced unless we go to displace him (see chapter 13).

In the same way that Jesus was sent by His Father into the world to transform it, so He sends His appointed ones into the world to finish the work that He started.

> **John 17:18 (NLT)**
> *Just as you sent me into the world,*
> *I am sending them into the world.*

This is a co-mission of the highest order between God and the believer. The emphasis and focus is on the Sender, not the sent ones. We are His ambassadors; we are carriers of His Presence, of His Glory of His authority, of his power, of His mission and His vision, and of His love.

This is the culture of Heaven that an apostolic center / hub / network will instil into its members.

John Eckhardt coined the phrase "apostolic companies of believers" in his book *Ordinary People, Extraordinary Power*. He said :-

> *It was never the will of God just to have apostles.*
> *God's intention is to have an apostolic company*
> *of believers.* [41]

Apostolic companies of believers are believers who are apostolic in character and supernatural authority. They will be raised up in the Open Heaven, dynamic Spirit-led environment of the apostolic center; and they in turn will produce large crops of eternal fruit to the uttermost ends of the Earth and train others to do the same. They will be sent into the world by the apostles, who have been sent by the Father and the Son.

There will be an apostolic impartation that will work through them, and it will result in supernatural fruitfulness and also cause the enemy to flee in terror **(Deuteronomy 28:7)**.

Apostolic Networks

An apostolic network will include apostolic centers and hubs, national and regional 24/7 prayer and worship centers, local ekklesias, and other ministry centers or ministries located anywhere on the seven mountains. It could include Kingdom businesses (businesses that exist to fund the expansion of the Kingdom of God) and Kingdom business networks, and Christian schools.

An apostolic network can include any organization with a Kingdom vision or that wants to develop one. There is no stipulation that a local church needs to become an apostolic center to become part the network. In fact, the diversity of the member organizations within an apostolic network is a cause for great rejoicing.

Apostolic centers and apostolic hubs are epicenters of revival. When revival comes to a city or region, if an apostolic network, formed through agape-love-based, Holy Spirit strengthened relationships is already in place, then revival will spread rapidly, and the harvest can be brought in by all believers working together as one **(Ephesians 4:1-6)**. Where there is unity, God commands the blessing.**(Psalm 133)**.

Here is another quote from Alain Caron's *Heaven's Headquarters – Apostolic Centers* :-

> *There are therefore two types of healthy churches*
> *in the New Testament and both are apostolic!*
> *We have apostolic churches, where pastors remain*
> *aligned with an apostle, and we have apostolic centers,*
> *where the apostle is residing with his team.*
> *Those apostolic centers are resource centers*
> *for the apostolic churches that surround them*
> *in a region or territory.* [42]

In our modern era, a typical local ekklesia that is run by a pastor may have never had an opportunity for the blessing that flows from apostolic connections and alignment, depending upon the denominational affiliation, governmental structure, and other factors. An apostolic network offers that opportunity. Local ekklesias are a vital part of an apostolic network and they are embraced and welcomed just as they are. Denominational affiliations can also remain exactly as they are – the apostolic network is cross-denominational, and it will purposefully link denominations and provide resources for the entire Body of Christ.

We can see from the Scriptures that Paul and the other apostles and team members didn't just establish an ekklesia and then leave it isolated and to take care of itself. The missionary journeys not only brought the Gospel to places where it had not yet been heard. They were also an opportunity for Paul and his teams (and the other apostles and their teams) to encourage and strengthen the established fellowships.

Acts 14:21-23 (AMP)
[21] They preached the good news to that city and made many disciples, then they returned to Lystra and to Iconium and to Antioch, [22] strengthening and establishing the hearts of the disciples; encouraging them to remain firm in the faith, saying, "It is through many tribulations and hardships that we must enter the kingdom of God." [23] When they had appointed elders for them in every church, having prayed with fasting, they entrusted them to the Lord in whom they believed [and joyfully accepted as the Messiah].

Acts 15:36, 40-41(AMP)
- Paul's Second Missionary Journey

36 After some time Paul said to Barnabas,
"Let us go back and visit the brothers and sisters (believers)
in every city where we preached the message of the Lord,
and see how they are doing."

40 But Paul chose Silas [who was again in Antioch]
and set out [on his second journey], commended
by the brothers to the grace and favor of the Lord.
41 And he traveled through Syria and Cilicia,
strengthening the churches.

Acts 20:4 (NIV)

4 He was accompanied by Sopater son of Pyrrhus
from Berea, Aristarchus and Secundus from Thessalonica,
Gaius from Derbe, Timothy also, and Tychicus and Trophimus
from the province of Asia.

(also see **Acts 15:29-33; Acts 16:3-5**)

One of Paul's main purposes in writing many of his epistles was to strengthen the existing relationships and to encourage the believers. He would often speak about how much he longed to see them, and often ended them with very personal greetings.

(Romans 1:11; Romans 15:23; Philippians 1:8;
Philippians 4:1; Colossians 3:14-18; 2 Timothy 4:19-22)

Spiritual Governance

The apostolic network exists to release the fullness of the Gospel of the Kingdom everywhere. When functioning correctly, such a network in effect sets up a spiritual governance structure within a nation.

It forms a powerful spiritual network that will influence the spheres of human culture and even cause shifts within the national political government to align itself with Heaven's purposes, due to its inherent Divine authority and resultant spiritual power. This is beginning to occur in some nations of the world.

Unifying Influence

A true apostolic network will embrace and bring together people from *every* Christian stream. It has no denominational affiliation - yet it is a spiritual resource for every denomination.

It is "ecclesiastical" in the purest sense; the ekklesia being God's people coming together in unity, and operating in the full authority of Heaven, and filled with overflowing, multiplying Spirit life according to the Promise of the Father.

One net – one harvest – many boats.

(Matthew 14:33, Zephaniah 3:9 NIV)

Commanded Blessing, and Lasting Change

We have seen God pour out His commanded blessings and influence a wide region through the apostolic center as described in Chapter 14, with far-reaching impact upon and through individuals, villages, children, local government, and even the national government. There are many more similar examples within our network - and of course many of the other apostolic networks that exist throughout the world will have even more powerful testimonies.

We firmly believe that we are being true to the Divine patterns for the ekklesia that were sent from the Father, imparted by the Son, empowered by the Holy Spirit, implemented by the first apostles, and documented in the Book of Acts, by raising up apostolic centers, hubs, and networks in our time as the Holy Spirit leads.

We further believe that the co-ordination of apostolic prayer, worship, training, equipping, and sending strategies at local and national levels is essential if we are going to see true and lasting change within our nations.

Chapter 20

Apostolic Hubs – Kingdom Worship and Resource Centers for the Nations

An apostolic hub is an apostolic center that is operating at a higher level of influence. For example, an apostolic center may influence a local region, but an apostolic hub may influence a number of states or provinces of a nation, or an entire nation. The apostolic centers will be resource centers for the local ekklesias, and for local or regional networks of ekklesias. The apostolic hubs will be resource centers for apostolic centers, for national and global networks, and for Kingdom business and other networks across all seven mountains, and beyond.

There may only be a handful of apostolic hubs within a nation.

For a nation of up to a population of say 10 million, one or two may be sufficient. For a nation such as the United States with a population of around 350 million, there could be a network (or networks) consisting of many apostolic hubs resourcing hundreds of apostolic networks.

An apostolic hub may attract leaders from other networks or ekklesias who would attend training and equipping sessions there and then return to their local apostolic center or local ekklesias, bringing the training and anointing back home with them – and imparting it there.

There will be an impartation and replication of apostolic and prophetic anointing; authority and foundations; of prophetic worship and intercession; and of miracle working power.

This impartation and replication is not limited by the border of the apostolic hub's home nation; it will cross political and geographical borders and continue in the nations that each assembly is influencing through their missions outreaches and programmes. Hallelujah.

The apostolic centers at Ephesus, Corinth, and Antioch may have functioned at this level. It is also possible that some apostolic centers will mature and then begin to function at the level of a hub.

The apostolic hub, like the apostolic center, is intended to be a meeting point where the spiritually hungry can easily access an Open Heaven, and experience the heights, depths, and glorious Presence released though prophetic and apostolic worship. It is a place where people can absorb the apostolic hub's Kingdom culture and replicate it at the home base, and be trained and equipped and strengthened in Christ for the edification and building up of the body - citywide, nationally, and globally **(2 Corinthians 12:19b; Psalm 96:3).** These things will also occur at apostolic centers, but it will all be at another level at the apostolic hub.

From the apostolic hub, abundant life flows out through the apostolic network, until every connected fellowship is vibrantly alive with the Presence, Holy Fire, and Glory of the LORD **(Isaiah 40:5; Isaiah 4:5; Habakkuk 2:14; Zechariah 14:8-9; Ephesians 4:1-6, 11-16).**

This happens through relationships and spending time together in agape fellowship, just as much as through the teaching, learning, and worship scenarios.

Acts 2:42 (NIV) -The Fellowship of the Believers
They devoted themselves to the apostles' teaching
and to fellowship, to the breaking of bread and to prayer.

This is not about a once off, one day or one weekend experience, but a place that can be visited at any time, or attended over time, for equipping and activating, strengthening and encouraging.

It's about strengthening connections between ekklesias and denominations, by regularly coming together from across the body to pray, worship, learn, and experience the tangible Presence of the LORD together.

Bringing the Body Together

We all need each other, and we can learn much from each other.

We all need apostolic and prophetic input and alignment, as the Word of God tells us that the gathering together of the saints and *"family members of God"* (οικειοι του θεου (oikoei tou Theou) (**Ephesians 2:19**) is to be based upon the foundations that the apostles and prophets have set.

I think it's wonderful that the expression "family members of God" is used here, because it underscores the loving, family building, and spiritual parenting roles that apostles and prophets should minister from.

Bringing the body together means connecting the leaders from diverse churches and denominations, and also sphere leaders from Kingdom organizations from each of the seven mountains of human culture, through the apostolic hub. (**1 Corinthians 12:27; Colossians 1:17**)

Why ? Because God is going to continue to intensify the outpouring of His Spirit, Glory, and love at the hub. He will continue to download apostolic and prophetic revelation at the hub for the benefit of an entire nation.

Balance in ministry is crucial. In the foreword I wrote about the importance of the old and familiar bringing balance to the new and fresh, and vice versa. Accountability helps to bring balance. Without spiritual accountability, an individual, ekklesia, or even a denomination or movement is in danger of becoming unbalanced in their revelation, interpretation, and application of the Word of God.

Cross-network exposure, such as that which occurs at an apostolic hub, adds another layer of accountability in the sense of the exposure to different revelatory streams that may challenge us to rethink, adjust, and realign our own paradigms for the Glory of God and the benefit of those whom we are called to serve and also lead into the fullness of God.

Having said that, during 2020, when restrictions on face-to-face meetings and international travel were introduced, other means of meeting together had to be devised. I have seen instances where a small, local apostolic nucleus has been able to reach into nations using video conferencing. In some instances many more people are being trained and equipped this way than previously. The container is flexible, and interaction, impartation, impact, and influence are still the priorities. This is yet another potential form of apostolic hub and apostolic network that could become extremely viable as we move further into the digital age.

Reaching Other Mountains

I also believe that in the near future, God will raise up apostolic hubs that will strategically focus on training government, economic, educational, media, and other leaders of cities, regions, and nations, in the ways of the LORD.

What if one of the functions of the apostolic hubs were to become a school of preparation for the emerging presidents and prime ministers of nations, and a place where they were commissioned and set apart for increase by the apostles for their governance role ?

There is no reason why an apostolic hub could not become a premier training and equipping and sending center – a Kingdom advancement center - for leaders and emerging leaders from every sphere of influence within a nation.

Whereas, the apostolic center may focus more on building relationships with regional leaders, the apostolic hub may focus more on forming relationships with national government members and national business leaders.

When government, economic, and spiritual mountains become aligned with Kingdom purposes, Kingdom reforms of every kind become possible.

The remainder of this chapter is examining things that have been seen in the Spirit and verified by Scripture. Some are in the prayer, planning, and development stages, but not yet completely seen in terms of their implementation. My prayer is that some who are reading will take these templates and run with them as God leads.

Kingdom Worship Centers

There have been many centres of 24/7 prayer and worship throughout the centuries. There were monastic movements from almost the earliest days of Christianity that were devoted almost exclusively to prayer and worship. Some examples of these are Cyprian and Athanasius of Africa in the 1st to 3rd centuries; "Alexander the Sleepless" and a 24/7 company in the 4th century Bangor, Ireland, in the 6th to 9th centuries; Clairvaux, France in the 12th century; the Moravian movement of the 18th and early 19th centuries.

There have been many others. Most of these movements birthed powerful revivals, some of which crossed the oceans and touched other nations and continents. At the present time though, there is more 24/7 prayer and worship rising from the earth than at any other time in human history. As we pray for every tribe, tongue, and nation, they will come.

> **Isaiah 56:6-7 (NASB)**
> *6 "Also the foreigners who join themselves to the Lord,*
> *To minister to Him, and to love the name of the Lord,*
> *To be His servants, every one who keeps from*
> *profaning the sabbath and holds fast My covenant;*
>
> *7 Even those I will bring to My holy mountain*
> *and make them joyful in My house of prayer.*
> *Their burnt offerings and their sacrifices*
> *will be acceptable on My altar; for My house*
> *will be called a house of prayer for all the peoples."*

One time when I was conducting a day and night worship and intercession seminar at our apostolic centre in Rigo District Papua New Guinea, right in the middle of one of the sessions, the Heavens literally opened, and I had to excuse myself to the people who were gathered and stop teaching to absorb the Open Heaven vision. When the vision first manifested, I saw four pairs of wings with a pillar of holy fire and Glory in the middle of the wings. Then, out of the fire and the Glory, the outlines of a building appeared. The building had four radiating arms, aligned to the north, east, south, and west, with a raised section in the middle.

The building that I was shown in the Spirit was the representation of an apostolic hub that would reach to the four corners of a nation through the praise and worship that would rise, Glory of God that would manifest and be imparted there, and by the people who would be trained and sent out from there.

The building had a name written on it : "Kingdom Worship Centre".

Overlaid on top of that, I could see the twelve tribes of Israel encamped around the Tabernacle of Moses with the pillar of Fire and Glory rising from their midst. The encampment of the Israelites was historically laid out in the shape of a cross, facing the pillar of fire and the Glory cloud of the Almighty – focused at all times on the Person and Presence of the Almighty. I believe God was revealing a Divine pattern for something that would be very powerful if implemented in our day.

> **Hebrews 8:5b (NKJV)**
> *" ... as Moses was divinely instructed*
> *when he was about to make the tabernacle.*
> *For He said, "See that you make all things*
> *according to the pattern shown you on the mountain."*

Function

The Kingdom Worship Center is a type of apostolic hub – an expression of the ekklesia - with a specific focus on restoring the centrality of the Presence and Glory of God to a nation, through the implementation of 24/7 intercession and worship at the center.

For the ekklesia in general, the centrality of the Presence and Glory of God is vital (see Chapter 12 "The Role of the Ekklesia"; **Deuteronomy 4:10; 1 Chronicles 13:2-4**). The Kingdom Worship Center has a specialist role to fulfill in terms of training, equipping and resourcing a nation so that the centrality of the Presence of God can become a reality everywhere.

One single assembly cannot fulfil this; but nationally co-ordinated intercession and worship, directed by highly skilled and anointed ministers of prayer and song, can lead an entire nation into the Presence of God.

I can see this, can you ? And I want to shout it from a mountain top – the Glory of the LORD *will* cover the Earth as the waters cover the sea, and the anointed, skilful yet genuinely humble, God-exalting singers and musicians will be there leading the way **(Psalm 68:24-25)**. Hallelujah !

The Kingdom Worship Center will serve as an example to the nation through the quality and anointing of the prayer and intercession that will continually rise from it, and the quality and anointing of Godly ministers that it produces – people with literally no other agenda other than to declare the glory and majesty of God through their pure, devoted intercession and worship, and to display His attributes through their surrendered, worshipping, Christlike lives **(Romans 12:1-2)**.

The Greek word translated as "worship" or "service" in **Romans 12** is "latreia" and includes amongst its meanings, Divine service involving sacrifice; in other words, a life poured out in the service of the King of Kings.

At the time of Christ, slaves were sold in the marketplace and the term of their service was seven years. But their master generally treated them very well, even like family, so that at the end of the seven years when they were given the option to go free, many would choose to stay in the house of their master and continue to serve him because of the great love that they had developed for their masters. The sacrificial service of "love servants" of the Most High – those who serve simply because they adore Him - is the kind of worshipful service that will open the floodgates of Heaven that will precede the end times revival.

It will be one of the greatest privileges to be called and chosen by the LORD to become an end times worshipper or intercessor.

The Kingdom Worship Center, therefore, has an absolutely crucial role to play in terms of equipping the end times army of worshippers and intercessors who - as we will see in the next section - will play a crucial role in the end times harvest of souls.

The Tabernacle of David Restored

The prophesied restoration of the Tabernacle of David has many levels of interpretation. One of those is that the restoration of 24/7 intercession and worship at the end of days (as it was in the days of King David) will coincide with, and be a key factor in, the greatest harvest of souls that the world has ever seen. It will occur *"so that the rest of mankind may seek the LORD"* (**Acts 15:17**).

Dick Eastman wrote the following in his powerful book entitled *Intercessory Worship* :-

> *I want to emphasize the totality of the Amos prophecy that James later cites during the Council of Jerusalem. Central to the prophecy is the restoration of David's Tabernacle "so that the rest of humanity might find the Lord, including the Gentiles" (Acts 15:17, NLT).*

> *This means that just as the prophecy of Israel's return from exile as recorded by Amos has been fulfilled quite literally, so will the part about David's Tabernacle being restored be fulfilled. Further, this restoration will involve an unprecedented harvest of souls being brought into the Kingdom.*

> *Could it be that the ultimate restoration of the Tabernacle of David, as described in Acts 15:16-18, actually refers to a supernatural tent, or covering, of worship and intercession that will be raised up by the Church in our generation over every tribe, tongue, people and nation on earth as pictured in Revelation 5:8-10 and Revelation 7:9-12 ?*

246

Could it be that the global Church is on the threshold
of a true worship reformation? If so, what can we learn
from worship in David's day that we might expect will mark
this movement?

"Reform" simply means "to change for the better"
or "to improve."

It's not that all worship in the Church today is deficient,
but perhaps God wants to take us to higher heights and deeper
depths of His glory. What reforms, then, might be required
to see the restoration of His Tabernacle become a practical
reality?

How will all of this bring in history's greatest harvest ? [43]

He then goes on to discuss seven worship reforms in the seven chapters that follow : continuous, skilful, creative, extravagant, expressive, open, and strategic; all based upon solid Scriptural precedents. These are foundational and extremely powerful spiritual attributes for worship that will indeed shift nations.

Now is the time to begin to step into the fullness of that worship - personally, corporately, and nationally. The Kingdom Worship Center will lead the way in this restoration through training and equipping, and through leading by example.

Resourcing the Nation

The Kingdom Worship Center will exist to resource the entire nation. It is a national centre of excellence; and a national centre for training, equipping, activating, and setting apart for increase world class intercessors and worshippers to restore the covering of Glory to the Earth **(Numbers 14:21; Habakkuk 2:14).**

Excellence and skill are important to God and release a higher level of anointing for the following reason; He honors our commitment, our time, our focus, and our heartfelt desire to be the very best that we can be for Him in every way, so that we can honor Him at the very highest levels.

Psalm 33:3 (TPT)
Compose new melodies
that release new praises to the LORD.
Play His praises on instruments with the anointing
and skill He gives you. Sing and shout with passion;
make a spectacular sound of joy ...

The Kingdom Worship Center will be instrumental in co-ordinating national prayer and worship. It will be a vehicle to unify the nation through the intentional inclusion of all tribes, people groups, and denominations at the center as one body, and by involving all denominations at every level. The Kingdom worship center will reproduce itself in terms of leadership and anointing at the provincial or state level.

A Kingdom Worship Center could well become a national center for the production of audio resources (praise and worship CDs, radio and Internet broadcasts, audio recordings of services) and video resources (live streams and recordings of prayer and worship services, recording of relevant messages, and production of Christian movies and media of all kinds) for the purpose of saturating the airwaves of the home nation, the surrounding nations, with the *message* of the Gospel of the Kingdom through the vehicles of anointed praise, worship, and intercession.

It will become a national learning resource through the establishment of a library of Kingdom resources - written, audio, video, podcasts etc.

National and Global Influence

In earlier chapters **(08, 09, 10, and 11)** we looked at the importance of the role of 24/7 intercession and worship to release the righteousness, mercy, and justice of God at every level of society.

Our primary example is King David and his establishment of 24/7 intercession and worship, with the corresponding generational blessing, peace, and prosperity of the nation for which, under God, he was responsible to rule.

Mike Bickle made the following observations regarding 24/7 prayer and worship during the time of David and its relationship to our times.

> *The quality that best defines David as a man after*
> *God's heart is his extravagant commitment to worship.*
> *After he conquered Jerusalem, his first act recorded*
> *in Scripture was that he brought the ark to Jerusalem*
> *and set singers and musicians before it to minister*
> *to the Lord.*
>
> *1 Chronicles 15-16 describes the historic day in Jerusalem*
> *when David brought the ark to Jerusalem and established*
> *a new worship order on earth that reflected the Lord's*
> *worship order in heaven.*
>
> *David vowed to dedicate his life to establishing*
> *a "dwelling place" for God. His vow included living*
> *in extravagant devotion to seek God with all his strength*
> *and resources (time, talents, and treasures).*
>
> *It included his time (Psalm 27:4), fasting (Psalm 69:7-12)*
> *and finance (1 Chronicles 22:14).*
>
> *This vow is at the heart of the end times 24/7 prayer*
> *and worship movement.* [44]

Psalm 132:1-5 (NKJV)
[1] Lord, remember David
And all his afflictions;
[2] How he swore to the Lord,
And vowed to the Mighty One of Jacob:
[3] "Surely I will not go into the chamber of my house,
Or go up to the comfort of my bed;
[4] I will not give sleep to my eyes
Or slumber to my eyelids,
[5] Until I find a place for the Lord,
A dwelling place for the Mighty One of Jacob."

1 Chronicles 18:13b (AMPC)
*And the Lord preserved and gave victory to David
wherever he went.*

1 Chronicles 18:14 (AMP)
*So David reigned over all Israel, and he administered
justice and righteousness to all his people.*

Prophecy - The End Times Sound of Heavenly Glory

Exodus 19:16, 19   (NKJV)
*[16] Then it came to pass on the third day,
in the morning, that there were thunderings and lightnings,
and a thick cloud on the mountain;
and the sound of the trumpet was very loud,
so that all the people who were in the camp trembled.*

*[19] And when the blast of the trumpet sounded long
and became louder and louder, Moses spoke,
and God answered him by voice.*

The sound of God was accompanied by thunder and lightning and a thick cloud; and had great effect upon the people.

See also **Revelation 5:8-14.** The sound that is made by the ekklesia depends upon the instruments – and we are God's chosen instruments of worship.

We will see God gathering the apostles, prophets, pastors, teachers, evangelists, prophetic worshippers, and intercessors in one place and at one time, so that He may fulfil His Mighty and Glorious purposes through them - and through you. This is one of the main purposes of an apostolic hub.

End times gatherings of believers, of which apostolic hubs are a vital part, are called to produce a sound. It's the Sound of Glory; it's the Sound of Heaven; it is a transformational sound; it is a revelatory sound; and it is a revolutionary sound.

It will not be what we have come to call worship in terms of set numbers of songs sung at set tempos and in set ways. This is a powerful, prophetic sound of Heaven, captured and released by singers and musicians who are attuned to Heaven's frequencies.

It is a sound that releases the fullness of the creative and redemptive power of God's Word.

It's a sound that releases mercy and justice.

It's the sound of a marching army; it's the sound of the end times.

It's the Sound of Heaven, coming down, and resonating inside of you, to the ends of the Earth, and back up to Heaven.

It causes the Golden Heavenly Harps to resound and the Golden Heavenly Bowls to be filled. In response, the Heavenly Hosts release the song that ushers in the end time harvest.

This incredible call and response between Earth and Heaven will build an unstoppable momentum and release wave after ever increasing wave of Glory to cover the Earth as the water cover the sea.

Revelation 5:8-14 (NKJV) - Worthy Is the Lamb

[8] Now when He had taken the scroll, the four living creatures and the twenty-four elders fell down before the Lamb, each having a harp, and golden bowls full of incense, which are the prayers of the saints.

[9] And they sang a new song, saying:

> *"You are worthy to take the scroll,*
> *And to open its seals;*
> *For You were slain,*
> *And have redeemed us to God by Your blood*
> *Out of every tribe and tongue and people and nation,*
> *[10] And have made us kings and priests to our God;*
> *And we shall reign on the earth."*

*¹¹ Then I looked, and I heard the voice of many angels
around the throne, the living creatures, and the elders;
and the number of them was ten thousand times ten thousand,
and thousands of thousands,*

¹² saying with a loud voice:

> *"Worthy is the Lamb who was slain
> To receive power and riches and wisdom,
> And strength and honour and glory and blessing!"*

*¹³ And every creature which is in heaven and on the earth
and under the earth and such as are in the sea,
and all that are in them, I heard saying:*

> *"Blessing and honour and glory and power
> Be to Him who sits on the throne,
> And to the Lamb, forever and ever!"*

*¹⁴ Then the four living creatures said, "Amen!"
And the twenty-four elders fell down
and worshiped Him who lives forever and ever.*

This *mighty sound* – a synchronous and antiphonal symphony involving heavenly and earthly singers and musicians - will coincide with an ever-expanding establishment of Open Heaven after Open Heaven here on the earth, and an unprecedented outpouring of God's Spirit and a covering of Glory.

As we learn to understand and flow in and release the Heavenly sounds and songs that will flow, the fruit of this end times sound of Heavenly Glory will overflow into nations. Get ready to hear the sounds of Heaven and to release them for the Glory of God.

Joshua 6:16 (NASB)
*At the seventh time,
when the priests blew the trumpets,
Joshua said to the people :
"Shout ! For the Lord has given you the city!"*

Kingdom Resource Centers

The Kingdom Resource Center is similar in concept to a Kingdom Worship Center, but with a different focus and a broader scope.

It is a high level, national leadership training centre of Kingdom learning for people from all denominations; a place of impartation and activation with a focus on the transformation of the seven mountains of human culture. It is an apostolic hub that will focus on resourcing the nation, not just with the *message* of the Gospel of the Kingdom, but also with *strategies* in terms of how to implement it.

It will become a national center of excellence, and a national centre for training, equipping, and setting apart for increase five-fold ministers, and also for Kingdom politicians, Kingdom economists, Kingdom entrepreneurs, and other local, provincial, and national Kingdom leaders.

Like the Kingdom Worship Center, the Kingdom Resource Center could well become a national center for the production of resources, but these resources will focus on the strategies for the implementation of the Gospel of the Kingdom.

The Kingdom Resource Centre will reproduce itself in terms of leadership and anointing at the provincial/state level. This training will develop supernatural, Christlike function and kingly authority in the life of the leader, and equip the leaders with Divine strategies to transform their nations according to Kingdom principles.

The Kingdom Resource Center and Kingdom Worship Center could share the same physical location. The important thing is to understand the very different but equally vital and complementary functions. Also, they could be large or small, in terms of the number of people attending – but if correctly implemented, the impact and influence of these Kingdom centers will be great.

Influencing the Seven Mountains of Human Culture

The Kingdom Worship and Resource Centres will influence all seven mountains of human culture by training equipping and releasing servants of God to operate at the very highest levels.

Intercessors and worshippers equipped through the Kingdom Worship Center, while primarily operating from the mountain of spirituality, will cause significant shifts on all the other mountains because of their anointed and strategic ministry.

Emerging government leaders and others trained at the Kingdom Resource Center will influence government policy and decision making. Kingdom economists and Kingdom entrepreneurs will engage in Godly resource and economic management. They will also influence others to operate with integrity.

The emerging generation of educators will be equipped to teach Kingdom principles to our children and grandchildren, and develop Kingdom strategies to overturn the war against the family that rages within many educational institutions around the world.

The Body of Christ should take the responsibility to impart Kingdom precepts to those whom God will choose to stand before kings and other rulers. Kingdom Resource Centers are the ideal place to do this.

> **Proverbs 22:29 (AMP)**
> *Do you see a man skilful and experienced in his work?*
> *He will stand [in honour] before kings;*
> *He will not stand before obscure men.*

LORD, Your Kingdom come, and Your will be done. Amen.

> **Matthew 6:10 (NASB)**
> *"Your kingdom come.*
> *Your will be done, on earth as it is in heaven."*

Chapter 21

The King's Economy

When we speak of transforming nations, we have seen that there are major spiritual and paradigm shifts that need to occur so that this transformation can take place. We have discussed these in the preceding chapters of this book, beginning at the personal level, and working through to the restoration of the ekklesia and, ultimately, the spiritual transformation of nations from grassroots to government.

However, there are also a series of financial shifts that also must occur so that the move of God can impact every sphere of society.

When Israel became a nation, God put some things into place in the areas of spiritual and economic leadership that have a definite and specific application for the 21st century ekklesia.

Following the Presence of the LORD in Divine Order

For the duration of their journey out of Egypt and into the Promised Land, the nation of Israel followed the Presence and Glory of the Almighty. In the Septuagint we see the word *ekklesia* being used to describe the gathering of the entire nation around the Presence of the LORD (see Chapter 12 – the Role of the Ekklesia).

There was a definite order to this gathering; and also a definite prioritization and order to the movement of the nation once the Presence of God began to move. In **Numbers Chapter 2**, the LORD spoke to Moses and Aaron, and gave them specific directions about the positioning of the twelve tribes in relation to His Presence, and in relation to each other. The Israelites were to *"camp around the Tent of Meeting at a distance"* **(Numbers 2:2)**.

On the east side of the tabernacle, Judah were to set up their camp closest to the Tent of Meeting; with Issachar next to them, and Zebulun next to them **(Numbers 2:1-9)**.

Reuben, Simeon, and Gad were on the south side **(Numbers 2:10-16)**. Ephraim, Manasseh, and Benjamin were on the west side **(Numbers 2:18-24)**; and Dan, Asher, and Napthali were on the north side **(Numbers 2:25-31)**.

Numbers 2:9 tells us that when it was time to break camp, i.e., when the fire and Glory of God began to move, Judah, Issachar, and Zebulun were to lead the way for the rest of the tribes, including Levi.

In **Numbers 10:11-17** we can read that the cloud of God's Presence and Glory lifted from the tabernacle and settled in the wilderness of Paran; and so the Israelites moved out as a nation, following the cloud, and led by Judah, Issachar, and Zebulun in that order.

Numbers 10:13-16 (NASB)
13 So they moved out for the first time according to the commandment of the Lord through Moses. 14 The standard of the camp of the sons of Judah, according to their armies, set out first, with Nahshon the son of Amminadab, over its army, 15 and Nethanel the son of Zuar, over the tribal army of the sons of Issachar; 16 and Eliab the son of Helon over the tribal army of the sons of Zebulun.

Exodus 40:36-38 (NASB)
*36 Throughout all their journeys whenever
the cloud was taken up from over the tabernacle,
the sons of Israel would set out;
37 but if the cloud was not taken up, then
they did not set out until the day when it was taken up.*

*38 For throughout all their journeys,
the cloud of the Lord was on the tabernacle by day,
and there was fire in it by night,
in the sight of all the house of Israel.*

Judah

Judah was the fourth son of Leah, born after Reuben, Simeon, and Levi.

Genesis 29:35 (NIV)
*She conceived again, and when she gave birth
to a son she said, "This time I will praise the Lord."
So she named him Judah.*

The name "Judah" means "praise" or "let Him be praised."

King David, King Solomon, and the King of Kings - Jesus Christ - were all descended from this tribe. Jesus is referred to as *"The Lion of (or from) the Tribe of Judah"* **(Revelation 5:5)**.

The territory of Judah included Jerusalem. Jacob blessed Judah by proclaiming that Judah would *"rule over his brothers"*; be *"like a lion's cub"*; and that *"the sceptre will not depart from Judah"* **(Genesis 49:8-10)**.

You could call Judah the kingly tribe
– they knew how to walk as rulers, and they produced kings.

We can relate the Tribe of Judah to the domata function of apostle.

Issachar

Issachar means "reward or "recompense."
Issachar was Leah's fifth son.

> **Genesis 30:18 (AMP)**
> *Then Leah said, "God has given me my reward*
> *because I have given my maid to my husband."*
> *So she named him Issachar.*

The land that was allotted to the tribe of Issachar was the most fertile land of any of the twelve tribes, and they *"saw the land was pleasant"* **(Genesis 49:14-15)** and worked it.

They were also noted as *"men who understood the times and knew what Israel should do."* **(1 Chronicles 12:32).** They perceived, they saw, and they understood the times.

We can relate the Tribe of Issachar to the domata function of prophet.

> **1 Chronicles 12:32 (NASB)**
> *[32] Of the sons of Issachar, men who understood the times,*
> *with knowledge of what Israel should do ...*

Zebulun

Zebulun, Leah's sixth son, was born after Issachar. Issachar and Zebulun are often mentioned together in Scripture. Zebulun's birth is recorded in **Genesis 30:19-20**.

> **Genesis 30:19-20 (AMP)**
> *[19] Leah conceived again and gave birth to a sixth son*
> *for Jacob. [20] Then Leah said, "God has endowed me*
> *with a good [marriage] gift [for my husband];*
> *now he will live with me [regarding me with honour*
> *as his wife], because I have given birth to six sons."*
> *So she named him Zebulun.*

The name "Zebulun" means "gift" or "to exalt or honor."

Moses blessed Issachar and Zebulun as follows :-

Deuteronomy 33:18-19 (NASB)
[18] *Of Zebulun he said,*
"Rejoice, Zebulun, in your going forth,
and, Issachar, in your tents.

[19] *"They will call peoples to the mountain;*
There they will offer righteous sacrifices;
For they will draw out the abundance of the seas,
And the hidden treasures of the sand."

The Amplified Bible says :
"Rejoice, Zebulun, in your interests abroad".

Jacob's blessing is also insightful
regarding the economic prowess of Zebulun.

Genesis 49:13 (NASB)
"Zebulun shall dwell at the seashore;
And he shall be a haven for ships,
And his flank shall be toward Sidon."

The Tribe of Zebulun were international traders, and suppliers and distributors of wealth; whereas Issachar stayed home, they worked their fields, and they studied the Word of God and stayed in the Presence of God *("in their tents").*

Zebulun supplied Issachar to enable them to linger in the Presence and discern the times.

The Tribe of Zebulun were also renowned for being mighty in warfare and leaders in battle **(Judges 5:14)**, and also for supplying large numbers of troops in proportion to the size of their tribe. Zebulun had a reputation for fighting strategically, fiercely, and loyally.

1 Chronicles 12:33 (NASB)
Of Zebulun, there were 50,000 who went out in the army,
who could draw up in battle formation with all kinds
of weapons of war and helped David with an undivided heart.

It is really not surprising that the tribe that excelled in warfare was also the tribe that excelled in enterprise and economics. The tenacity and strategy that served them so well on the battlefield also served them well in the marketplace.

How does this relate prophetically to our time ? Firstly, skilful spiritual warfare is a key to successful Kingdom economic strategy.

The stronghold of mammon has such a grip upon the children of men, that when we step on to the economics mountain to reclaim it in the Name of Jesus, we also step into a fiercely contested, no-holds-barred spiritual battle zone.

Only those who are called and seriously committed to spiritual warfare and the objectives of the Kingdom of God will be able to make headway, and then retain the ground that they take.

Strategic Partnerships

The economics mountain is not to be taken alone. Just as Judah, Issachar, and Zebulun moved together, so apostles, prophets, and modern day Zebuluns should do the same. Each has so much to offer to the other. The tribe of Judah excelled in worship and kingship. The Divine patterns of worship revealed to King David of the Tribe of Judah have set the precedent for worship, from his time until the return of Christ. Judah's worship was mighty and qualified them for kingship.

Zebulun shared their wealth with Issachar so that they could fulfil their prophetic duties of knowing the times and seasons. Issachar's prophetic knowledge enabled Judah to reign and lead more effectively, by revealing the Kairos timing of the LORD, and thereby synchronizing the strategies that Judah had received with Heaven's timing. Issachar blessed Zebulun with spiritual insight, which would have increased their success in economics and warfare.

Judah, through Divine revelation and kingly authority, knew how to lead the nation. Issachar revealed the times and seasons. Zebulun was the channel for Divine provision. These strategic partnerships ensured victory, security, and prosperity for the nation of Israel as a whole.

Chuck Pierce made the following powerful statements in an article entitled *Understanding Issachar : Interpreting the Times and Seasons.*

> *When God brought this people out of slavery in Egypt*
> *to move toward the Promised Land, each tribe*
> *was a warring army with a redemptive gift.*
>
> *Without each tribe warring for their portion,*
> *the full plan of God for the land promised to His people (Israel)*
> *could not be fully manifested in the earth.*
>
> *They moved toward their promise*
> *as the trumpet sounded.*
> *His presence, which was central, shifted them*
> *toward their destiny.*
>
> *God wants us to understand and interpret our times*
> *so we can prosper in every season, and possess the wisdom*
> *to advance.* [45]

Establishing and Maintaining Source and Supply

In any theatre of war, an effective strategy for an attacking army is to surround the opposing forces with the objective of cutting off their lines of supply. Once the supply lines are interrupted, those forces will be quickly rendered ineffective, since without supply of necessities, the fighting force cannot continue, and surrender will inevitably follow unless the supply lines can be re-established.

In terms of transforming nations, the same is true, and it applies spiritually and also economically. We've already looked at the importance of restoring and maintaining spiritual foundations in earlier chapters. But there are economic dynamics that must be implemented so that the Divine supply lines will not be interrupted.

When Jesus said, *"Seek first the Kingdom of God and all else will be added to you"* **(Matthew 6:33)**, He meant it.

Our hearts must be firmly, one hundred percent established in Him – that is an issue that simply needs to be settled.

We are who we are entirely because of who He is. We must leave all fear behind, and begin to truly believe that in He is all and is in all **(Colossians 3:11)**.

He will provide everything that is needed to fulfil our Divine purposes - as well as our daily needs - if we are willing to put His Kingdom and His righteousness first, and then step out into the unknown in faith.

> **Matthew 6:33 (AMP)**
> *"But seek first His kingdom and His righteousness, and all these things will be added to you."*

Fear of lack will disrupt the economic supply lines of the Kingdom of God if we allow it to. This fear is generated when we choose to focus on the limited resource of mammon rather than the limitless supplies of our King. Jesus plainly stated that we *"cannot serve God and mammon"* **(Matthew 6:24b NKJV)**.

The New Living Translation puts it this way :-

> **Matthew 6:24 (NLT)**
> *"No one can serve two masters.*
> *For you will hate one and love the other;*
> *you will be devoted to one and despise the other.*
> *You cannot serve God and be enslaved to money."*

A word study of **Matthew 6:24** in the original Greek yields so much. Very briefly, the word rendered "serve" (δουλεύειν (douleuein) *Strong's G1398*) means to be a slave, or to be subjected to. "Master" (κυρίοις (kyriois) *Strong's G2962*) means the one (implying the One) who has supreme authority over your life. The root word translated as "money" (μαμωνᾷ (mamōna) *Strong's G3126*) has its roots in a Chaldean word that does not just imply wealth but also avarice or greed.

The word rendered "hate" (καταφρονήσει (kataphronēsei) *Strong's G2706*) means "to detest" and therefore the other object of desire is esteemed less, or loved less.

The paragraph that contains this verse **(Matthew 6:20-24)** is subtitled "Treasures in Heaven" and in **verse 21** Jesus succinctly states, *"For where your treasure is, there your heart will be also"* **(Matthew 6:21 NIV).**

We can choose to be a love-slave of Jesus, or a fear-slave of mammon. Love-slaves of the Kingdom have been granted unlimited access to the limitless resources of the Creator of the universe. If we do not put Jesus first in the area of finances, ultimately, we will love Him less, and resent or ignore His desire to use us as conduits of Kingdom blessing.

Our increasing - or diminishing - levels of sowing will reflect the focus and desire of our heart. Fear of lack should not coexist in a heart where the Christ, the Hope of Glory, also resides; and it cannot exist in a heart where He truly reigns.

God of the Mountain

For the sake of Kingdom advancement, our spiritual, cultural, and financial paradigms will need to change. Financially speaking, Egypt represents slavery to the world system or to mammon. For most people, the paradigm shift from a mammon-dominated mindset to a Kingdom economic mindset is huge, and often confronting.

Apostles, prophets, and Zebuluns must lead the way to lift the Body of Christ out of dependency on the world's financial paradigms and restrictive systems, and into Kingdom financial freedom, just as Judah, Issachar, and Zebulun led the Israelites out of Egypt and into the Promised Land.

The secret is to seek His face in love, not His hand as beggars. When we seek His face with pure hearts, He opens His hand. Our God is always more than enough.

He is El Shaddai - the All Sufficient One, the Overpowerer **(Genesis 17:1; 28:3; 35:11).** Each of the times that God revealed Himself with this powerful name was a time when He was promising fruitfulness that was impossible to fulfil in the natural.

Abraham was ninety-nine years old when God told him that he would become the father of many nations.

Genesis 35:11 in particular is an incredible promise of supernatural multiplication, after God had already blessed Jacob and made him exceedingly, supernaturally wealthy.

God changed Jacob's name to Israel and said :-

> **Genesis 35:11 (TLV)**
> *God also said to him:*
> *"I am El Shaddai. Be fruitful and multiply.*
> *A nation and an assembly of nations will come from you.*
> *From your loins will come forth kings."*

God declares His Name and then declares the generational fruitfulness that will follow that declaration, which included the foundation of nations and the establishment of kings.

Another interpretation of the name "El Shaddai" is "God of the Mountain." This is powerful when we are considering His lordship over every mountain of human culture. It is only by His favour and Divine provision in every area that our mountains are made strong **(Psalm 30:7).**

He is also Jehovah Jireh, the LORD Who Provides. God revealed Himself this way when Abraham was about to sacrifice his son, his all, his beloved, in simple, unquestioning obedience to his God. God provided the sacrifice and made Abraham the father of many nations. Abraham demonstrates the unshakeable trust and straightforward faith that God desires for us to have in the realm of Kingdom finances.

If we understand that the LORD provides out of His own storehouse, then giving will excite us, because we will know that the replenishment from the Divine storehouse may well overtake the seed that has been sown, both in timing and in quantity **(Luke 6:38; Amos 9:13).** Giving has very little to do with what we "have," but everything to do with us giving freely based upon the King's desires that He has placed within our heart **(Psalm 37:4).**

All of His riches are in His Glory **(Philippians 4:19)**. Worship, once again, is the powerful key that our Creator has placed into our hand that unlocks the chambers of His heart, and all that is contained therein, towards us. The destination of the spirit-and-truth worshipper is the realm of Glory where the Almighty dwells.

The point is that is when God promises to provide, He *will* provide.

The reality is that we are giving freely from His riches. When we cannot see the solution with our natural eyes, it's time to get excited, because God is hovering, waiting for His servants to access His unsearchable riches and limitless resources.

"Delay" does not signify "denial." It could signify spiritual opposition to breakthrough as recorded in the Book of Daniel **(Daniel 10:10-14)**, which again should draw us into a deeper realm of seeking the face of the Almighty, and into spiritual warfare as led by the Holy Spirit.

Like the domata gifts and call, the Zebulun call is a marathon of endurance, not a quick sprint to the finish line, with many spiritual and life lessons to be learned along the way.

Every believer who learns to live a life of continually seeking the Kingdom above all else will experience some level of supernatural outpouring of resources from our Creator. Note that 99 percent of the time, the cheerful, obedient, faith-fuelled and extravagant giving of the children of the King will precede the King's extravagant gifts to His children !

But when someone is called and specifically anointed in the realm of Kingdom finances – in other words, when they are called to be a modern day Zebulun, the finances and provision are going to happen at a completely different and undeniably miraculous level.

Psalm 144:13 (TLV)
Our storehouses are full,
supplying every kind of produce.
Our flocks increase by thousands
and ten thousands in our fields.

Joseph is an excellent example of a Kingdom economist.

He had to overcome incredibly intense adversity to succeed **(Genesis 39:2-6a)**. During his times of persecution and imprisonment, he sought the face of God, and became exceptionally strong in the LORD and was highly favoured by those who ruled. He became an advisor to them, and the steward of their wealth.

Ultimately, the Divine wisdom with which he implemented Kingdom economic strategies saved not only his own nation, but also the surrounding nations, during a time of unprecedented famine and lack **(Genesis 41:53-57)**.

The World System

The problem with the world's financial system is that it is fear based. When our love or desire of money exceeds our love for God, there will be a tendency to hang on to our financial resources – whether great or small - or even to fearfully hoard them. With that mindset, it is easy to become enslaved to the world system, and also to accrue all kinds of unnecessary debt. This is turn leads to a lack of effectiveness in the Kingdom of God, because instead of being free to give, there will be a fear of lack that will be created if we do give, a fear of becoming enslaved to debt, a fear of poverty, and ultimately, poverty itself – spiritual and material.

> **1 Timothy 6:10 (TLV)**
> *For the love of money is the root of all kinds of evil*
> *- some, longing for it, have gone astray from the faith*
> *and pierced themselves through with many sorrows.*

I believe that fear-based financial thinking is one of the major enemies and obstacles that hinders the extension of the Kingdom of God.

Fear is the enemy of faith, and love is the antidote.

Perfect love casts out fear **(1 John 4:18)**.

We cannot please God without faith **(Hebrews 11:6)**.

Giving is not about calculating what we can "afford" to give.

When we understand that we are temporary custodians and stewards of His limitless wealth, the equation changes, and it is easy to give even what we do not seem to have, because we realize that we are sowing from His supply - not ours – into His work – not ours.

Give Jesus two fish and five loaves of bread, and watch it multiply in His hands ! Love was His motivation to give His life in exchange for ours. Love should be our motivation when, as His ambassadors, we freely give of the substance that He has entrusted us to steward.

Why is Zebulun Important in our Time ?

We have seen that the apostles are like the Judahs of our time, and the prophets are like the Issachars. **Ephesians 2:19-20** speaks of the household of God being built upon the foundation of the apostles and the prophets.

So why is Zebulun important ? Just as the Israelites would not move to follow the Glory until they saw that Judah (apostolic), Issachar (prophetic) and Zebulun (warfare and economy) had moved first, so we must, in our time, re-establish the spiritual connection between those who are appointed to lay the spiritual foundations (the apostles and prophets) and those whom God has appointed to supply at a supernatural level (the modern day Zebuluns).

The Word of God instructs us all to sow into the work of the Kingdom. That is not being disputed, but what we are unpacking here is that there is a "Zebulun company" of believers, headed by Kingdom economists and Kingdom entrepreneurs, who are called to source and supply wealth at another level, which is needed to fund great and mighty exploits within the Kingdom of God. This includes resourcing the Divine patterns and blueprints to transform nations that are given to the apostles and prophets.

God will connect these Zebuluns – these mighty spiritual and financial warriors - with His apostles and prophets so that His end time purposes will be fulfilled on time, and not frustrated or delayed through lack of supply.

Characteristics of Modern Day Zebuluns

An effective modern day Zebulun will be a Holy of Holies worshipper. The progression from the Outer Court, to the Holy Place (or Inner Court), to the Holy of Holies was a physical journey in the times of the Old Testament priests **(Hebrews 9:1-12).**

The Outer Court was a distance from the Ark of the Presence; it was noisy and illuminated by natural light. The Holy Place or Inner Court could only be entered by the priests. It was lit by candlelight. The Holy of Holies could only be entered by the high priest at specific times. The only light in the Holy of Holies emanated from the Glory of God.

There are so many parallels that can be drawn from the Outer Court to Holy Place to Holy of Holies progression, to the modern Christian's walk. I just want to say that the plans that are birthed in the Glory realm of the Holy of Holies are going to be incredibly fruitful compared to those that are drawn from the natural realm or those which are drawn from a mixture of the two.

The Outer Court experience of God will yield a measure of fruit; the Inner Court experience will yield more, but those who abide in and draw from the Holy of Holies will be extraordinarily fruitful. The handprints and holy seal of the Divine will be all over any and every business or ministry idea that is revealed and imparted there.

Think 30-fold, 60-fold, 100-fold, and just keep going from there, because our God is omnipotent omniscient and omnipresent. He has no limits ! He has all the supply that is needed to fulfil His glorious purposes. I could tell you many testimonies of miraculous supply for the fields of God's choosing in my own life, and yet I know that He has so much more to impart.

As much as Zebuluns will love the Holy of Holies, they will also love spiritual warfare, and be people of action. They will delight to implement the Divine financial strategies received in the Throne Room. Some of these strategies will be received by them, but others may have been received by apostles or prophets.

However the Zebuluns will have the marketplace skills. At times, they my even raise up specific businesses or income streams to fund specific projects. To succeed, it is a given that Zebuluns will be guided by Biblical financial principles, and therefore demonstrate high levels of wisdom and acumen in the way that they handle their day to day finances, and in the operational aspects of their Kingdom businesses and associated ministries.

I have had people knock on my door with envelopes with the exact amount (usually one or more thousands of dollars) that exactly met the needs of missions projects that they had no prior knowledge of.

This is wonderful of course. But I've also sat with more than one apostle to whom God had given a mission field and told them to plant and build; and then, seemingly out of nowhere, a Zebulun has contacted them, knowing nothing of the Divine plans given to the apostle, but offering whatever was needed to fund and then complete the mission.

We are talking about millions, tens of millions and more dollars at a time, including equipment, resources, vehicles, buildings, and financial resources - and all being released for the radical, large-scale extension of the Kingdom of God. Those relationships, initiated by the Holy One, will tend to become ongoing. This is an example of the strategic apostolic-Zebulun partnership bringing Kingdom expansion and victory.

Kingdom Entrepreneurs

What will a Kingdom entrepreneur look like ? Kingdom entrepreneurs and Kingdom economists are both of the Zebulun company. Kingdom entrepreneurs will demonstrate supernatural business skills, and if the nature of their Kingdom enterprise requires it, they will also have unusual networking skills. They will be passionate about, and contend for, Biblical mercy and justice.

They will have a "hand up" focus and mindset to eradicate poverty as opposed to a "hand out" approach, which will not improve the long-term plight of the poor. They will be actively involved in raising up the next generation of Zebulun companies of believers.

A Word on Small to Medium Enterprises

The following quote is from the World Bank.

> *Small and medium enterprises (SMEs)*
> *are the economic backbone of virtually every*
> *economy in the world. SMEs represent more than*
> *95 percent of registered firms worldwide, account*
> *for more than 50 percent of jobs, and contribute*
> *more than 35 percent of Gross Domestic Product*
> *(GDP) in many emerging markets.* [46]

In developed nations with strong economies, the small-to-medium enterprise sector will typically account for 65 percent or even more of the available jobs. However, in developing nations it is typically less than 20 percent, or even as low as 3 to 5 percent. Where the SME sector is small or nearly non-existent, poverty is rampant. That is why the SME sector has been referred to as the "missing middle" of the economy of developing nations.

As soon as we understand this, we can see that part of the mandate to transform nations must be to raise up Kingdom entrepreneurs who understand the importance of establishing SMEs, and who are willing to share and reproduce their expertise where it is most needed.

The Moringa Project

We have established one such project in a south Asian nation, in an area of high-level poverty. We have purchased ten acres of land, and we are preparing and planting them one acre at a time with moringa seedlings. The moringa tree has a multitude of well documented healing properties. These include boosting the immune system to develop resistance to malaria and many viruses.

The process involves removing all weeds and scrub from the land and levelling it, excavating 1,200 holes per acre for planting, laying irrigation pipes, applying organic manure, and finally, planting the moringa seedlings. This creates jobs for the local people and also stimulates the local economy through the purchase of local materials.

Those who are working preparing the fields will be lifted out of generational poverty by future income from the global export sales that will be generated from the leaves and fruits of the trees that they are helping to establish. This is Kingdom enterprise in action.

We have also set up a micro finance institution that gives out small loans to local people ($USD50 – 300) to enable them to start their own enterprises. The loans are paid back from the first fruits of the enterprises that are started. The moringa project is one that we want to replicate in other nations, as it is relatively easy to set up and has great potential to impact generations. This project is a living, breathing demonstration of the transformative nature of the Gospel of the Kingdom, and it has also opened previously closed doors to share the Gospel of salvation in the region.

Kingdom Economists

A Kingdom economist will go to another level. They will most likely have degrees in economics and/or political science. They will probably have CEO experience and understand the macro economic issues that affect the cash flow and prosperity of nations and beyond. They may be sought by kings, presidents, and prime ministers for economic and strategic advice. They will be interested in acquiring natural resources such as oil, natural gas, and gold on a kingly scale.

Speaking prophetically now, I believe that Kingdom economists will receive Divine strategies that will release Divine provision and create Divine storehouses and strategies that will provide for both the present and the future, just as Joseph did. Nations will look to the Kingdom economists and their Divine Storehouse Strategies when the world systems crash, just as the nations looked to Joseph for economic survival and to feed their people in Old Testament times.

Kingdom economists will have the wisdom, strategy, and balance to ensure overflows of abundance even in times of global lack. They may set up parallel financial systems that will not rely on the world financial system, and so they will flourish even when the world system crashes. They will innovate, using cutting edge technologies, and also set up investment strategies and micro and large scale financial institutions.

We are fortunate to have emerging Kingdom entrepreneurs and Kingdom economists who are connected to our network, and we highly value their input and the example set by their lives within their spheres of influence.

Convergence

When apostles, prophets, Kingdom economists, and Kingdom entrepreneurs come together, powerful Kingdom strategies will be birthed that will transform nations from grassroots to government. This coming together, and working together, is vital for Kingdom advancement.

Kingdom entrepreneurs and economists truly need the spiritual input and impartation from the apostles and prophets; and the Divine patterns that the apostles and prophets are called to release benefit greatly from the Kingdom financial dynamic that is brought by the Kingdom entrepreneurs and economists.

God will raise up more and more modern day Zebuluns - Kingdom economists and Kingdom entrepreneurs - financial kings and queens who are moving in the realms of millions and also billions of dollars, and who will understand and delight in their roles as distributors of supply for the apostolic builders of the Kingdom of God.

I have met a financial king who lives in my home city. He is a passionate worshipper, connected to many well known national leaders, speaks all over the world, and at any one time has tens of billions of dollars' worth of property development that he is working on for the extension of God's Kingdom. This is real, and it is happening in our day and in our time.

These are people who are highly connected and established in the 3rd Heaven through their worshipful lives, and therefore experiencing great favor in all their business dealings, including favor from heads of governments and CEOs of multinational corporations. God is setting them up as a precursor to the release of Kingdom finances on a massive scale for the advancement of His Kingdom Purposes to the very ends of the earth.

There are seven principles of Kingdom economy that will form a firm foundation in the inward lives and outward relationships of those whom God will call and choose to become conduits for His overflowing blessing.

(1) Strategic Planning and **Partnerships** based upon **(2) Divine Wisdom** and **(3) Integrity** are essential to initially **(4) Create/Access** and then **(5) Multiply,** and **(6) Distribute/Manage** Kingdom financial flows.

(7) Protection of these finances and the people and processes associated with them is essential, as Kingdom financial systems provide a direct challenge to existing, mammon-based financial systems, particularly where corruption, etc., has taken hold. Because of this, there can be increased levels of spiritual interference and warfare around the establishment Kingdom finances, and also around those called to raise them up, particularly during the establishment phases of Kingdom ministries, businesses and networks.

Ultimately, God and His people shall prevail.

> **Deuteronomy 8:18 (AMP)**
> *But you shall remember [with profound respect] the Lord your God, for it is He who is giving you power to make wealth, that He may confirm His covenant which He swore (solemnly promised) to your fathers, as it is this day.*
>
> *see also*
>
> **Psalm 73:24; Proverbs 3:19** (wisdom);
> **Proverbs 11:3; Psalm 41:12)** (integrity);
> **Proverbs 15:22; 16:31** (strategic planning);
> **Genesis 1:12; 22:14, Philippians 4:19** (creation);
> **Genesis 1:28, 22:18; 39:2-5; Leviticus 9:26;**
> **Proverbs 10:22; Luke 6:38** (multiplication);
> **Genesis 41:53-57; Ezra 7:13-20;**
> **Proverbs 11:25, 19:17, 22:9, 58:6-8;**
> **Acts 2:45-46, Galatians 2:10** (distribution)
> **Psalm 32:7; Luke 10:19; Romans 8:31** (protection)

Judah

Issachar

Throne Room
Revelation &
Divine Patterns

Transformation
of Nations
From Grassroots
to Government

Apostle

Prophet

Kingdom
Strategies

Knowing
the Times
& Seasons

Kingdom
Economist

Kingdom
Entrepreneur

Zebulun

Kingdom
Enterprises

Mercy & Justice
Projects

Amos 9:11-13
Numbers 14:21
Habakkuk 2:14
Deuteronomy 4:10

Micah 6:8
James 1:27
Ephesians 2:20
Philippians 4:19

Apostolic & Prophetic
Worship & Intercession

Part 04

Final Thoughts

Philippians 4:8 (AMP)
8 Finally, believers, whatever is true,
whatever is honorable and worthy of respect,
whatever is right and confirmed by God's word,
whatever is pure and wholesome,
whatever is lovely and brings peace,
whatever is admirable and of good repute;
if there is any excellence,
if there is anything worthy of praise,
think continually on these things
[center your mind on them,
and implant them in your heart].

Chapter 22

Final Thoughts

During the time that this book was being written, our small but vibrant apostolic network, Global Influencers, increased in size by more than a factor of 10. Much of that growth occurred during a three-day period that occurred right after Chapters 19 and 20 had been completed.

The network grew through the addition of local ekklesias; schools, Kingdom business schools, prayer teams and networks of ekklesias run by pastors and apostles, across three nations, very much as had been outlined in chapter 19. The Kingdom influence and advancement that has come about as a result of that growth has been nothing short of phenomenal in some of the regions where we are involved.

I couldn't help but think that the Habakkuk 2 principle expounded in Chapter 1 was being confirmed by the Almighty; write down the vision, and God will breathe upon it and cause others to run with it.

Within these pages, we have examined revival, beginning on a personal level and continuing through to national transformation.

We have underscored the importance of Holy Spirit led intercession and worship to restore and then maintain the spiritual foundations that will pave the way for the spiritual revelation and revolution that the ekklesia, the glorious Bride of Christ, is destined to release.

In particular, we examined the Divine patterns that will restore the ekklesia as God's chosen vehicle to not only save souls, but to transform nations from grassroots to government.

We looked at the ancient paradigms that are being released today for the global ekklesia, and some of the practical, Biblical forms through which these paradigms can take shape and be most effective in the 21st century.

Throughout the journey, testimonies of supernatural Heavenly encounters and earthly missions have been shared that testify to the Author and Finisher of the subjects that have been discussed. We are about the Master's work, and if we choose to plant and water according to the Master's Divine patterns, He will cause a supernatural increase that will manifest in glorious and miraculous ways to the very ends of the earth.

While the principles discussed in Parts 01 to 03 apply to all believers, it is those functioning as apostles who will establish the practical patterns that will facilitate the identification, equipping, activation, and release of the wider Body of Christ into the fullness of their God-given destinies. Therefore, establishing connections between local ekklesias and apostolic networks is vital for the health of the worldwide body of believers. All the fivefold functions are vital, as are the Zebulun functions of Kingdom economists and entrepreneurs.

There are many wonderfully detailed and beautifully written books that describe the function of apostles and the implementation of apostolic strategies in more detail than has been covered here, and from other perspectives. Some of those volumes (and/or websites) are listed in the "Further Reading" section located at the end of this book. I encourage you to read them to broaden your understanding of the Divine patterns and Kingdom strategies that the Holy Spirit is releasing in our day and in our time.

On that note, I would like to once again convey my heartfelt thanks to all of the authors who gave their kind permission to be quoted within this work – especially those who took the time to respond personally.

May God bless you and your beloveds and your ministries, and may we all be found standing shoulder to shoulder in the fields of God's choosing when the end times revival begins to sweep the globe.

Chapter 23

Global Influencers

Global Influencers is a global community that is joined together in agape love and growing through the truth of God's Word and the fire of the Holy Spirit.

Our heart's desire is to help each member to identify their God-given calling, to see them walking in the absolute fullness of it, and then to set them apart for increase to accomplish the fulfilment of it.

The Global Influencers Vision

    a. Restore Kingdom culture from grassroots to government in the villages, cities, regions, and nations of the world **(Matthew 6:10).**

    b. Build a vibrant, agape-filled, Christ-centred, and Holy Spirit led global network of inter-connected communities that makes Kingdom hearted and Kingdom minded disciples **(Acts 2:42-47).**

    c. Eliminate generationally entrenched poverty in all its forms through applied agape love that consists of strategic application of Kingdom principles, and generous distribution of Kingdom resources **(Luke 4:18-19; Galatians 2:10).**

d. Work with local Kingdom communities
    all over the world to equip them to fulfil
    their own God-given purposes and destinies
    (Zephaniah 3:9).

The Global Influencers Network

Our network consists of local assemblies, prayer teams, schools (grade education, ministry, and Kingdom business), and leaders of influence (sphere leaders and partners). We believe that God is raising up this network at this specific time to release the fullness of the Gospel of the Kingdom from grassroots to government in the fields of His choosing around the globe.

The network has four main branches :-

1 - Global Influencers
The main relational network consisting of ekklesias,
schools (grade education, ministry, and Kingdom economics),
people of influence, and a distribution hub for worship,
training and equipping resources;

2 - Outpouring Ministries
Our not-for-profit missions and projects branch;

3 - Global RestoreNet
Our global prayer and intercessory network;

and

4 - Global Influencers Invest
Our Kingdom investment branch

Global Influencers Leadership

The leaders of Global Influencers (sphere leaders and sphere partners) are drawn from many different backgrounds, They are all passionate lovers of God, innovators, forerunners, and people of influence within their spheres.

For more information about our Kingdom work in developing nations, to support a project, and for enquiries regarding the schools of ministry, bookings, and membership, please contact :-

www.globalinfluencers.org

admin@globalinfluencers.org

God bless you thoroughly and completely
with his overflowing fullness.

Steve Harris
Founder
Global Influencers

GLOBAL INFLUENCERS

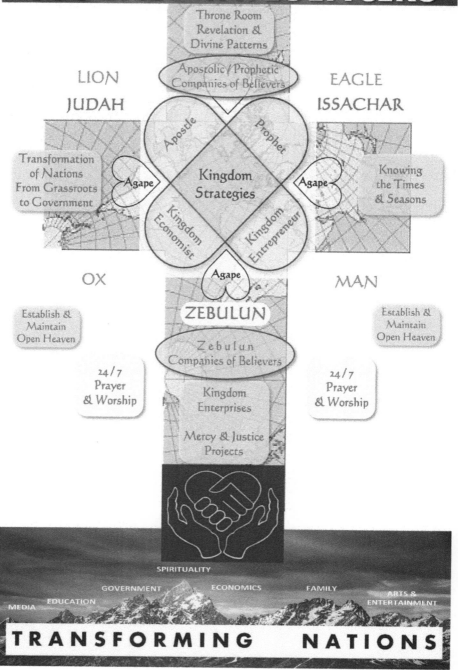

Throne Room
Revelation &
Divine Patterns

Apostolic / Prophetic
Companies of Believers

LION
JUDAH

EAGLE
ISSACHAR

Apostle

Prophet

Agape

Kingdom
Strategies

Agape

Transformation
of Nations
From Grassroots
to Government

Knowing
the Times
& Seasons

Kingdom
Economist

Kingdom
Entrepreneur

Agape

OX

MAN

ZEBULUN

Establish &
Maintain
Open Heaven

Establish &
Maintain
Open Heaven

Zebulun
Companies of Believers

24 / 7
Prayer
& Worship

24 / 7
Prayer
& Worship

Kingdom
Enterprises

Mercy & Justice
Projects

SPIRITUALITY

GOVERNMENT   ECONOMICS   FAMILY

MEDIA   EDUCATION

ARTS &
ENTERTAINMENT

TRANSFORMING NATIONS

Part 05

Resources, References, and Further Reading

2 Timothy 2:15 (AMP)
*Study and do your best
to present yourself to God approved,
a workman [tested by trial]
who has no reason to be ashamed,
accurately handling and skilfully
teaching the word of truth.*

Resources

Prayer
Global RestoreNet (Global Prayer
Team)
Prayer Requests / Join the Team
www.globalinfluencers.org/
communities/
prayer@globalrestorenet.org

GLOBAL RestoreNet
Nehemiah 2:20
Revelation 3:7-8
Revelation 5:8-10

Worship *(see Worship Projects section)*
www.globalinfluencers.org/resources/
steveharris.hearnow.com

Communities
Global Influencers
Global RestoreNet
www.globalinfluencers.org/
communities/

Projects
Global Influencers
Outpouring Ministries
www.globalinfluencers.org/comm
unities/

Learning, Equipping and Activation
Global Influencers School of Ministry
Sanctuary Supernatural Discipleship School (SSDS)
www.globalinfluencers.org/curriculum/

General Enquiries
www.globalinfluencers.org/contact/

Bookings, Seminars and Enquiries
www.globalinfluencers.org/contact/
admin@globalinfluencers.org

Worship Projects

Steve Harris has been a pianist and keyboardist for over 40 years. He has worshipped with Ron Kenoly, Olivia McClurkin, and Pastor Benny Hinn, amongst many others. 100% of the proceeds from the sales of these CDs will fund projects in developing nations such as wells, schools and other children's programmes, sewing and computer schools, and a variety of Kingdom enterprise projects designed to lift communities out of generationally entrenched poverty.

Overflow

Featuring the incomparable vocals of Olivia McClurkin, this is an anointed CD filled with Gospel & African grooves and mellow worship sounds, and saturated with the atmosphere of Heaven.

It was a once in a lifetime privilege to be able to gather such an extraordinarily gifted and anointed group of singers and musicians for this project.

Presence Music – Beyond the Veil

This is an instrumental 'soaking' worship album, used all over the world to fill the atmosphere with the presence of God. Many people around the world have received healing miracles while listening to this CD.

We should not be satisfied with spending time in the outer courts... we need to draw away from the busyness of day-to-day existence and seek face to face encounters with God. Beyond the veil, in the Holy of Holies, God is waiting for you. Will you meet Him there?

Journey to the Secret Place

Take the journey into the realms of Glory through the vehicle of prophetic worship.

Featuring anointed, world–class singers and musicians, and richly textured music encompassing many genres, this album will take you to the Throne Room. It was produced over a long period of time spent lingering in the deep places of God; and each track releases a different dimension of the Presence of the Holy One.

Worship Resource Links

www.globalinfluencers.org/resources/

steveharris.hearnow.com

References

Foreword

1 – Scribe

Anciently, scribes held various important offices in the public affairs of the nation. The Hebrew word so rendered (sopher) is first used to designate the holder of some military office (Judges 5:14; A.V., "pen of the writer;" RSV, "the marshal's staff;" marg., "the staff of the scribe"). The scribes acted as secretaries of state, whose business it was to prepare and issue decrees in the name of the king (**2 Samuel 8:17; 20:25; 1 Chronicles 18:16; 24:6; 1 Kings 4:3; 2 Kings 12:9-11; 18:18-37**). They discharged various other important public duties as men of high authority and influence in the affairs of state.

"These dictionary topics are from M.G. Easton M.A., D.D., *Illustrated Bible Dictionary, Third Edition*, published by Thomas Nelson, 1897. Public Domain." https://www.biblestudytools.com/dictionaries/eastons-bible-dictionary/scribes.html   *accessed 2020.03.20*

Part 01 : Foundations

Chapter 02 - One Net, Many Boats

2 – Kabod

Strong's H5513
כָּבוֹד kâbôwd, kaw-bode'; rarely כָּבֹד kâbôd; properly, weight, but only figuratively in a good sense, splendor or copiousness:—glorious(-ly), glory, honour(-able). *Strong's Exhaustive Concordance of the Bible*, ed. James Strong (Nashville, TN: Thomas Nelson Publishers, 1977)

3 – Anointing

Strong's H4886
mashach : a primitive root; to rub with oil, i.e., to anoint; by implication, to consecrate; also to paint--anoint, paint. *Strong's Exhaustive Concordance of the Bible*, ed. James Strong (Nashville, TN: Thomas Nelson Publishers, 1977)

Brown-Driver-Briggs Hebrew Lexicon
mâshach: 1) to smear, anoint, spread a liquid
1a) (Qal); 1a1) to smear; 1a2) to anoint (as consecration) 1a3) to anoint, consecrate;
1b) (Niphal) to be anointed

https://www.blueletterbible.org/lang/lexicon/lexicon.cfm?t=KJV&strongs=H488
6*accessed 2020.03.20*

Chapter 03 – Glorious Regiments

4 – Kevin J. Conner - *The Foundations of Christian Doctrine*
© 1980 KJC Publications PO Box 300 Vermont Victoria 3133 Australia p85

5 – ibid. p87
Quoted with publisher's permission.

Chapter 05 – Habitation or Visitation?

6 – Latter and Former Rain

Adapted from *One for Israel – Yoreh and Malkosh*
https://www.oneforisrael.org/bible-based-teaching-from-israel/the-former-latter-rains-in-israel/
accessed 2020.04.04

Chapter 07 Repentance, Forgiveness, Humility, and Unity

7 - Repentance
Strong's g3341: metanoia: change of mind, repentance
Original Word: μετάνοια, ας, ἡ
Definition: change of mind, repentance
Usage: repentance, a change of mind, change in the inner man.

Strong's Exhaustive Concordance of the Bible, ed. James Strong (Nashville, TN: Thomas Nelson Publishers, 1977)

Part 02 : Restoration

Chapter 10 – Altars

8 - Apostasy

Strong's g646
apostasia: defection, revolt

Strong's Exhaustive Concordance of the Bible, ed. James Strong (Nashville, TN: Thomas Nelson Publishers, 1977)

9 – Sanctuary (Living Sacrifice)

Music & Lyrics: Steve Harris
available on the "Overflow" worship project
https://steveharris.hearnow.com/overflow

10 Taken from *Charting the Bible Chronologically*, Copyright © 2016 by Ed Hindson and Thomas Ice, p. 62
   Published by Harvest House Publishers, Eugene, Oregon 97408.
www.harvesthousepublishers.com
   Quoted with publisher's permission

11 ibid. p63
   Quoted with publisher's permission

12 – Jebusites
Strong's h947
bus: to tread down, trample

Strong's Exhaustive Concordance of the Bible, ed. James Strong (Nashville, TN: Thomas Nelson Publishers, 1977)

NASB Translation: loathes (1), squirming (2), trample (1), trample down (1), trampled (1), trampled down (1), tread down (2), treading down (1), trod down (1), trodden it down (1).

NAS Exhaustive Concordance of the Bible with Hebrew-Aramaic and Greek Dictionaries Copyright © 1981, 1998 by The Lockman Foundation. All rights reserved.

13 – Four Streams of Poverty

Dr. Ed Silvoso - *Ekklesia – Rediscovering God's Instrument for Global Transformation*
Chosen books, © 2014, 2017. p25-26

In the section entitled "Paradigms for Changing the World," under the 5th paradigm, Dr. Silvoso mentions four streams of poverty as follows:

5. The elimination of systemic poverty in its four dimensions - spiritual, relational, motivational and material - is the premier *social* indicator of transformation.

Chapter 12 – The Role of the Ekklesia
14 – Ekklesia in the Septuagint

Kyle Pope - *The Use of the Word Ekklesia in the Greek Old Testament*
http://www.olsenpark.com/Sermons07/CongregationOfTheLord.html
accessed 2020.05.01
Quoted with kind permission of the author

15 – ibid.
16 – ibid.

17 - qahal

Strong's H6950
קָהַל qâhal, 'kaw-hal';
a primitive root; to convoke - assemble (selves) (together), gather (selves) (together).

Strong's Exhaustive Concordance of the Bible, ed. James Strong (Nashville, TN: Thomas Nelson Publishers, 1977)

KJV Translation Count — Total: 39x
The KJV translates **Strong's H6950** in the following manner:
(gather, assemble) together (14x), gather (16x), assembled (9x)

Outline of Biblical Usage

1. To assemble, gather
    1. (Niphal) to assemble
        1. for religious reasons
        2. for political reasons
    2. (Hiphil) to summon an assembly
        1. for war, judgment
        2. for religious purposes

https://www.blueletterbible.org/lang/lexicon/lexicon.cfm?t=KJV&strongs=H695
0*accessed 2020.05.01*

18 – Kyle Pope - *The Use of the Word Ekklesia in the Greek Old Testament*

http://www.olsenpark.com/Sermons07/CongregationOfTheLord.html,
        accessed 2020.05.01
Quoted with kind permission of the author

19 – Definition of Church from Merriam-Webster Dictionary (online)

1 : A building for public and especially Christian worship
2 : The clergy or officialdom of a religious body the word church
3 : A body or organization of religious believers such as:
        a : The whole body of Christians, the one church, is the whole body gathered together from all ages.
            - J. H. Newman
        b : Denomination the Presbyterian church
        c : Congregation they had appointed elders for them in every church—Acts 14:23 (Revised Standard Version)
4 : A public divine worship goes to church every Sunday.
5 : The clerical profession considered the church as a possible career.
Merriam-Webster Online Dictionary copyright © 2015 by Merriam-Webster, Incorporated https://www.merriam-webster.com/dictionary/church#
accessed 2020,.04.20

20 – The Two Great Commissions

Dr. Ed Silvoso - *Ekklesia – Rediscovering God's Instrument for Global Transformation*
Chosen books, © 2014, 2017. p44
Published by Chosen Books 11400 Hampshire Avenue South, Bloomington, Minnesota 55438
Quoted with publisher's permission

21 – Recovering All That Was Lost

Ibid. p45
Quoted with publisher's permission

Chapter 13 - Seven Mountains, Seven Spheres

22 – Dr. Bill Bright and Loren Cunningham – Seven Mountains
https://christianinternational.com/blog/2016/7/8/origin-of-7-mountain-concepts-and-7mki?rq=7%20mountains accessed 2020.05.01

23 – Johnny Enlow - *The Seven Mountains Prophecy – Unveiling the Coming Elijah Revolution*
Published by Creation House - A Charisma Media Company
600 Rinehart Road, Lake Mary, Florida 32746 www.charismamedia.com

24 – ibid. Introduction
25 – ibid. Appendix : The Seven Mountains Quick Reference Chart
26 – ibid. Appendix : The Seven Mountains Quick Reference Chart
Quoted with kind permission of the author

27 – Dato Dr. Kim Tan - *The Jubilee Gospel*
© 2008 Authentic Media, PO BOX 6326, Bletchley, Milton Keynes, MK1 9GG, UK
www.authenticmedia.co.uk
Quoted with kind permission of the author
The indented paragraphs are adapted from Dr. Tan's brilliant book that
looks at the fifty years' Jubilee cycle and its relevance for today in great detail.

Dato Dr. Tan is the co-founder of the Transformational Business Network, which
does wonderful work in many nations eliminating poverty through the
establishment of small to medium enterprises.
https://www.tbnetwork.org/
https://www.tbn.asia

Chapter 16 – End Times Kingdom Paradigms

28 – *The Qanat System – A Reflection on the Heritage,* p.47
N. Sanaan Bensi
© The Author(s) 2020
C. Hein (ed.), *Adaptive Strategies for Water Heritage,*
https://doi.org/10.1007/978-3-030-00268-8_3
accessed 2020.05.01
Quoted with kind permission of the author

29 – ibid., p49
30 – ibid. p41 [paraphrased]
31 – ibid. p53 [paraphrased]

Chapter 17 - Domata

32 - J. Rodman Williams - *Renewal Theology – Systematic Theology from a Charismatic Perspective"*
Volume 2 : Salvation, the Holy Spirit, and Christian Living, pp. 324-325
Copyright © 1992 by J. Rodman Williams, Zondervan,
Grand Rapids, Michigan 49530 All Rights Reserved. Used with permission.

33 - *The Power of Covenant Prayer* - Francis Frangipane, Charisma House, © **1998. p. 42.**
Copyright © 1998 by Francis Frangipane All rights reserved
Published by Charisma House – A Strang Company 600 Rinehart Road Lake Mary, Florida 32746www.charismahouse.com ISBN: 0-88419-548-1

34 - ibid. p42.

35 - Meaning of diakonia, and close connection to faith

Strong's Concordance
diakonia : service, ministry
Usage: waiting at table; in a wider sense: service, ministration.

HELPS Word-studies
Cognate: 1248 diakonía – ministry; active service, done with a willing (voluntary) attitude. See 1249 (diakonos).

For the believer, 1248 /diakonía ("ministry") specifically refers to Spirit-empowered service guided by faith (4102 /pístis, "the Lord's inbirthed persuasion").

[Observe the close connection of faith (4102 /pístis) and 1248 (diakonía) in Acts 6:1-7, 21:19, 20; Romans 12:3, 7; 1 Corinthians 16:13, 15; Ephesians 4:12, 13; 1 Timothy 1:12, 14; 2 Timothy 4:5, 7.] *Strong's Exhaustive Concordance of the Bible,* ed. James Strong (Nashville, TN: Thomas Nelson Publishers, 1977)

Chapter 18 – Apostolos

36 - J. Rodman Williams - *Renewal Theology – Systematic Theology from a Charismatic Perspective*
Volume 3 : The Church, the Kingdom, and Last Things, p.164-170
Copyright © 1992 by J. Rodman Williams, Zondervan,
Grand Rapids, Michigan 49530 All Rights Reserved. Used with permission.

37 – Apostolos
   https://www.biblestudytools.com/dictionary/apostle/
      accessed 2020.05.01
38 - Ibid.

Chapter 19 - Apostolic Centers, Hubs, and Networks

39 - Human Development Index (HDI)
United Nations Development Programme - Human Development Reports "The Human Development Index (HDI) was created to emphasize that people and their capabilities should be the ultimate criteria for assessing the development of a country, not economic growth alone. The HDI can also be used to question national policy choices, asking how two countries with the same level of GNI per capita can end up with different human development outcomes. These contrasts can stimulate debate about government policy priorities.

"The Human Development Index (HDI) is a summary measure of average achievement in key dimensions of human development: a long and healthy life, being knowledgeable and have a decent standard of living. The HDI is the geometric mean of normalized indices for each of the three dimensions."

http://hdr.undp.org/en/content/human-development-index-hdi
accessed 2020.03.20

40 - Alain Caron – *Heaven's Headquarters – Apostolic Centers,* pp. 31-32
© Alain Caron 2016
Published by Hodos, 480, rue de Vernon Gatineau (Québec) J9J 3K5 Canada
(819) 778-2681
ISBN : 978-2-924586-14-3 (print)
ISBN : 978-2-924586-15-0 (digital)
Quoted with kind permission of the author

41 - John Eckhardt - *Ordinary People, Extraordinary Power*
Published by Charisma House
Charisma Media/Charisma House Book Group, 600 Rinehart Road, Lake Mary, Florida 32746
www.charismahouse.com

42 - Alain Caron – *Heaven's Headquarters – Apostolic Centers,* p33
Quoted with kind permission from the author

Chapter 20
- Apostolic Hubs – Kingdom Worship and Resource Centers for the Nations

43 - Dick Eastman – *Intercessory Worship – Combining Worship & Prayer to Touch the Heart of God*
© *2011 Dick Eastman*
Published by Chosen Books, 11400 Hampshire Avenue South, Bloomington, Minnesota 55438 chosenbooks.com
Chosen Books is a division of Baker Publishing Group, Grand Rapids, Michigan.
www.bakerpublishinggroup.com
Chosen edition published 2014   ISBN 978-1-4412-6809-9
Quoted with publisher's permission

44 - Mike Bickle - IHOP Session 21 - *David's Tabernacle: Extravagant Worship*
https://ihopkcorg-a.akamaih/d.net/platform/IHOP/748/467/LOD21_Davids_Tabernacle-Extravagant_Worship_(1_Chr._15-16).pdf
accessed 2020.05.01

Chapter 21 – The King's Economy

45 – Chuck Pierce – *Understanding Issachar: Interpreting the Times and Seasons*
Article first published on the Elijah List 2010.06.24
https://www.elijahlist.com/words/display_word.html?ID=8886
Quoted with kind permission of Glory of Zion Ministries
Accessed 2020.05.01

46 – Missing Middle
Alibhai, Salman; Bell, Simon; Conner, Gillette. **2017.** *What's Happening in the Missing Middle?*

Lessons from Financing SMEs. **World Bank, Washington, DC.** ©

World Bank. https://openknowledge.worldbank.org/handle/10986/26324 License: CC BY 3.0 IGO." *accessed 2020.07.19*

Further Reading

Alain Caron

Apostolic Centers – Shifting the Church, Transforming the World
© 2013 Alain Caron Published by Arsenal Press P.O. Box 26178 Colorado Springs, CO 80936 719-278-8422 www.arsenalbooks.com

Heaven's Headquarters – Apostolic Centers
(Apostolic Live Series Book 1)
© Alain Caron 2016 Published by Hodos, 480, rue de Vernon, Gatineau (Québec) J9J 3K5 Canada

Bringing Back the Glory – The Apostolic Mandate
(Apostolic Live Series Book 2)
© Alain Caron 2017 Published by Hodos, 480, rue de Vernon, Gatineau (Québec) J9J 3K5 Canada

God's Barak – Apostolic Prosperity
(Apostolic Live Series Book 3)
© Alain Caron 2015 Published by Hodos, 480, rue de Vernon, Gatineau (Québec) J9J 3K5 Canada

Dato Dr Kim Tan

The Jubilee Gospel
© 2008 Authentic Media,
PO BOX 6326, Bletchley, Milton Keynes, MK1 9GG, UK

Dato Dr Kim Tan & Lord Brian Griffiths

Fighting Poverty Through Enterprise
Transformational Business Network Fifth Floor, 11 Leadenhall Street London EC3V 1LP © Lord Brian Griffiths and Dr. Kim Tan, April 2007 The authors assert the moral right to be identified as the authors of this book. Third Edition Published by Anchor Recordings Ltd
72 The Street Kennington Ashford Kent TN24 9 HS

Social Impact Investing: New Agendas to Fight Poverty
Transformational Business Network Fifth Floor, 11 Leadenhall Street London EC3V 1LP @ Dr Kim Tan and Lord Brian Griffiths, February 2016. The authors assert the moral right to be identified as the authors of this book. First Edition, 2016 Printed in Malaysia

Ed Silvoso

Ekklesia - Rediscovering God's Instrument for Global Transformation
Chosen books, © 2014, 2017.
Published by Chosen Books
11400 Hampshire Avenue South, Bloomington, Minnesota 55438

Francis Frangipane

The Power of Covenant Prayer
Copyright © 1998 by Francis Frangipane All rights reserved
Published by Charisma House A Strang Company
600 Rinehart Road, Lake Mary, Florida 32746 www.charismahouse.com

Glen Gerhauser

Desperate for Jesus : A Call to Revival
© Glen Gerhauser 2001 Published by Holy Fire Fellowship Brisbane Australia

Johnny Enlow

The Seven Mountain Prophecy: Unveiling the Coming Elijah Revolution
© 2008 by Johnny Enlow Published by Creation House - A Charisma Media Company
600 Rinehart Road, Lake Mary, Florida 32746
www.charismamedia.com

The Seven Mountain Mantle : Receiving the Joseph Anointing to Reform Nations
© 2009 by Johnny Enlow Published by Creation House - A Charisma Media Company
600 Rinehart Road, Lake Mary, Florida 32746
www.charismamedia.com

Stephen Bennett

The Power of Apostolic Music: The Proper Order of David's Tabernacle Rebuilding in These End Times
First edition 2004 © Copyright 2001 Stephen Bennett, Awesome City Music Pty Ltd.

Published by Awesome City Music Publishing PO Box 1312 Dee Why NSW Australia 2099

Notes

Lightning Source UK Ltd.
Milton Keynes UK
UKHW010627160921
390678UK00001B/72

9 780645 034301